Stateless Subjects

T0385661

Stateless Subjects

Chinese Martial Arts Literature
and
Postcolonial History

PETRUS LIU

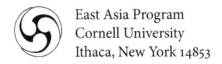
East Asia Program
Cornell University
Ithaca, New York 14853

For my parents,
Shyi-Huei Liu and Mei-Fang Lee

The Cornell East Asia Series is published by the Cornell University East Asia Program (distinct from Cornell University Press). We publish books on a variety of scholarly topics relating to East Asia as a service to the academic community and the general public. Standing Orders, which provide for automatic notification and invoicing of each title in the series upon publication, are accepted.

Address submission inquiries to CEAS Editorial Board, East Asia Program, Cornell University, 140 Uris Hall, Ithaca, New York 14853-7601.

This publication is supported by a generous grant from the Hull Memorial Publication Fund of Cornell University.
Cover design by Brian Y. Lin.

CONTENTS

ACKNOWLEDGMENTS

Much of the pleasure I have derived from writing this book came from the conversations I have had with the extraordinary scholars I have met. I am deeply grateful to my dissertation advisors, Judith Butler, Lydia Liu, Andrew Jones, and Colleen Lye. I would like to thank Anindita Banerjee, Dan Boucher, Calum Carmichael, Debra Castillo, Samuel Cheung, Walter Cohen, Chris Connery, Jonathan Culler, Brett de Bary, David Eng, Ed Gunn, TJ Hinrichs, Peter Hohendahl, Christine Hong, Wengqing Kang, Bill Kennedy, Dominick LaCapra, Barry Maxwell, Kathleen McCarthy, Natalie Melas, Jonathan Monroe, Timothy Murray, Lisa Rofel, Nancy Ruttenburg, Neil Saccamano, Naoki Sakai, Paul Stasi, Amy Villarejo, Sophie Volpp, Andy Chih-ming Wang, Ding Xiang Warner, and Kenneth Wu for their encouragement and advice throughout the writing process.

I would like to thank Anne Allison, Leo Ching, and Hank Okazaki for inviting me to present an early version of Chapter Four at the 2005 "Martial Arts/Global Flows" conference at Duke University. Chapter Two was presented as an invitational lecture in Berkeley in 2007.

Completion of this manuscript was made possible by grants provided by the Berkeley Institute for East Asian Studies, Cornell Society for the Humanities, the Telluride Association, and Cornell University Hull Memorial Publication Fund.

Various friends and colleagues have assisted me in my research at the Center for the Study of Sexualities, the Center for the Study of Martial Arts Fiction, Academia Sinica, the National Central Library, and the Shanghai Municipal Library. I would also like to thank Chiu-Hua Chiang, Chu Yu-Li, Cui Zi'en, Kuan-Hsing Chen, Naifei Ding, Josephine Ho, Ruhong Lin, Huang Fushan, Hans Tao-Ming Huang,

Lin Baochun, Wah-Guan Lim, Liu Jen-peng, Jiazhen Ni, Amie Parry, and Wang Ping for their assistance.

I am grateful to my research assistants, Sue Besemer, Han Xin, Enajite Onos, Wu Xian, Aaron Hodges, Sean Connolly, Sheri Englund, and Shao Wenteng. Anthony Reed and Madeleine Casad read the entire manuscript and provided invaluable comments and editorial suggestions. I would like to thank the anonymous referees and my marvelous editor at Cornell East Asia Series, Mai Shaikhanuar-Cota, for their critical comments and guidance in the preparation of the final manuscript.

My family and friends supported me through the years in ways that no words of gratitude can describe: Jean Liu, Kevin Huang, Sandy Liu, Itzik Giat, Rebecca Giat, Sharon Giat, Mario Choi, Loan Dao, Bobby Diep, Alvin Hung, Stephen Lau, Brian Lin, Helen Lin, Manuel Gonzales, Amy Hsiao, Yenling Tsai, Pearl Tseng, and Tony Wu. My parents, Shyi-Huei Liu and Mei-Fang Lee, have been my first and best teachers of literature. This book is dedicated to them.

INTRODUCTION

STATELESS SUBJECTS

"If once upon a time a good harvest was the mark of a
good king, now it is the sustained raising of industrial
productivity which signified a sound regime."
—Gopal Balakrishnan, *Mapping the Nation*

The past decades have seen a broad transformation of China
studies into the new Sovietology.[1] In the international sphere, this
change has involved, in equal measure, frenzied media denunciations
of China's human rights violations, pollution, and military buildup—
and at the same time, popular, sensationalist images of mummies,
angels, and kung fu–fighting pandas. A culture of martial arts has
come to play a surprisingly important role in shaping China's global
identity, delineating the contours of its cultural influence, helping to
predict its political transformations, and suggesting ways to interpret
its historical formation as a nation-state. Far from being a trivial matter
of popular culture, Chinese martial arts are persistently linked—in the
imagination of academic critics, political gurus, business entrepre-
neurs, and social activists—to the master narratives of the twentieth
century: capitalism, colonialism, and globalization.

Above all, nationalism has emerged as the most common
explanatory paradigm for the study of Chinese martial arts film and
literature. Virtually every currently available scholarly work on martial
arts fiction connects the genre's historical rise, aesthetic conventions,
and popular appeal to the emotional freight of representing the
Chinese nation. For example, the first English-language monograph
on a twentieth-century Chinese martial arts novelist, Chris Hamm's

Paper Swordsmen: Jin Yong and the Modern Chinese Martial Arts Novel (2005), uses the status of Hong Kong as a British colony to explain the author's popular appeal to the masses, characterizing his martial arts novels as the embodiment of "a heroic and erotic nationalism." According to Hamm, Jin Yong's writings signify the increasing dominance of "an essentialized and celebratory Chinese cultural identity" over a "consciousness of loss and displacement," which serves as "a point of reference and token of continuity amidst the uncertainties of existence" for the citizens of Hong Kong.[2] Hamm points out that all of Jin Yong's novels were originally serialized in Hong Kong's newspapers before appearing in book form, and he argues on this basis that Jin Yong's martial arts fiction exemplifies Benedict Anderson's theory of "print-capitalism"—the ability of serialized fiction to create sentiments of diasporic nationalism by allowing readers who have never met each other to imagine themselves as members of a coherent national community: cultural China. In the final analysis, Hamm's explanation is a psychologizing one. His argument suggests that martial arts literature is a result of the colonial inferiority complex of the citizens of the British Crown Colony. The popularity of the genre is explained by its ideological persuasive-ness rather than its intellectual depth.

This common explanation of martial arts fiction as the ideological instrument of Chinese nationalism, however, has generated a bewildering array of contradictory conclusions. Recent martial arts films such as *Hero* (2002), *Kung Fu Hustle* (2004), *House of Flying Daggers* (2004), and *Crouching Tiger, Hidden Dragon* (2000) have led critics to characterize the genre as a paean to Chinese authoritarianism, a representation of diasporic consciousness, an apologia for Chinese unification, cultural resistance to Sinocentrism from the margins, an instrument of China's "kung fu diplomacy," an index of the exploitation of third-world labor by a Hollywood-centered, capitalist regime of "flexible production," or the reverse cultural colonization of America by Asia—an "Asian invasion of Hollywood."[3] While these interpretations contradict one another in their assessment of particular texts' relation to Chinese nationalism, they share one thing in common: the assumption that martial arts fiction is a by-product of China's colonial and postcolonial histories, and that therefore the economic and political organizations of China, Hong Kong, and Taiwan (semicolonial, postcolonial, capitalist, socialist, or postsocialist) should serve as the prevailing analytical framework for our interpretation of this literature.

Stateless Subjects: Chinese Martial Arts Literature and Post-colonial History is the first full-length English-language study of the literary genre of *wuxia xiaoshuo*.[4] It explores the forgotten history and aesthetics of a genre whose vital contributions to the development of modern Chinese culture have been suppressed and marginalized as merely popular entertainment. Traditional "state-centered" interpretations emphasize the problem of Chinese identity and the role of the nation-state in the production of the martial arts text. Far from signifying a singular attitude toward the Chinese nation, however, martial arts literature has demonstrated a remarkable ability to unify ideological opposites, an ability that is compounded with the genre's antisystemic, rhizomatous dispersion across many registers of social discourse. In the popular imaginary, martial arts are commonly associated with ideas of harmony, inner peace, Zen, meditation, alternative medicine, and respect for all sentient beings. They also suggest a human tendency toward aggression and bear an affinity with the realist or pragmatist school of political science that argues for the inevitability of conflict and violence in human civilization. It is also true that images of kung fu readily invoke traumatic memories of war, nationalism, banditry, and political chaos. The malleable nature of martial arts fiction allows it to be assimilated to political claims about the "Sick Man of Asia" and "China rising" with equal ease. Punitive readings emphasize China's degenerative tendency, citing martial arts as evidence that traditional thinking still holds sway in a country that stubbornly refuses to modernize and open its door to the West. Early twentieth-century Chinese intellectuals, such as Qu Qubai, characterized martial arts fiction as an escapist fantasy, "the dreams of flying swords and kung fu" that deflected the Chinese people's revolutionary consciousness and receptivity to Marxism.[5] Similarly, contemporary Chinese scholars such as Cao Zhengwen explain the rise of the martial arts novel in early twentieth-century China as psychological compensation for foreign imperialism, warlordism, and ineffectual government.[6] By contrast, triumphant accounts of the "East Asian Economic Miracle" discover in martial arts a presumably unique cultural ethic that is responsible for China's accelerated growth in the postsocialist period. Those who applaud the virtues of martial arts read the cinematic and literary depictions of a willingness to endure the trials and tribulations of "cruel training" as evidence for the existence of a "Confucian ethics" analogous to Weber's postulation of the Protestant spirit of capitalism, arguing that this cultural spirit of sheer determination and hard work has allowed a formerly third-world country to overwrite the historical laws of colonial subjugation to reemerge as the epicenter of global finance and industrial output—the international equivalent of the "model minority myth" in the U.S. domestic context.[7]

Just as the ideological message of martial arts literature is anything but unambiguously nationalist, its cast of characters encompasses a wide spectrum of social and class roles, ranging from monks with white eyebrows flying on magical carpets to hypermuscular ex-socialist athletes. Whereas the image of the emaciated peasant militia accompanies many a history textbook's representation of modern China as a backward nation torn by war, strife, and third-world underdevelopment, the martial Chinese body is also a recurring image in the media that exemplifies an exceptional racial form of muscular prowess, agility, uniformity, and numerical superiority, one that presages the decline of the West and the coming of the "Pacific Century."[8] The discursive spaces occupied by martial arts characters are just as likely to be ancient bamboo forests as the postmodern Olympic complexes of Beijing's Water Cube and Bird's Nest. What travels under the name of martial arts forms the kernel of a perplexing series of narratives from and about China. To write the political history of martial arts is to investigate these persistent images as vehicles for what we have alternately taken to be a hopelessly stagnant and archaic civilization and a spectacularly rising site of postmodern consumerism.

That the same genre—and often the same works—can animate

mutually contradictory views about China's relation to the world is one of the most curious features of martial arts aesthetics. I argue in this book that a persistent desire to read martial arts narratives as national allegories has prevented us from developing a historical account of precisely what is interesting and complex about these works. Specifically, no sustained account of twentieth-century martial arts literature *as literature*—that is, as a historically determinate discourse with a unique set of aesthetic conventions, philosophical basis, institutional history, and thematic coherence—has been forthcoming. The lack of critical attention to the aesthetics of martial arts narratives stems, no doubt, from a widespread perception of martial arts fiction as potboilers for mass culture consumption that have little to say about serious politics. This perception itself rests on the even more fundamental assumption that politics is always state politics, which is precisely what, I will argue, the martial arts novel as a modern literary movement sets out to challenge. If one aim of the present book is to produce a descriptive account of the distinctive aesthetic properties of the genre, another is to resituate this genre as an interventionist and progressive cultural movement in twentieth-century Chinese intellectual history that invented the most important model of *nonstatist* political responsibility.

Classical European theories of the state since Hobbes, Rousseau, Smith, Hegel, and Marx explain the state as the bureaucratic institution designed to resolve the problem of private property. These theorists are keenly aware of the fact that, left to themselves, "the people" would destroy themselves through the pursuit of individual gain. The modern state purports to represent the general will of the people but in reality constrains it. The theory of classical jurisprudence represents an advance over an earlier model of natural law theory, which casts the state as the formal expression of an abstract form of harmony that originally emanated from God, nature, or some other higher moral authority.

The Chinese martial arts novel represents a radically different political philosophy of the state. In this aesthetic tradition, the state is neither the arbiter of justice nor the sphere of moral constraints that prevents civil society from destroying itself through its own rapacity. On the contrary, the martial arts novel invents scenes of stateless subjects to explain the constitutive sociality of the self. Its discourse of *jianghu* (rivers and lakes) defines a public sphere unconnected to the sovereign power of the state, a sphere that is historically related to the idea of *minjian* (between the people) as opposed to the concept of *tianxia* (all under heaven) in Chinese philosophy. The martial arts novel presents the human subject as an ethical alterity, constituted by and dependent on its responsibilities to other human beings. It is through the recognition of this mutual interdependence, rather than the formal and positive laws of the state, that humanity manages to preserve itself despite rampant inequalities in privilege, rank, and status. As recounted by martial arts novels, the human subject is made and remade by forces that cannot be defined by positive laws of the state—rage, love, gender, morality, life and death. The formation of this stateless subject is incompatible with the liberal conception of an autonomous rights-bearing citizen.

Max Weber defined the state as the apparatus that monopolizes the legitimate use of violence. The Chinese martial arts novel shifts the arbiter of justice from the state to a special group of martial arts master idiomatically termed *xia*. This genre does not so much promote private use of violence as it opens up a nonstatist field of political considerations. Chinese martial arts novels dramatize scenarios of moral dilemmas beyond the purview of the nation-state and without recourse to its guarantees. The Chinese martial arts novel, in other words, can be seen as a thought experiment on this question: If we lived in a world where the meaning of politics were not reduced to the ballot-box, revolutions, fiscal crises, wars, and other trappings of governmentality, what would it mean to be a person of public responsibility? The fact that modern Chinese cultures produced such a thought experiment deserves a historical analysis, and the emergence of stateless literature in twentieth-century China provides a powerfully concrete counterexample to the widely accepted thesis that China's response to foreign imperialism has always been the establishment of a strong modern nation-state.[9]

The Martial Arts of China's Culture War

Certain critics use "martial arts fiction" to refer to both pre–twentieth-century and modern works.[10] We should note that late imperial works are called *xiayi* rather than *wuxia* fiction in Chinese and the two genres maintain different statuses in literary history.[11] Stimulating works on *xiayi* have been produced—David Wang, for example, has powerfully argued that *xiayi* is an expression of the true but "repressed" origins of modern Chinese culture.[12] There is much to gain, however, from a consideration of martial arts literature proper, the distinctiveness of its features, and its fate in modern China, and this move requires that we conceptually separate *wuxia* from its premodern predecessors.

Despite the global hypervisibility of martial arts cinema, no systematic study of this visual culture's literary basis in Chinese fiction is available in English. *Wuxia xiaoshuo*, the literary tradition that gave rise to these cultural images and political paradoxes of martial arts, is a novelistic genre unique to Chinese literature that has no satisfactory translation in English.[13] Known in the West primarily through poorly subtitled films, Chinese martial arts fiction is one of the most iconic and yet the most understudied forms of modern sinophone creativity. Current scholarship on the subject is characterized by three central assumptions that I argue against in this book: first, that martial arts fiction is the representation of a bodily spectacle that historically originated in Hong Kong cinema; second, that the genre came into being as an escapist fantasy that provided psychological comfort to the Chinese people during the height of imperialism;[14] and third, that martial arts fiction reflects a patriotic attitude that celebrates the greatness of Chinese culture, which in turn is variously described as the China-complex, colonial modernity, essentialized identity, diasporic consciousness, anxieties about globalization, or other psychological difficulties experienced by the Chinese people during modernization. Contrary to these perceptions, *Stateless Subjects* re-interprets martial arts literature as a progressive intellectual critique of modernization theory. I will strive to demonstrate that martial arts culture was first invented as a poetic relation between words rather than a visual relation between bodies. Not only did the historical rise of martial arts literature predate the rise of martial arts cinema but the culture of martial arts, even in its cinematic incarnations and adaptations, is explicitly concerned with *literariness*, the question of what makes literature distinct from other types of discourses.[15] Over and against commonly accepted interpretations of martial arts fiction as an apolitical form of escapist fantasy, this book presents it as a mode of intellectual intervention that has shaped the course of modern Chinese history.

The historical reason for the genre's exclusion from the Chinese canon lies precisely in its distance from and incompatibility with Chinese nationalism, which since the Qing dynasty has been a campaign to reform literature with criteria derived from European experiences of modernity.[16] The expansion of modernization discourse into the sphere of literary production in the May Fourth period had rendered alternative (nonmodernization-based) philosophical and literary discourses illegitimate, and martial arts fiction, which has resisted Western models of instrumental reason and rational bureaucracy, was quickly branded as the feudal ideology of "Old China," an obstacle that must be eradicated from the field of cultural production. While May Fourth intellectuals advocated Western thought as the basis for rapid modernization, martial arts novelists continued to draw upon China's indigenous intellectual sources— Taoism, Buddhism, Confucianism, and premodern literary models such as linked-chapter fiction. The martial arts novel in Chinese is renowned for the density of its classical poetic devices, historical allusions, philosophical precepts, and sophisticated plots. Indeed, the martial arts novel is the only genre in modern Chinese literature to be written in a semiclassical language after the early twentieth century, when the spoken vernacular Chinese (*baihua*) replaced Classical Chinese (*wenyan*) as the official language of literary communication.[17] Unlike the "universal language" of cinema, the semiclassical language of the martial arts novel is in fact inaccessible to the masses—a fact that bedeviled early twentieth-century Chinese revolutionaries' attempts to frame the genre as merely "popular fiction."[18] Viewing the difficulty of the Chinese language as the cause of mass illiteracy, Chinese intellectuals after May Fourth movement systematically advocated the Europeanization of Chinese syntax or even the replacement of Chinese characters with Romanizations as a recipe for rapid modernization. As a result, martial arts novelists were quickly demonized as "traditionalists" who were holding China back from economic and military modernization. In lieu of martial arts fiction, Chinese reformers sought to create a "New Fiction" (*xin wenxue*) that could bridge the educational gap between the literary elite and the common masses. For Hu Shi, Chen Duxiu, and Mao Dun, the explosive growth, commercial successes, cultural influence, and greater number of martial arts novels posed a threat to the modernization project undertaken by New Fiction. The chief strategy adopted in the May Fourth crusade against martial arts fiction was to collapse the genre with "mandarin ducks and butterflies" (*yuanyang hudie pai*) fiction, stories about love published in *Saturday* and other less respected venues.

The label of popular fiction was nonetheless strictly a May Fourth construction. Before the rise of modernization discourse and developmental thinking in China, martial arts narratives were not seen as popular or even middle-brow fiction, but part of China's high literary canon. The culture of martial arts has always been a normative and privileged theme in Chinese literature. In this light, it was perfectly natural for twentieth-century authors to continue developing this theme and capitalize on what had always been understood as a cultural achievement in Chinese letters. As indicated by James Liu's important and massive 1967 study, *The Chinese Knight-Errant*, the philosophy of martial arts has permeated and dominated virtually every form of premodern Chinese literature for over two thousand years: philosophical treatises, *shi* and *ci* poetry, dynastic histories, *zawen* ("miscellaneous writings"), songs, Tang *chuanqi* (legends), Ming drama, and prose fiction.[19] Indeed, two of the so-called Four Great Classical Novels of Chinese Literature (*sida qishu*) are explicit representations of the culture of martial arts: *Water Margin* and *Romance of the Three Kingdoms*, and despite being proto-martial arts novels, the two fourteenth-century classics have never been relegated to the status of popular fiction.

We can see that what May Fourth reformers objected to was not martial arts narratives *as such*, but the existence of such narratives in the twentieth century. Both Mao Zedong and Lu Xun wrote approvingly of premodern narratives of outlaws and martial valor, which they considered to be an expression of the people's heroic struggles against feudal values, while accusing the modern descendants of the same works of corrupting the minds of the Chinese masses and blocking their revolutionary consciousness.[20] After 1932, martial arts film was banned in China. Martial arts fiction was banned by both the Communist Party in China and the Nationalist government in Taiwan after 1949. In post-1949 mainland China, members of the League of Leftist Writers assumed leading positions in the PRC's cultural bureaucracy and published literary histories that canonized (socialist) realism as "modern Chinese literature." Nonrealist trends in early twentieth-century China, such as martial arts fiction, were removed from literary history.[21] The story of modern Chinese literature and Chinese modernity was subsequently told as a unilinear movement toward realism and Europeanized syntax, a feat accomplished through the translations, introductions, and appropriations of Western thought.[22] With the decline and censorship of the genre on the mainland, Hong Kong became the new center for martial arts film and literature after 1949, although Taiwan also produced a significant number of talented and prolific authors despite censorship. The literary historian Lin Baochun actually considers the early period under martial law (1961–1970) to be Taiwan's "golden age of martial arts literature."[23]

One of the most salient characteristics of the martial arts novel is its length. The extraordinary number of *wuxia* works across the twentieth-century makes the genre an unprecedented phenomenon in Chinese literary history. By a conservative count, more than two hundred major novels in the Republican period were published as *wuxia xiaoshuo*, usually of extraordinary length—Huanzhu Louzhu's entire corpus consists of no less than an astronomical 10,000,000 words, thirty times the length of Proust's *Swann's Way*.[24] His unfinished magnum opus, *Shushan jianxia zhuan* (Swordsmen from the Shu Mountains), was serialized in the newspaper *Tianfeng Bao* over a span of seventeen years (1932 to 1949), and the project was aborted only because of the Communist Revolution in 1949. The extant chapters of *Shushan jianxia zhuan* were later published in book form in fifty-five separate volumes, with 329 chapters chronicling the rise and fall of more than a thousand different fictional characters.[25] By the end of 1949, at least 170 major authors had published *wuxia* stories in different periodicals.[26] The most prolific martial arts novelist, Zheng Zhengyin, published 102 different titles. Huanzhu Louzhu has thirty-six works to his name, while Gu Mingdao and Wang Dulu each wrote more than twenty novels before they were forced to abandon their craft under the new government.

Martial arts texts' concern with literariness is foregrounded by the recurring motif of the "Secret Scripture" (*miji*). A standard formula in *wuxia* films and novels, the Secret Scripture is a lost or carefully guarded ancient text that endows its owner with superhuman combat abilities; the competition or quest for this book forms the main plot of many *wuxia* stories. Significantly, the Secret Scripture is not a training manual with pictorial illustrations of martial moves, but a verbal text written in Classical Chinese (or sometimes in Sanskrit). The Secret Scripture contains instructions that guide the protagonist through a series of inner or spiritual transformations, which is, however, possible only if the protagonist is literate—that is, if the character has access to what in the real world would be termed the educational capital of the dominant class. The narrative tradition of the Secret Scripture is the subject of Stephen Chow's critically acclaimed 2004 parody of the genre, *Kung Fu Hustle*, in which Yuen Wooping (Yuan Heping), the legendary action cinema choreographer behind *Matrix* and *Kill Bill*, plays the character of a beggar who sells "fake" manuals that turn out to be real Secret Scriptures for the protagonist, played by Stephen Chow himself. The inside joke for those who recognize Yuen is that the action choreographer is the creator of fantastic martial arts, while the wirework, trampolines, and computer-generated images are the real Secret Scriptures. The joke draws its comedic power from a local knowledge of the genre's tendency to reference textual artifacts.[27] Accordingly, the protagonist of the stories is almost always a scholar rather than a fighter.[28] This choice of protagonist is, of course, consistent with the genre's advocacy of book learning as the source of martial power.

Wuxia is a self-consciously literary discourse that draws attention to the aesthetic properties of language. Its aim is to translate classical Chinese literary and cosmological concepts into a large corpus of easily quotable, memorable phrases. These *wuxia* phrases have by now become endemic in speech situations unrelated to martial arts, such as "*shenhuai jueji*" (a skilled but self-effacing person), "*yitong jianghu*" (unify the nation), "*jinpen xishou*" (close one's business), and "*tuichu jianghu*" (retire from politics). These elegant phrases are composed of four Chinese characters chosen according to classical rules for syntactical and tonal parallelisms. Martial arts novels have also created a battery of less poetic, but still archaic-sounding, idioms in modern Chinese. "*Shiba ban wuyi juquan*," an expression that originally refers to the mastery of all "eighteen types of martial arts and weapons," is now commonly used as a compliment on a person's versatility and resourcefulness in cooking, schoolwork, or professional development. The martial technique unique to the Murong family in Jin Yong's *Tianlong Babu*, "*yi bi zhi dao, huan zhi qi shen*," has become a Chinese expression for "an eye for eye." The standard formula for the exchange of pleasantries, greetings, or declarations of combat in martial arts dialogues have also been integrated into contemporary Chinese. "*Mingnian de jintian jiushi ni de jiri*" (exactly one year from today will be the anniversary of your death) is a convoluted way of predicting an opponent's doom that is parodied over and over again in contemporary novels, advertisements, magazines, and TV shows. "*Houhui youqi*" (a date has been selected by heaven for our next meeting in this life) has become a facetious way of saying goodbye in the Chinese language. The widespread use of martial arts phrases out of context in modern Chinese testifies to the affinity between martial arts and language.

The martial arts novel's motifs have also had a discernible impact on modern Chinese language. *Zhaoshi*, martial "stances" or "techniques," are commonly used to refer to mahjong games, political campaign strategies, and tips for students at cram schools. Commercial presses publish study guides and try to sell study guides to students by referring to them as "*miji*" (Secret Scriptures). In the media, Jin Yong's and Gu Long's characters are frequently used as shorthand for the archetypes of politicians: "Yue Buqun" (from Jin Yong's *State of Divinity*) is a twofaced, backstabbing weasel who pretends to be a Confucian gentleman. "Zuo Lengchan" is a politician who prefers brute, naked domination and often fails in the end. "Heibai Langjun" is somebody who finds joy in others' failure, *Schadenfreude*. Martial arts culture has become a significant element of Chinese cultural semiotics beyond the confines of film and consumer culture.

China's Homeric Epic

Since the 1990s, the martial arts novel has undergone a significant reversal of fortune in the opinion of Chinese critics and cultural authorities.[29] Doctoral dissertations on the topic mushroomed across Chinese universities; research centers, archives, and international conferences have come into being. The study of the best-selling martial arts novelist, Jin Yong, is now a newly baptized subbranch of academic studies—"Jin-ology" (*jinxue*)—in a manner analogous to *hongxue*, the dedicated specialization in the study of *Hongloumeng* (Dream of the Red Chamber), or to Shakespeare Studies in the West.[30] A full series devoted to Jin-ology has appeared from Yuanliu Press, which includes both monographs on Jin Yong's individual works and global exegeses of his philosophy, worldview, and stylistics. An asteroid was named after Jin Yong, and the martial arts novelist was the first living person in China to be honored by a bronze statue—a two-million-yuan structure erected on an island in his birth province, Zhejiang.[31] Jin Yong is currently the best-selling living Chinese author, with an official record of 300 million copies sold, and untold numbers of bootleg copies. Jin Yong has been nominated for the Nobel Prize. Excerpts of his novels are now included in the official textbooks in secondary education in mainland China. In 1994, an authoritative new history of modern Chinese literature written by professors in Beijing identified Jin Yong as China's fourth greatest author (after Lu Xun, Shen Congwen, and

Ba Jin).[32] Of the four "masters" of modern Chinese literature recognized by critics in Beijing, Jin Yong is not only the sole living author from the post-1949 period, but also the only "Hong Kong" author. The fin-de-siècle canonization of Jin Yong is a testament to the exceptional cultural power of *wuxia*, which is even more striking when we consider the limited (by *wuxia* standards) number of Jin Yong's works. Jin Yong has written only fifteen martial arts novels in his life, although they have spawned endless remakes in the media since the 1970s. Every year there is a new television series based on one of his novels. As with Jane Austen's legacy in the Anglophone world—only six novels to work with, but the movies never quit coming—Jin Yong's works offer an emotional richness that seems inexhaustible, a vitality that continues to speak to men and women of the twenty-first century, decades after the original stories were conceived and published.

The "Jin Yong phenomenon," as critics are now calling it, signifies more than an emerging literary canon or merely changing conditions of literary evaluation. Comprehended historically, the rise of martial arts studies has profound implications for postcolonial studies and our understanding of what constitutes a colonial situation. While a previous generation of scholars tended to understand colonialism in a more literal sense as territorial occupation, we are now much more aware of colonialism's discursive workings in the production of identities and subject positions. Newer postcolonial theory has taught us to recognize the ways in which colonialism reproduces itself as the anticolonial nationalist elite's attitude toward their own past. As the subaltern studies scholar Partha Chatterjee argues, the dominant West not only colonizes non-Western peoples and territories, but their imagination as well.[33] Martial arts literature provides an opportunity for us to reevaluate the assumption, promulgated since the May Fourth period, that Chinese modernity could only be attained through the negation and destruction of its own traditions. Martial arts literature challenges our conventional sense that literary modernity belonged to those "iconoclasts" who promoted the Europeanization of the Chinese language. The submerged political history of martial arts literature reveals one of the modes in which a desire for the West and its rationalism colonized Chinese intellectuals' consciousness in their self-appointed roles as saviors of the nation. For Liu Zaifu, Jin Yong's achievements and the reasons for his newfound canonicity reside precisely in his ability to develop an "anti-Europeanized Chinese writing" against the May Fourth enlightenment ideology and Europeanized sentence structures, and Jin Yong's writing has succeeded in preserving China's "accumulated cultural treasures."[34] Li Tuo takes the argument further to suggest that Jin Yong has invented a new vernacular that is *sui generis*, distinct from both the Europeanized syntax of modern Chinese and traditional vernacular Chinese, where the inventiveness of Jin Yong's language provides the most vital resistance to the ossification of literary creativity between May Fourth and the rise of "Maoist discourse" (*Mao wenti*) during the Cultural Revolution era.[35] Wang Ban's view summarizes the significance of the Jin Yong phenomenon: "From this literary lineage, Jin Yong's work arose as a challenge to this lopsided view that China could only become modern by discarding traditional culture."[36] In a pioneering book, Song Weijie argues that martial arts novels serve as the repository of what Paul Ricoeur, Richard Dyer, and Fredric Jameson have called "the Utopian impulse" of society: the collective desire for a classless society that the development of capitalism fails to suppress.[37] Building on these views, I argue in this book that martial arts literature offers an important form of subaltern resistance to the logic of internalized colonialism. If what made the martial arts novel aesthetically disreputable half a century ago is also what makes it a privileged object of cultural studies today, we have in this genre a unique opportunity to understand the lost organicity of Chinese culture before the bureaucratic rationalization of modernity. The mythical time of the *wuxia* imaginary belongs to the time of pre-capital; it constitutes an idealized space in which the subject and the object of social life are still unified before their fragmentation by the advent of capitalist modernity. What was once considered the result of an infectious, commodified mass culture is today China's Homeric epic.[38]

What difference, then, does it make when we cease to view this form of literature as the stuff of cheaply produced B-list midnight movies and the window on the colonial psyche of the Chinese people, and instead begin to view it as a serious mode of social thought, as an intellectual resource of importance for contemporary theory and cultural practice from which all global citizens have something to learn? Inspired by Guattari and Deleuze's notion of "minor literature," Meaghan Morris characterizes martial arts film as "minor cinema" that serves as a critical pedagogical tool in the classroom for the study of class consciousness.[39] While "major cinema" is "global" (difference-denying), "minor cinema" is "transnational" (community-building).[40] For Morris, martial arts cinema is a historical example of how a minor cinema from a distant culture (Hong Kong) can reshape world culture through the preservation of spaces that are rapidly disappearing—urban slums, motels, buses, factories, and other "any-space-whatever" filled with distressed futures and chronic dereliction and loss—against the apocalyptic, spectacular, U.S. patriotic ("saving the world") or global folkloric design of Hollywood's big-budget major cinema. Similarly, Vijay Prashad observes in an important book on Afro-Asian connections that, historically, martial arts culture has produced political solidarity and interracial cross-identification between oppressed peoples across the globe—a strange "alliance between the Red Guard and the Black Panthers" from the Cultural Revolution in China to the Civil Rights movement in the States—that is otherwise unthinkable.[41] What Prashad cleverly terms "Kung Fusion" indicates a form of "polycultural" communication that is distinct from the multi-culturalist celebration of diversity (similar to Morris's distinction between the transnational and the global). Amy Abugo Ongiri argues that by recognizing the historical role played by kung fu visual icons in the formation of a Black aesthetic that she calls "spectacular Blackness," and by recognizing the interconnections and dialogues between Asians and African Americans, we can refuse America's racial ideological landscape that constructs these communities as polar opposites in debates surrounding affirmative action and the model minority myth.[42] These are only a few examples of critical uses of the lessons of martial arts today. The boundless political possibilities of critical martial arts are something we are only beginning to imagine now.

NOTES

1. Bruce Cumings describes the end of the Cold War and the collapse of Western communism as a crisis of political management for the American university-state intelligence-foundation nexus: "Lacking a clear enemy and worried about their budgets, forces within the [Clinton administration] national security state sought to reposition China as another Soviet Union requiring 'containment.'" *Parallax Visions*, 178–179.

2. Hamm, *Paper Swordsmen: Jin Yong and the Modern Chinese Martial Arts Novel*, 79.

3. See Robert Eng, "Is HERO a Paean to Authoritarianism?" for an analysis of the relation between Zhang's film and Chinese nationalism. John Eperjesi argues in "*Crouching Tiger, Hidden Dragon*: Kung Fu Diplomacy and the Dream of Cultural China" that "kung fu" has taken the place of "pandas" as tokens of culture in maintaining peaceful Sino-American relations. Eperjesi believes that martial arts film allows the Chinese diaspora to imagine themselves as members of a "cultural China," a thesis that is similar to Chris Hamm's interpretation of the ideological role of Jin Yong's serialized novels. Both Tina Klein's and Sheldon Lu's works pay special attention to the material conditions of the production of martial arts films, which are often financed by major U.S. companies but shot on sites with abundant cheap labor, such as China. Both Sheldon Lu in his "Crouching Tiger, Hidden Dragon, Bouncing Angels" and Minh-Ha T. Pham in "The Asian Invasion in Hollywood" see the rise of martial arts cinema as "the end of national cinema" in film theory and history.

4. The phrase *wuxia xiaoshuo* first entered the Chinese language in 1915, in a magazine called *Xiaoshuo daguan*. The first *wuxia* story, "Fumeishi," was written by the famous translator and scholar Lin Shu in Classical Chinese, although the full-length *wuxia* novels were written in Modern Chinese. Chinese scholars call the *wuxia* novels written on the Mainland during the Republican period (1912–1949) "*jiu pai*," Old School martial arts novels, in contrast to works by the "*xin pai*," New School luminaries in postwar Hong Kong and Taiwan. The major Old School authors are Pingjiang Buxiaosheng (born Xiang Kairan, 1890–1957), Zhao Huanting (1877–1951), Gu Mingdao (1897–1944), Wang Dulu (Wang Baoxiang, 1909–1977), and Huanzhu Louzhu (Li Shoumin, 1902–1961). The New School is spearheaded by Wolongsheng (Niu Heting, 1930–1997), Sima Ling (Wu Siming, 1933–1989), Zhuge Qingyun (Zhang Jianxin, 1929–1996), Jin Yong (Zha Liangyong or Louis Cha, 1924–), Gu Long (Xiong Yiaohua, 1936–1985), and Liang Yusheng (Chen Wentong, 1926–).

5. Qu Qiubai, "Jihede de shidai" (The era of Don Quixote).

6. Cao Zhengwen, 99–100.

7. Tu, Weiming, *Confucian Ethics Today*.

8. The relation between Asian American racialization in the domestic context and American ascendancy in the Asia Pacific has been brilliantly explored by Colleen Lye. "[T]he domestic signification of Asian Americans [as capable of upward mobility without the aid of state-engineered correctives] has its counterpart in the global signification of Asia. While the new visibility of an Asian-American middle class was being used to support a neoconservative-led 'retreat from race' in domestic public policy, the expanding economies of the newly industrialized countries of East Asia— the 'Asian Tigers'—were being heralded by free market critics of import-substitution as evidence of the conceptual and political 'end of the Third World.'" *America's Asia*, 2–3.

9. For a historical study of China's responses to Western encroachments as a series of state, nation, and party building projects, see Fitzgerald, *Awakening China*.

10. For an example of a work that considers late imperial works (such as *Three Knights and Five Gallants*) as martial arts fiction, see Paize Keulemans's excellent *Sounds of the Novel*.

11. Leo Lee and Perry Link point out that another key difference was that *xiayi* fiction often depended on public performances such as operas and local storytellers for their transmission, while *wuxia* novels were from their inception inseparable from the rise of the modern information structure. "The Beginnings of Mass Culture," 360–395.

12. David Wang, *Fin-de-siècle Splendor*, 117–182.

13. "The martial arts novel" is the preferred translation used in this book. Other critics have used names such as Chinese knight-errant fiction, Chinese gallant fiction, tales of swords and chivalry, fiction of swordplay, among others.

14. Several histories of martial arts literature published in the late 1980s and 1990s popularized the interpretation of the rise of martial arts literature as a wish-fulfillment for a colonial need for pleasure and escape. These include Cao Zhengwen's *Zhongguo xia wenhua shi*, Ye Hongsheng's "Zhongguo wuxia xiaoshuo shi lun," Luo Liqun's *Zhongguo wuxia xiaoshuo shi*, Chen Pingyuan's *Qiangu wenren xiake meng*, and Wang Hailin's *Zhongguo wuxia xiaoshuo shi lüe* (1988). These scholars maintain that, since the late nineteenth century, China was ravaged by imperialist countries and plagued by a corrupt, ineffectual Qing court. As the traditional distinction between good and evil afforded by Confucian and Buddhist cosmologies collapsed, people

formed collective fantasies about martial heroes and hoped they would mend the ills of society. As Cao put it, martial arts fiction was created to serve a nostalgic, compensatory, and escapist function under colonialism. They characterize the genre as "adult fairy tale" (*chengren tonghua*), "utopian impulse" (*wutuobang chongdong*), "popular fiction" (*dazhong wenhua, tongsu wenhua*), and "mass entertainment" (*yule meijie*).

15. For a definition of literature as self-conscious artifacts that call attention to the workings of language ("literariness"), see Jonathan Culler, *The Pursuit of Signs*.

16. See, for example, Edmund Fung, *The Intellectual Foundations of Chinese Modernity*, esp. 37–45.

17. For technical analyses, see Ed Gunn, *Rewriting Chinese*. For intellectual and social backgrounds, see Chow Tse-tsung, *The May Fourth Movement*, esp. 277–278. For a historical investigation of the international factors that produced the "problem" of the Chinese script (such as Soviet influence and Japan's *genbun itchi* movement), see John DeFrancis, *Nationalism and Language Reform in China*.

18. See Perry Link, "Traditional-Style Popular Urban Fiction" and *Mandarin Ducks and Butterflies: Popular Fiction in Early Twentieth Century Chinese Cities*.

19. See James Liu, *The Chinese Knight-Errant*.

20. Lu Xun, *Zhongguo xiaoshuo lun* (A History of the Chinese Novel).

21. See Catherine Vance Yeh, "Root Literature of the 1980s: May Fourth as a Double Burden," 246–248.

22. Against the scholarly tendency to read May Fourth translations of Western thought as a reactive formation, Lydia Liu has powerfully reinterpreted Chinese modernity as "co-authorship," emphasizing modernity's complex and overdetermined routes of cross-cultural dissemination and reinventions. See *Translingual Practice*.

23. Lin Baochun, *Taiwan wuxia xiaoshuo fazhan shi* (The development of martial arts fiction in Taiwan).

24. See Cao, Zhengwen, *Xia wenhua* (The culture of *xia*), 103–105; and Hu, Zhongquan, *Wuxia xiaoshuo yanjiu cankao ziliao* (Research materials on *wuxia xiaoshuo*), 15–24.

25. For a detailed discussion of the genealogy of the characters and their differential representations of Taoist, Buddhist, and Confucian strands of thought, see Ye Hongsheng, *Shushan jianxia pinglun* (Commentary on *Shushan jianxia*), 1–27.

26. Cao, Zhengwen, Ibid., 104.

27. On the distinctively local structure of address that is responsible for the

film's success, see S.V. Srinivas, "Kung Fu Hustle: A Note on the Local."

28. Jin Yong's *Divine Eagle, Gallant Knight*, for example, argues that the culture of *wuxia* expresses the unity of *wen* (letters) and *wu* (might): "Literature and martial arts are different means that serve the same aim" (Vol. II, 21).

29. For an analysis of the canonization of martial arts fiction as China's "new cultural revolution," see Yan Jiayan, *Shiji de zuyin*, 185–189.

30. The phrase "Jinxue yanjiu" was first invented by Shen Deng'en. See Chen Shuo, *Jingdian zhizao*, 82.

31. *China Daily* (April 11, 2005).

32. Wang Yichuan, *Ershi shiji Zhongguo wenxue dashi wenku, xiaoshuo juan* (Twentieth-century Chinese literature: The novel).

33. Partha Chatterjee, *The Nation and Its Fragments: Colonial and Postcolonial Histories*, 6.

34. Liu Zaifu, "Jin Yong and Twentieth-century Chinese Literature," 36.

35. Li Tuo, "The Language of Jin Yong's Writing: A New Direction in the Development of Modern Chinese."

36. Wang Ban, "Forward," xi.

37. Song Weijie, *Cong yule xingwei dao wutuobang chongdong*.

38. My analysis of martial arts literature and social fragmentation parallels Lukács's interpretation capitalism as the atomization of the organic totality of humanity in *History and Class Consciousness*. While Lukács identifies a dichotomy between two historically successive artistic forms—the Greek epic, which has neither a beginning nor an end, and the novel, whose formal features allow for the representation of the bourgeois individual—my analysis engages two contemporaneous narrative forms in a colonial context.

39. See also her "Learning from Bruce Lee: Pedagogy and Political Correctness in Martial Arts Cinema."

40. Morris, "Transnational Imagination in Action Cinema: Hong Kong and the Making of a Global Popular Culture," 190.

41. Vijay Prashad, *Everybody was Kung Fu Fighting: Afro-Asian Connections and the Myth of Cultural Purity*.

42. Amy Ongiri, "He Wanted to Be Just Like Bruce Lee: African Americans, Kung Fu Theater and Cultural Exchange at the Margins." For another illuminating analysis of the connection, see Gina Marchetti, "Jackie Chan and the Black Connection."

Chapter 1

THE VICISSITUDES OF ANTICOLONIAL NATIONALISM

"The Way (*dao*) that can be spoken (*dao*-ed) is not constant Way (*dao*)."

—*Lao Zi*

Hearing the term "martial arts fiction" today, one often assumes that it refers to a cinematic rather than literary genre. If such a thing as a "martial arts novel" exists in Chinese, one assumes it must be an effort to capture in written words the spectacles and actions one sees on the screen. Film is understood to be the natural and original medium for the construction of the martial arts imaginary, whereas literature is seen as derivative and secondary. As Leon Hunt puts it in a widely read study, "The kung fu film can be seen as what Steven Shaviro (1993) and Linda Williams (1995) call a 'body genre' ... alongside pornography, horror and the 'weepie' ... Kung fu is a genre of bodies; extraordinary, expressive, spectacular, sometimes even grotesque bodies."[1]

The claim that the "kung fu craze" was created by film is, nonetheless, an anachronism. Historically, the rise of martial arts fiction predates martial arts cinema. Today's visual culture of martial arts—motion pictures, graphic novels, comic books, and video games—arose as a historical consequence of the influence of martial arts literature. More important, the Chinese understand *wuxia* primarily as a function of language instead of a bodily practice. Before the appearance of martial arts films in the 1920s, the *xiayi* novels from

21

the Qing dynasty had already created a distinctive and idiomatic representational apparatus to help its readers imagine the fantastic martial arts that were only later seen in movies. Long before martial arts cinema, the Qing novel *Three Heroes and Five Gallants*, for example, already contained detailed descriptions of fantastic skills such as lightness kungfu, concealed weapons, and nerve attack that would later become the staple of modern *wuxia*.

The common perception of the martial arts aesthetic as a visual fantasy about bodies is intimately connected to another assumption—that the genre reflects a nationalist fantasy. According to this view, the martial arts genre projects onto the screen a powerful Asian hero whose superhuman, spectacular body denies the technological superiority of the West. This projection allows the genre to function as an ideological fantasy that compensates for the real and historical oppression of racial minorities. Martial arts fiction is here understood in terms of what I call the "inversion-thesis": the ideological inversion of colonial reality that allows a primitive visual fantasy to provide mass entertainment and psychological comfort to the defeated.

The inversion-thesis has become the standard argument in all Chinese-language histories of the genre. The current perception of martial arts fiction as the political ideology of anticolonial nationalism originates from an early twentieth-century Chinese view of the genre as the "opium of the people" that prevented the feudal-minded, common masses from accepting Marxism and taking arms against landlords and foreign imperialists.[2] Early Chinese Marxist intellectuals explained the rise of the genre by claiming that feudalism and imperialism created the psychological need and longing for a "superman-like deus ex machina" (*xiaoren yiyang de xiake chu lai*) to "alleviate their feelings of despair and hopelessness."[3] Most contemporary Chinese scholars of the genre hold this view. The most famous nickname for martial arts fiction in Chinese is "adult fairytale," a term invented by the mathematician Hua Luogeng. Cao Zhengwen, in one of the earliest historical studies of martial arts fiction, argues that the genre emerged as the result of an "objective" factor and a "subjective" factor. The "objective" factor was that "the late Qing government was corrupt and weakened, and the nation was on the verge of disintegration after the war with the Eight-Nation Alliance." In the face of a weakened state, "the people rose to defend their own nation," and "ordinary men and women, dissatisfied with a corrupt government, placed their hope on an imaginary class of martial heroes." Cao's "subjective" factor was that during this time, editors of commercial newspapers saw a golden opportunity in this climate and exploited it to their fullest advantage by specializing in serialized martial arts stories.[4] Ye Hongsheng, a well-respected editor and cultural critic in Taiwan, states a similar view in another historical study. Writing specifically on Pingjiang Buxiaosheng (whose work I address in this chapter), Ye proposes that martial arts literature contains four distinctive characteristics. One is the "emphasis on the moral integrity of the [Chinese] ethnos, the spirit of chivalry, and the shame brought by the name of the 'Sick Men of Asia'; [Pingjiang's work] empowers the Chinese race and inspires the people to strengthen their bodies, strengthen their genes, and strengthen their nation (*qiangshen, qiangzhong, qiangguo*)." Another characteristic is the "opposition between old thought and new thought at the end of the Qing dynasty, a time of chaos. Pingjiang possessed a unique insight into the cultural psychology of the 'anti-foreign' group and the 'pro-foreign' group alike. Pingjiang was not merely a novelist, but a shrewd social historian as well."[5] Beijing University Professor Chen Pingyuan emphasizes the commercial character of martial arts fiction:

> As a form of popular culture, martial arts fiction rose to fulfill the needs of an urban bourgeoisie for pleasure and entertainment. No wonder, the historical centers for the production of this type of fiction, in order of importance, were Shanghai, Tianjing, Hong Kong and Taipei, namely the cities in which commerce was more developed. To the urban readers who were under-educated and therefore lacking in the ability to appreciate real, refined arts, martial arts fiction was particularly attractive.[6]

Hunt, Cao, Chen, and Ye represent four divergent approaches to martial arts literature that nonetheless agree on the idea that the genre arises as an ideological distortion that appeals to a collective inferiority complex in the time of Western imperialism. More nuanced is Lingnan University's Siu-Leung Li's work, which characterizes the martial arts genre as a dialectical struggle with the consequences of industrialization. Li suggests that the martial arts genre "envisions a contest between tradition and modernity with a self-denial of modernity caught in a liminal temporal space imagined somewhere in modern history" so that the genre can "reimagine the myth of kung fu as all powerful and yet at once self-reflexively point to the uselessness of kung fu in the modern era of Western firearms."[7] Although attentive to the dialectical difference between power and powerlessness in this imaginary, Li's analysis nevertheless conveys the impression that, since martial arts became a technologically obsolete form of combat after the advent of mechanized warfare, the continuous thematization and invocation of such arts in Chinese culture must be a compensatory and escapist narrative. Whether martial arts fiction is read psychoanalytically as a figure of hope, suture, or lack; ideologically as a *point de caption*; or sociologically as mass entertainment, the dominant interpretations emphasize the *unreal* or fantasized dimension of this genre, seeing it as a simplistic, low-brow entertainment that temporarily restores pride and relief to the oppressed and must be explained in psychological or ideological terms as a form of *false* consciousness.

From the perspective of the inversion-thesis, the term "martial arts fiction" most commonly conjures the image of a hero who uses his unarmed body to defend China's honor by defeating foreign champions from China's technologically advanced invaders— Germany, Russia, Japan, and the United States. The most iconic version of this scene is, needless to say, Bruce Lee's *Fist of Fury* (also known as *The Chinese Connection*, directed by Lo Wei in 1972). In the film, Lee's character, Chen Zhen, fights a horde of Japanese students in their dojo after the Japanese insult Chen and his master, Huo Yuanjia, with a tablet that decries the Chinese as the "Sick Men of Asia."[8] Set in early twentieth-century Shanghai International Settlement, Bruce

Lee's character then wanders to the Huangpu Park and is denied entry by the guard, who points to the sign, "No dogs and Chinese allowed," which Chen Zhen quickly smashes with a flying kick.

Other Bruce Lee films are similarly concerned with the theme of minority empowerment in the face of foreign oppression, casting the star as the defender of diasporic Chinese in Thailand (*The Big Boss*, 1971) and Italy (*Way of the Dragon*, 1972). A uniquely successful Asian male movie star in 1970s America, Bruce Lee rose to fame in a prejudicial film industry that was not only marked by a conspicuous absence of male Asian celebrities, but burdened by an entrenched perception of Asian men as emasculated.[9] Bruce Lee's own brilliant, short-lived, and much mythologized career took off during the transition era in the United States from official exclusion to cultural assimilation of Asian immigrants and influences.[10] Consequently, Lee's personal life served as a real-life success story that mimics the idea of minority self-empowerment that he portrays in his films.[11] The model minority myth is mutually reinforced by Bruce Lee and his fictional characters. So emblazoned in the popular consciousness, the phenomenon seems to be inextricably tethered to a contradiction between the reality of racial oppression and the ideological fantasy of nationalism.

The history of Hong Kong cinema is full of examples that can easily be mobilized to illustrate these standard explanations. Chang Cheh's 1972 *Boxer from Shantung* depicts a low-class manual laborer suffering from the problem of social invisibility. He rises to the status of fame and social respectability after defeating a Russian boxing champion, physically twice his size, to the sound of cheers from his fellow countrymen. Donnie Yen's *Ip Man* (2008) is a semifictional story of Bruce Lee's teacher, a Chinese coolie during the Sino-Japanese War. Ip competes in an arena with Japanese karate masters and defeats ten of them effortlessly in a single match. Similar examples include Wang Yu's *The Chinese Boxers* (1970), Chang Cheh's *Duel of Fists* (1971), and Chu Yuan's *The Lizard* (1972). The recurring scene of a minority hero's martial triumph over "foreign devils" has also inspired other Asian cinemas, giving rise to works such as *Ong-bak* (2003), arguably the most sensational international block-

buster from Thailand in recent decades, where Tony Jaa showcases
his Muay Thai as he kicks Australian, Japanese, and Burmese boxers
flying through the air.

The significance of the Huo Yuanjia–Chen Zhen story to kung
fu cinema cannot be overstated: the legend of Huo Yuanjia and
Chen Zhen defines kung fu cinema. Indeed, the Bruce Lee story
about Huo Yuanjia and Chen Zhen in *Fist of Fury* has seen so many
reincarnations since its making that the entire industry of kung fu
cinema seems to be mere variations on the same theme. Virtually
every major Chinese martial arts actor in Hong Kong, China, and
Hollywood owes his career to a role related to this legend. Lo
Wei's 1976 *Xin Jingwu men* (*New Fist of Fury*) gave Jackie Chan
his first major role in a kung fu movie as Chen Zhen's heir. Jet
Li reprised Chen Zhen's character in the 1994 *Jingwu yingxiong*
(*Fist of Legend*) before playing the role of Huo Yuanjia himself
in *Fearless* a decade later, where he challenges foreign fighters
in the arena during the height of imperialism.[12] Hong Kong's
Asia Television Limited (ATV) produced *Daxia Huo Yuanjia*, a
drama series based on Huo in 1981, which was remade twice
by mainland Chinese companies (2000–2001, 2007). ATV also
produced *Fist of Fury* in 1995, a thirty-episode series featuring
Donnie Yen. Donnie Yen reprises his roles as Chen Zhen in the
2010 *Legend of the Fist: The Return of Chen Zhen*, and as Ip Man in
Ip Man II. *Fist of Fury* also inspired the popular Hong Kong singer
and actor Stephen Fung's *House of Fury* (2005) (the second film
produced by Fung; his début directorial work was *Enter the Phoenix*
[2004]), as well as Taiwan singer Show Luo's 2006 hit single, "Fist
of Fury."

The literary and historical roots of the legend of Huo Yuanjia
and Chen Zhen remain an important but underexamined aspect of
modern Chinese cultures. Frequently attributed to the cult of kung
fu created by Bruce Lee in 1970s transnational cinema, the story
was actually a popular legend first formally recorded by Pingjiang
Buxiaosheng in his 1923 novel, *Jianghu qixia zhuan* (Stateless Heroes
of Marvels). Pingjiang's work, moreover, is an explicit subversion
of the ideology of nationalism in that it insists on the distinction

between *wuxia* and kung fu. Not only were the origins of Huo Yuanjia literary rather than cinematic, this figure was specifically conceived as part of a dual discourse *about* the opposition between literary and bodily types of martial arts. Our analysis of the Huo Yuanjia legend must therefore begin with a historicist understanding of the peculiarities of Chinese anticolonial thought in the 1920s instead of the 1970s.

Film scholars sometimes distinguish between *wuxia* and *kung fu* by translating the former as "Chinese swordplay movies" and the latter as "kung fu movies." It is more common, however, for scholars to conflate *kung fu* and *wuxia* as interchangeable examples of "martial arts cinema."[13] *Wuxia pian* are films typically set in an ancient or mythical China, and the martial arts represented are fantastic ones, such as the ability to fly onto rooftops or walk on water ("lightness kungfu"); throw darts, needles, abacus beads, or other "concealed weapons" (*anqi*); morph into other human beings (*yirong shu*); deploy one's internal energy to shield one's body (*jinzhong zhao*); send messages to friends and foes miles away by producing acoustic waves in the air (*qianli chuanyin*); transfer one's *qi* to others as a healing or empowering mechanism; use writing and musical instruments as lethal weapons; and paralyze an opponent by freezing their acupuncture points (*dianxue*).

The distinction between *wuxia pian* (martial arts films, "swordplay films") and *gongfu pian* (kung fu films) is of historical significance to the original producers and consumers of these works. In *wuxia pian*, the main spectacle is the flying sword and not the acrobatic body of the martial artist. In the early Chinese-language reviews of this genre, *wuxia pian* was considered a subgenre of *wuxia shenguai pian* (films of martial arts, chivalry, ghosts-spirits, and strange events). The *wuxia-shenguai pian* depict magic and incantation, Taoist immortals, talking animals, dreams and prophecies, visitors from the underworld, and kung fu all in one breath. *Wuxia* was the generic name for strange events and superhuman abilities, and magic (*shenguai*) and martial arts (*wuxia*) were indistinguishable. The ur-text for this cinematic development is the large canon of vernacular Chinese fiction, which has traditionally associated martial arts with such themes. *Gongfu pian* (kung fu films), on the contrary, have not drawn extensively on literary sources. They have developed instead as part of action cinema in a broader sense that includes a wide range of non–martial arts materials such as gangster films, detective stories, suspense, "military-education" (*jun-jiao*) movies, and slapstick comedy that proved to be popular in the postwar period. *Gongfu* films are not always set in imperial times; they refer to contemporary or even futuristic events. In the course of the twentieth century they have developed an impressive arsenal of stock characters ranging from schoolgirls/undercover agents to kung-fu fighting robots. Although both *gongfu* and *wuxia* have played central roles in the development of Hong Kong cinema, it was the flexibility of the former's temporal and geographical imaginations, rather than the latter's rigidity and classicism, that brought about the transpacific popularization of Hong Kong action cinema. The differences between these two traditions remain important to Chinese critics because the object of representation in a *wuxia* text is precisely the difference between body and language—between our physical existence and our literary relations to "fiction."[14]

A *xia*, similarly, is not a martial artist, but an imagined class of human beings in Chinese literary and philosophical texts. As elaborated by fiction, *xia* designates both the ethical responsibilities of the martial world and the carrier of those responsibilities. These responsibilities include obvious virtues such as the protection of the powerless and loyalty to one's own clan, but *xia* also refers to the genre's own specific rules of social conduct, such as the prohibition against making a second attempt on another person's life in the same day, socially acceptable ways of challenging a person of higher status, the taboo of calling a woman by her name in public, the maximum number of years before an insult or a favor must be returned, legitimate use of poison and other concealed weapons, and the differentiation between transferable and nontransferable types of rights and obligations from master to disciple. Because martial arts novelists prioritize the narrative construction of the social order and ethical alterity over the depiction of actions, the learning of martial arts is consistently subordinated to the attainment of the moral ideal of *xia*, the end to which *wu* is the means.

Pingjiang's works, including the legend of Huo Yuanjia, do not transparently represent nationalist thought through their display of spectacular bodies. Rather, they produce a distinction between bodies and language in order to deliver a critique of the teleology of nationalist thought that has appropriated notions of language as an instrument of progress. In Pingjiang's works, history is revelatory rather than backward or ossified, a potentiality rather than a liability. His works thematize the human capacity for self-realization, which presents itself as a historical exemplar rather than a messianic revelation through the hands of a prophet, the party, the state, or the revolution. To properly understand Pingjiang's works and the semiotics of martial arts fiction, we must therefore begin with the analysis of the specific context of Chinese nationalism. We must, in other words, situate the rise of martial arts fiction as a historically determinate interlocutor with Chinese nationalism in the Republican period rather than an ideological reflex of a colonial mentality or a transhistorical image on the screen.

The Peculiarities of Chinese Nationalism

The story that Chinese "modernity" began with the radical student protests following the Treaty of Versailles on May 4, 1919, has been told repeatedly in literary history books. According to the official script of Chinese nationalist historiography, these events precipitated the collapse of an archaic, now socially defunct, Confucian order, which was replaced by the radical, "iconoclastic" literary tradition inaugurated by Lu Xun, Ba Jin, Mao Dun, Lao She, and Ding Ling based on the modern vernacular language, collectively known as May Fourth literature. Influential works such as Chow Tse-tsung's *May Fourth Movement: Intellectual Revolution in Modern China* (1960) and Vera Schwarcz's *The Chinese Enlightenment: Intellectuals and the*

Legacy of the May Fourth Movement of 1919 (1986) characterize the May Fourth movement as China's Age of Enlightenment, positing a homology between the May Fourth and the European experience that had occurred two hundred years prior. According to this historical narrative, China had had no Enlightenment prior to the twentieth century, and it was thanks to the efforts of Lu Xun and other May Fourth literary authors that China finally came to understand what had already been discovered in Europe two centuries before— science, democracy, reason, revolution, and individualism.[15]

While the May Fourth movement presented itself as an anticolonial moment, it was in fact an instance of colonized consciousness. Jing Tsu's skillful literary readings argue that the underlying reason for the prominence of the themes of masochism and melancholia in May Fourth literature reveals the ways China's own "failure" depends upon the internalization of Western norms.[16] The trope of failure caused a violent internal split between perceptions of May Fourth "realism" as socially progressive and martial arts fiction as retrograde. May Fourth intellectuals invented a relationship to the movement's contemporary Other by "traditionalizing" martial arts literature, banishing that competing literary current to the abyss of unreason, opacity, and feudalism. The story of the early twentieth century is then told as a confrontation between "radical-iconoclastic" and "traditionalist" literatures, a dichotomy the advocates of May Fourth invented. This submerged history of martial arts literature, however, suggests that colonialism is neither simply territorial occupation nor cultural hegemony, but the incorporation of the defeated countries into the global mechanized arms race. The example of martial arts fiction and modernization discourse in China shows that colonialism universalizes the compulsion to constantly modernize the means of destruction, a treadmill effect that both colonizer and colonized have accepted as the prerequisite for their membership in the modern world.[17] The violent confrontations between those in control of "solid ships and effective guns" (*chuanjian paoli*) and those stuck with self-styled bulletproof monks began to be perceived first as a quantitative difference in the sphere ofproduction, the nation's "modernity." After 1919, May Fourth thinkers also began to grade the quantitative difference in degrees of industrialization as a qualitative difference between rationalized and irrational forms of governance. The relation between the industrialized West and the militarily weak China began to be read as the difference between progressive and retrograde literature within China. A sense of having been excluded from the military-industrial complex of the colonizers and a sense of nostalgia for the imperial glories of the once supreme Middle Kingdom generated a dichotomous reading of the social whole.

The perception of martial arts as a roadblock to Chinese modernization has its origins in the Boxer Rebellion of 1899–1901, when a group of self-proclaimed bulletproof "Fists of Righteous Harmony" attacked foreigners, especially Christians, in an attempt to rid China of foreign imperialism. Instead of saving the country, the Boxers generated a stronger wave of imperialism by providing the Eight-Nation Alliance with the perfect excuse to sack China's capital, which was followed by exorbitant indemnities, concessions, unequal treaties, and the general weakening of the Qing state. In both Western and Chinese historiography, the Boxers often stand as the incontrovertible evidence that China was still mired in magic and superstition, unable to develop techniques beyond martial arts to solve its ancient problems or meet the challenges of the modern world.[18] The Boxers thus serve as an important historical example of the deployment of martial arts in the binary construction of pre-1919 China as "feudalism" and post-1919 as "modernity."

Why, in striking against the martial arts novel, did Chinese intellectuals imagine themselves to be targeting Western imperialism? The peculiarities of Chinese nationalism causally related literature to the mastery of abstract principles of scientific modernity and the industrial use of the body. As the incursion of China's own barbaric past into the present, martial arts literature represented the failure of universal reason. The stigmatization of martial arts fiction was part of a general fear of fiction, with depictions of private violence particularly reprehensible.[19] Significantly, May Fourth proponents never sought to ban actual martial arts practice, which was considered compatible with the goal of promoting physical education in order to produce healthy children for the "Sick Men of Asia."[20] Nor did they object to premodern literary descriptions of martial artists and chivalrous deeds, such as those in *Romance of the Three Kingdoms*. What worried them was the existence of *fictional* tales of martial arts in *modern* China—*wuxia* literature. They attributed to martial arts fiction a curious power to produce that which it named, inducing people to actual street violence or seditious activities. Martial arts fiction was assumed to be particularly dangerous to the impressionable minds of children.

In the 1930s, Mao Dun argued that martial arts fiction was responsible for deflecting the revolutionary consciousness of the Chinese people. Martial arts *fiction* became demonized as the cause of foreign imperialism in China, the bourgeoisie's failure to take up arms, and the division of the country by warlordism. Hu Shi criticized martial arts literature for promoting violence, seditious activities, and antinationalist ideologies. At the same time, critics on both the Left and the Right were bedeviled by an inability to explain the resounding success of a literary theme that appeared as the spectral remains of a precapitalist history. To the anticolonial reformers, martial arts fiction appeared to be a fossil of useless knowledge from China's prerationalized imperial past, something the people should have discarded but for some reason had not, which stood in the way of China's modernization. After 1949, socialist realism became the official doctrine of Communist China, and martial arts novelists were forced by the state to give up their craft. Across the straits in Taiwan, martial arts writers were also persecuted by the government on empty charges; in one famous instance, several novelists were arrested by the Kuomintang (KMT) government for "spreading Communist propaganda." Jin Yong was forced to change the title of *Shediao yingxiong zhuan* (*The Eagle-Shooting Heroes*) from the original (*Damo yingxiong zhuan*) when the book was first published in Taiwan because the censorship bureau thought "eagle-shooting" was a reference to a poem by Mao Zedong. Hong Kong, which escaped much of the clash of Cold War ideologies, fostered a liberal culture and emerged as the new center of martial arts film and fiction in the postwar era. Hong Kong's reputation as the natural home to martial arts fiction, however, has been called into question by the recent rediscovery of pre-1949 mainland martial arts novelists such as Wang Dulu (author of the original story of *Crouching Tiger, Hidden Dragon*), and the reassessment of Taiwan's importance in the formation of postwar martial arts literary culture following the canonization of Gu Long.[21]

In this context, the main reason why martial arts literature never became a common subject of study in the Chinese education system before the 1990s turns out to have less to do with its status as "popular fiction" than its antithetical relationship to the nation-building project of May Fourth. The vast archive of martial arts literature disrupts the commonly accepted narrative that modern Chinese literature saw the progressive Europeanization of the Chinese language. A study of martial arts literature has the advantage of helping us immunize ourselves against the May Fourth epistemological and axiological paradigm of modernity. With our reconstructed knowledge of martial arts literature, we can begin to view twentieth-century Chinese literary history as the maturation, efflorescence, and explosive growth of the historical novel, whose most famous premodern prototype was defined by *Water Margin* and *Romance of the Three Kingdoms* and whose most successful modern incarnation is the martial arts novel.

In recent years, dissenting critics have begun writing alternative stories of the ways Chinese modernity came about. The eminent Chinese historian and intellectual Yu Yingshi, for example, argues in an important article that the May Fourth period was neither Enlightenment nor Renaissance.[22] Yu points out that the rhetoric of the May Fourth as the Chinese Renaissance was first propagated by the liberal thinker Hu Shi on a lecture tour in Great Britain in November 1926. The term was based on the title of a student magazine he founded, *Xin chao* (*New Tide*), which helped promote Hu as the "Father of the Chinese Renaissance" to Westerners. In subsequent years, the notion of "Renaissance" was replaced by "Enlightenment" (*qimeng*), a term espoused by the Communists in 1935, including Chen Boda, Ai Siqi, and Chen Duxiu. Hu Shi and

Chen Duxiu's charisma was largely responsible for the sanctioning of May Fourth as the inauguration of Chinese modernity. In addition to Yu, other cultural critics and historians have delivered trenchant, revisionist critiques of the May Fourth paradigm. Leo Lee and David Wang argue that the creation of a public sphere of reason and liberal-pluralist thought actually began in the late Qing, while the May Fourth period was marked by a higher degree of intolerance, elitism, and dogmatism.[23] Rudolf Wagner and Mau-sang Ng outline the Korean and Russian origins of concepts such as "*yundong*" (movement) that were appropriated by the New Culture leaders as their own inventions.[24] Wang Hui, in his massive multivolume *Xiandai Zhongguo sixiang de xingqi* (*The rise of modern Chinese thought*, 2004), rejects not only the conception of May Fourth as the watershed movement that separated premodern from modern Chinese history, but defies that periodizing distinction altogether. In his view, if the Chinese ever experienced an epochal rupture in their own worldview, their modernity was first conceived in the Song dynasty and not the twentieth century.[25] Although these theories of "alternative modernities" have been formulated against the May Fourth paradigm, revisionist scholars have not systematically challenged the desirability of the notion of "modernity" itself. In other words, although we have grown wary of the Eurocentric emanation model of modernity and succeeded in pluralizing modernities, we have not yet fully rethought the categories of "the traditional" and "the unmodern" and why these terms were constructed as something we should devalue and reject in the first place.

In the Chinese case, "traditional culture" was discursively produced as a matter of national embarrassment in anticolonial thought. In particular, this construction was accomplished through a systematic attack on martial arts fiction. The nationalism of May Fourth literature has two important historical consequences that I term the "traditionalization of martial arts fiction" and the "instrumentalization of language." By "traditionalization," I refer to the process whereby May Fourth literature produced its self-identity as modern and revolutionary by casting competing modernist literary trends as "traditionalist." By "the instrumentalization of language," I refer to the ways in which May Fourth thinkers made the reforms of literary forms and social consciousness the means to China's national survival and economic progress. May Fourth thought was based on a conception of literature as mediation for China's class mobility on the global scale. This social theory identified literature as a means of redressing and overcoming social inequality, both within China and between China and the imperialist nations. The most obvious example of this social theory is Lu Xun's well-known decision to give up the practice of medicine to become a writer because "it is more important to cure the soul of the Chinese than their bodies." The precise contributions of May Fourth literature to economic modernization is unclear—it is hard to say, for example, how many more railways were built in China because there was such a literature—but the dematerializing tendency of May Fourth social thought is noteworthy. May Fourth culture, despite its claims to affinity to Marxism, was ultimately an idealist and not a materialist doctrine. Both processes—the traditionalization of martial arts literature and the instrumentalization of language—deserve a detailed analysis before we can examine the responses from martial arts novelists.

The Traditionalization of Martial Arts Literature

In the 1920s, the leaders of the New Culture movement launched a campaign to marginalize the works of writers who resisted Westernization by grouping martial arts literature with urban romance fiction under the pejorative rubric of the "mandarin ducks and butterflies school," urban romance novels about love (as captured by the figures of mandarin ducks and butterflies, symbols of lovers in classical Chinese literature) and other matters held trivial by nationalist writers. Although May Fourth authors sought to stigmatize martial arts fiction as popular fiction, they also claimed that May Fourth literature was the true popular literature of the people, and started various movements to collect their traditional folksongs.[26] The status of "the people" in the May Fourth period was given a narrow political definition. While martial arts novels enjoyed a wide readership, they were dismissed as products of a decadent bourgeois culture by the dominant cultural personalities of May Fourth intellectualism who abrogated to themselves the authority to represent the "people." Zheng Zhenduo's 1938 *History of Chinese Popular Literature* (*Zhongguo su wenxue shi*), for example, explicitly claims that May Fourth realism, instead of the martial arts novel, was the real aesthetic of the Chinese people. His criticism of the martial arts novel consisted of charges that it was too popular and not popular enough—that it was too traditionalist and at the same time too modern and urban. The nationalist project was, indeed, an internally contradictory discourse built on the negation of the martial arts novel rather than a coherent intellectual agenda of its own.

The May Fourth rhetoric produced new discursive identities and temporalities. It identified itself as "modernist" (*xiandai*) and martial arts fiction as "traditionalist" (*chuantong pai*), even though the two were contemporaneous literary trends.[27] The appearance of a time lag between actually contemporaneous fields of literary production was an important strategy of legitimation for May Fourth authors. Linguistically, structurally, and thematically, the birth of *wuxia* in twentieth-century China struck May Fourth intellectuals as not just backward-looking, but perversely antimodern and unpatriotic. The linguistic hallmark of the *wuxia* genre was the hybridization of Classical Chinese and Vernacular usages, a style dismissively called "*buwen bubai*." The retention of Classical literary usages in martial arts novels was perceived to be at odds with early twentieth-century Chinese reformers' efforts to promote Modern Vernacular Chinese as the basis of a New Literature, a literature they hoped could narrow the gap between the linguistic capital of the educated elite and the ordinary speech of the Chinese masses. Formally, the martial arts novel followed the narrative organization of the *zhang-hui xiaoshuo*, "linked-chapter fiction," a literary form that developed during the Ming dynasty and rejects Western literary models.

Thematically, martial arts novels fell outside the narrative of New China in their preference for imperial history. These novels ignored leftist writers' call for literature to "reflect society and true life" in an era when realism and the representation of contemporary concerns were being codified as the correct and vital mode of literary writing.[28] To make matters worse, martial arts novels typically expressed a positive attitude toward "traditional" folk beliefs condemned by nationalist reformers. These novelists characteristically embellish their tales of martial adventures with citations of Classical Chinese poetry; esoteric elements of Confucian, Taoist, and Buddhist philosophies; and anecdotes about officials and emperors in ancient China (*baiguan yeshi*). In the early twentieth century, positive descriptions of the "habits of traditional China" were in many quarters deemed an evolutionary failure. To nationalist writers, the existence of martial arts fiction in modern Chinese culture seemed to be a perverse episode in China's march toward modernity, a residue of "tradition" that the Chinese nation should have left behind but somehow had not.

The construction of May Fourth culture as China's "modernity" logically presumes the existence of something that can be called "tradition." Indeed, May Fourth rhetoric of modernity was crucially accomplished through the discursive production of its Other, the designation of competing literary trends in the twentieth century as "traditionalist literature." As Rey Chow points out in her pioneering study on mandarin ducks and butterflies literature, May Fourth authors' self-appointed roles as guardians of modernity embodied a "desire for the new [that] quickly acquired the force of an ideological imperative that successfully rationalized China's contact with the West," producing a systematic moral condemnation of mandarin ducks and butterflies literature that denied its modernity and complexity. Instead of being a sign of stagnancy, mandarin ducks and butterflies literature should be read as a "mediated response to ... changes taking place in China around the turn of the century."[29] As the primary example of so-called mandarin ducks and butterflies literature, martial arts fiction provided the most important historical target for May Fourth literature's attack on tradition. For May Fourth authors, the martial arts novel was the fictional construction of a hierarchical social world of heroes, masters, and disciples of magical kung fu that supplied the strongest evidence that China had failed to evolve past superstitions, feudalism, and Oriental despotism.

In reality, however, martial arts fiction represents not an evolutionary failure but the most successful literary attempt to preserve and revitalize the idiom of classical Chinese literary culture in the twentieth century. The genre refashions China's indigenous intellectual resources into a modernist literature that could compete with Westernized May Fourth literature. We should now examine the linguistic characteristics of the genre to further understand its politically motivated exclusion from literary history in the twentieth century.

An Instrumental View of Language

Hu Shi, in his *Baihua wenxue shi* (*History of Vernacular Literature*, 1928), divided the Chinese language into Classical Chinese (*wen-yan*) and Modern Vernacular Chinese (*baihua*). He then argued that modern literature must abandon its indigenous roots and embrace Westernization in order to mobilize the common people. This proposal, grounded in the presumed affinity of Westernization to Chinese vernacular folk culture, was shared by liberal and Marxist thinkers in China, despite being an inversion of the base-superstructure concept in Western Marxism. Hu's theory situated language as the object of reform and in turn posited language as the determinant and explanatory paradigm of economic progress. The leaders of the New Culture movement, in fact, claimed that the difficulty of the Chinese language was the source of foreign imperialism. They argued that the complexity of its orthography, the mutual unintelligibility of its many dialects, and its status as an analytical, isolating language led to mass illiteracy and hence military weaknesses. By comparison, the inflected, agglutinative nature of the Japanese language was diagnosed as the secret of its rapid post-Meiji industrialization.[30] The modernization of China thus required the standardization of the national language, to be achieved through the systematic suppression of the use of non-Mandarin dialects, and the simplification of the written language. Some reformers even proposed to replace Chinese characters with total Romanization, which would in turn provide a more efficient disciplinary tool for the state to transform the illiterate peasant masses into productive citizens as befitting the modern industrial world.

Yet the emergence of the *wuxia* novel was a decisively modern event in Chinese history. While the culture of martial arts was commonly depicted in all forms of premodern Chinese literature, *wuxia* became a literary genre in its own right only in the twentieth century, precisely after the advent of mechanized warfare, the demise of the dynastic system, and the disintegration of the Middle Kingdom's heliocentrism. The beginnings of the twentieth century saw the machine replace the human body as the new source of productivity and military prowess, and saw technological and instrumental reason begin to dominate artistic creativity. It saw communities fragmented and dissolved, human beings alienated from their species-being, and statecraft rationalized. Industrialization was now the universal ideal, and the (postdynastic) state was the vehicle for its realization. The fact that the martial arts themes consolidated into a full-fledged novelistic form at this time struck the early Chinese reformers as an unexplainable perversity. While May Fourth reformers were busy advocating a New Fiction based on a simplified form of Chinese—one closer to the spoken language and conducive to mass mobilization against imperialism—martial arts writers began writing novels in traditional Chinese about heroes, kung fu, Confucianism, Taoism, Buddhism, and flying swords in a hierarchical world of masters and disciples. The immense popularity of the genre and its classicism posed a threat to the nationalist project, but the hostility of leftist writers to martial arts aesthetics can only be explained in light of the historical process whereby language itself became appropriated and instrumentalized as an object of national reform and as a vehicle for progress.

May Fourth Culture's Teleological Thinking and the Invention of Feudalism

Among May Fourth authors' most important strategies of self-legitimation was the invention of the notion of "feudalism." As Arif Dirlik and other historians have shown, while Chinese intellectuals had taken an interest in Marxist historiography as early as the 1910s, the invention of "feudalism" was a distinct product of the 1920s "social history controversy," which was from the start the result of a competition for state power between the Nationalists and the Communists—a pseudo-intellectual debate that "owed its origins to the conflicts over revolutionary strategies that broke out in 1927 pursuant to inter- and intraparty divisions within the United Front."[31] The Nationalists and the Communists each claimed to have discovered in the past the roots of modern conditions that their own political programs were designed to overcome. The idea of "feudalism" and "feudal mores" was popularized by works such as Tao Xisheng's *Zhongguo fengjian shehui shi* (*History of Chinese feudal society*, 1929) and Guo Morou's *Zhongguo gudai shehui yanjiu* (*Research on ancient Chinese society*, 1930). These works argued that foreign imperialism was caused by China's economic backwardness, which in turn was caused by the persistence of remnants of feudal culture such as Confucianism and martial arts. Theorists of feudalism, however, showed little interest in the actual nuances and details of imperial history. Guo summarized the entire history of China between the Zhou dynasty and the mid-nineteenth century as "feudalism" and offered only a confused amalgam of scattered observations on landholding, agricultural means of subsistence, the development of commercial capital, property relations, and political oppression. The debate between Guo and his contemporaries focused on the question of whether China in the Zhou dynasty had been a slave society that constituted an additional "stage" in the development from primitive gens to feudalism and capitalism. The historians of feudalism, whether adopting a three-stage or four-stage model, uniformly thought that no structural change took place in China for two centuries.

"Feudalism," spanning the entire period between the Zhou dynasty and the nineteenth century, was taken as a single mode of production, "a unit of two thousand years' duration."[32]

Chen Duxiu, cofounder of the Chinese Communist Party, notoriously asked in his 1917 essay, "On Literary Revolution," "Pray, where is our Chinese Hugo, Zola, Goethe, Hauptmann, Dickens, or Wilde?"[33] Chen did not ask why the West had never produced a Li Po or Du Fu. Construing Chinese literature as a lack, an absence, and a deficiency against Western norms, Chen represented the attack on Confucianism with the liberation of Chinese people from feudalism. It is worth noting that many Western Marxists at the time, such as Lenin and Rosa Luxemburg, were advocating an international explanation of the genesis of imperialism, seeing it as the result of the structural contradiction between the saturation of the European market and capitalism's need for constant expansion. Chen Duxiu, on the other hand, adopted an internal, nation-based explanation and identified China's own structural deficiencies as the *cause* of foreign imperialism. The classification of literature into modern and backward types naturalized not only the idea of progress, but that of the nation as a vehicle for modernity as well. Zheng Zhenduo writes:

> Under extreme political oppression, ordinary people (*yiban minzhong*) are filled with anger and frustration. Powerless to fight back, however, they resort to fantasies and in their childish minds (*youzhi xinli*) they project a "superman"-type of *xiake*, coming out of nowhere, to help them and fight for justice. This type of fantasy reflects the backward national character [of the Chinese people] (*genxingbilie*). It provides psychological relief and comfort to a hopeless people through ridiculous stories. This is the reason why martial arts fiction flourished during the chaotic times in the Tang dynasty when feudal lords rebelled against central authority and oppressed the people (*fanzhen bahu*),

and in the present after the Western nations invaded
China with their militaries.[34]

The construction of martial arts literature as the cause of foreign
imperialism, in other words, first required the political fiction of "feudalism" as a distinctive "stage" or a mode of production from which
the advent of Chinese Communism liberated the people. The most
influential Chinese Marxist literary critic, Qu Qiubai, compared the
Chinese *xia* to the knight in European feudalism in a 1931 essay, calling upon the masses to wake up from the dreams of flying swords and
kung fu, which to him supplied literary evidence of Chinese people's
willingness to be enslaved.[35] Another critic, Su Min, wrote, "The cheap
tricks of flying and swordplay appealed to the curiously superstitious
minds of China's middle and lower classes and women in general. As
soon as *The Burning of the Red Lotus Temple* was released, middle-
lower class people, women, and children all fell for it, discussing it as
a wonder in Chinese cinema with excitement."[36] In Su, the problem
posed by martial arts literature to Chinese revolutions became a class
issue. No statement on the phenomenon, however, was more influential than Mao Dun's 1933 essay entitled "the literature of the feudal
petty bourgeoisie."

> Since 1930, *wuxia xiaoshuo* has become extremely
> popular in China. By a conservative estimate, there
> have been a few hundreds of imitations of Pingjiang
> Buxiaosheng's *Stateless Heroes of Marvels*. At the
> same time, the domestic movie industry has been
> dominated by *wuxia* movies. Since *The Burning of the
> Red Lotus Temple* became the toast of the town, there
> have been dozens of new movies trying to lure viewers
> to the theater with the phrase "Burning" in their titles.
> Readers of this type of fiction are mostly the
> petty bourgeoisie—that is, people belonging to the
> small capitalist class. With even fewer exceptions, the
> fans of these movies are also the petty bourgeoisie,
> especially the young people in the petty bourgeois

class such as young students and shopkeepers. They cannot stop thinking about Jin Luohan and Honggu [characters in *The Burning of the Red Lotus Temple*] even while they are sleeping. This *wuxia* fever is not accidental. On the one hand, this is a reflection of the need for an escapist fantasy among feudal China's petty-bourgeois class. On the other hand, this is a potent drug feudal China gave to the petty bourgeoisie in tumultuous times.[37]

Mao Dun understood martial arts literature to be an impediment to China's march toward a classless society. However, he could not decide whether China's social formation was "feudal" or "bourgeois"—two entirely different concepts in Marxism. What is generally clear is that a class-vocabulary was attached to the content of martial arts novels because they appeared to be thematically unconcerned with national self-awakening, class struggle, and social productivity, and that this assignment of a social formation (feudal or bourgeois) to a category of literature was logically dependent on the presumed desirability of a rationally managed economy. Martial arts literature appeared to be a literary form that could not be harnessed to a productive national economy. The attack furthermore required a reflection theory of literature, one that began to identify literature as an instrument or epiphenomenon of a collective impulse toward change. It was only in this specific social context that literature came to be characterized as efficient or inefficient, exploitative or equitable, correct or incorrect, class-based or classless. The injunction to modernize produced a grid of aesthetic evaluation that classified works of art into ideologically progressive and retrograde expressions of the social body. It functioned not merely as a polarization of modern and traditional values, but also a selection of superior and inferior works, with prescriptions for achieving respectability on the international literary scene. These requirements of modernization gave birth to a dominant social theory that judged the value of literature on the values it represents, further conflating the aesthetic value of a work with the social values that it espouses or represents, and these social values with the class-consciousness of the people.[38]

The Dichotomy of Language and Action in the Martial Arts Novel

We are now ready to examine the political significance of the martial arts novel's concern with "literariness" in the context of May Fourth authors' attempts to revolutionize the Chinese language. The conception of martial arts as language rather than action is widely attested in Chinese literature and philosophy. The first etymologist of the Chinese, Zhang Taiyan, was among the first to identify martial arts as a linguistic problem for politics. While researching the materials for his *The Origin of Writing* (*Wenshi*), which would become the basis of modern Chinese philology, Zhang Taiyan wrote a series of essays on the relation between martial arts, the nature of the Chinese language, and ethical governance. In an 1897 essay, "Ruxia" (The Confucian and the martial arts master), Zhang posits a homology between martial arts and language. For Zhang, the Chinese concept of martial arts is unique in that *xia* is both a social agent and the social relations that define the identity of that agent. The problem Zhang is grappling with is reflected in the difficulty of translating in contemporary scholarship on the subject. *Xia* is rendered with a bewildering battery of infelicitous English equivalents that could be either a person or a value: the knight-errant, swordsman, kung fu master, chivalry, honor, gallantry, and others. *Xia* in Chinese is both the person (knight-errant) and the moral burden (chivalry) that accompanies the use of martial arts as an instrument of ethical violence. The fact that the person and the ideal translate into the same word in Chinese gives the philologist the unique insight that martial arts are structured like a language—inherently hierarchical, dispersed and embodied in everyday use without an apparent center, and necessarily embedded in concrete social relations. Indeed, it is more accurate to say that *xia* refers to the overcoming of the distinction between agent and structure, between the subject of political action and the objective conditions that compel and enable that subject to act in a politically responsible way. The linguistic particularities of *xia* allows Zhang to construct a theory of the systematic relation between subjectivity and Confucian theories of the state. Zhang argues that mankind is governed by a self-renewing moral order, one exemplified by *xia* as the spiritual, physical, and ethical training of a person. Martial arts do not monopolize the definition of ethical self-cultivation, but stand in an exemplary relation to it. The Confucian theory of the state works somewhat as a paradox. The perfect Confucian state expresses the moral and intellectual will of the people, but the will of the people is also what the state seeks to edify and cultivate once it comes into existence. For Zhang, the ambivalence of the concept of *xia* is not simply an idiosyncrasy of the Chinese language; it is the starting point of modern political science.

Zhang uses many examples from Chinese literature to illustrate the reciprocal relation between the state and its political subjects. The assassin Jing Ke, whom Sima Qian calls a *xia* in his monumental *Records of the Grand Historian*, serves two different lords, and the choice is not personal vagaries, but a reflection of the order of the universe, circumstances, and social determinants that constitute a person and his subjectivity. During the time of chaos (*luanshi*)—the time of division or illegitimate political rulers such as the period of the Warring States—the *xia* serves the people (*fu min*) and rises up against tyranny. During the time of peace (*pingshi*), the *xia* serves the law of the state (*fu fa*) and becomes the hand of swift justice for his lord. The process of self-cultivation is exemplified by the ideal of martial arts as spiritual and ethical training. In this view, the state is only a secular section of a greater cosmic order whose immediate realization is the training of the martial artist. Zhang specifically argues that the laws of *xia* are not the laws of the nation-state but forces that transcend the interstate system. To Zhang, martial arts and martial arts literature signify a stateless tradition of the people. In his essay "Fuchou shifei lun" (Revenge as a moral problem), Zhang argues that since language is always used socially, the emphatically social world of martial arts justifies the homology between language and martial arts.[39]

As a political reformer, Zhang Taiyan was not unique in attach-
ing such significance to martial arts in his formulation of theories
of the modern Chinese state. Liang Qichao composed *Zhongguo de
wushi dao* (*The Way of the Martial Artist in China*) and proposed
to use it as a textbook in the modern Chinese education system.
Liang's work is concerned with the philosophical tenets of
the Way (*tao/dao*) of the martial artist, which he discusses as
wushidao, his reverse translation of the Japanese kanji loanword,
bushido. *Wushidao* were originally Chinese characters borrowed
by the Japanese to describe the ethical code of the samurai that
developed in the late twelfth century, but in his own twentieth-
century redeployment of the term, Liang takes the resinicized
kanji compound to describe the clash of civilizations between
China, Japan, and the West. Liang's choice of the word *wushidao*
is not intended to emphasize the origins of martial arts in
China but to reinscribe China in a new discourse of East Asian
modernity, now centered on Japan and standing in opposition to the
West. Liang urges his countrymen to learn from the "warrior-like"
qualities of the Japanese civilization, which originated in China
in the time of the Yellow Emperor but has gradually declined on
the continent and migrated to the island country of Japan. Liang
writes,

> Westerners and the Japanese often say that China
> did not have a martial past (*bu wu*), and that the
> Chinese are not a martial people. I say, Shame on
> them. I am angry at these words. Their words have
> not convinced me. Our revered forefather, The Yellow
> Emperor, descended from Mount Kunlun to pacify
> the barbarians through countless battles. He bestowed
> the gift of valor and virtue (*wu de*) upon his children.
> From then on, hundreds of different races have settled
> on the Great Continent of Asia (*dongfang dalu*) in the
> course of 3,000 years, but none was more martial than
> our race, and that was the reason why we emerged as
> the master of the Continent.[40]

In the next few paragraphs, however, Liang quickly admits that the warrior instincts of the Chinese race have indeed been suppressed by the joint forces of "historical, geographical, and human circumstances" (*shi shi, di shi, ren shi*) (17).

Liang, writing in political exile in Japan because of a pamphlet he wrote at the time of Japan's spectacular ascension to world power with the Russo-Japanese War—the first time in modern global history a "yellow race" defeated a European power—was keenly aware of the rhetorical advantages of realigning China with Japan through a common discourse of *wushidao/bushido,* and of the possibility that the invocation might destabilize the binary opposition between a modern West and a backward Asia. The "miraculously" accelerated industrialization of post-Meiji Japan served as the basis of the discourse of Oriental exceptionalism, one that nourished the hope of Liang and other Chinese anticolonial intellectuals that China, too, could escape the law of historical development and effects of colonial subjection. The Way of the martial artist denotes the commonalities between industrial Japan and its historical sibling and predecessor, and the rearticulation of these two races promises a new world order that sees the rise of Asia and the decline of the West. Liang's pamphlet suggests that China, too, could undergo a miraculous modernization by virtue of a common East Asian culture evidenced by the shared tradition of martial arts.

What Liang calls "Asia" in his text is a social imaginary full of internal contradiction, oscillating between a cartographically bounded region, the spiritual and bodily practice of martial arts, the spread of Confucianism, racial and genetic features, and linguistic affinities. Likewise, martial arts in this text denote a modernization program that is simultaneously the signifier of an ancient tradition. At the beginning of *The Way of the Martial Artist in China*, Liang presents an apocalyptic vision of the clash of civilizations, a story populated by characters that are either nameless ("hundred of different races") or named ("The Continent of Asia," "Westerners," "the Japanese," and "the Chinese"). Liang advises his fellow countrymen that once China regains a consciousness of its own martial past just as Japan has, the Sick Man of Asia will regain its strength and restore sovereignty, pride, and glory to the nation and rise again in the inevitable clash between the yellow and white races. Liang's idea rests, paradoxically, on an expansive, pan-Asian ("The Continent of Asia") as well as a narrowly culturalist ("us" against "the rest," which included both Japan and the West) logic of racialization. Borrowing a Japanese word to describe a Chinese tradition, Liang attempts to prove the true origins of the practice in China by enumerating a long list of figures he calls *xia*. The list includes illustrious philosophers and patriots such as Confucius (1), Jing Ke the Assassin (43) as well as nameless commoners (The Woman of Liyang, A Fisherman [16]).

Liang's *The Way of the Martial Artist in China* contains literary commentaries on the classical Chinese novel *Water Margin*, and this text is where the term *wuxia* makes its first appearance in the Chinese language. The compound *wuxia* in the modern Chinese language, like *wushi dao*, is a reverse translation of a Japanese loanword from Classical Chinese, this time *bukyo*.[41] In early twentieth-century Japan, three novels by the popular writer Oshikawa Shunro (written between 1900 and 1907) use the word "bukyo" in their titles, and these works were quickly translated and introduced to the Chinese literary scene. The magazine Oshikawa founded, *Bukyosekai* (The world of martial arts), inspired the Chinese to make "martial arts" the basis for a literary genre.[42] In 1908, Xu Nianci published an essay called "My View on Literature" in *Xiaoshuo Lin*, which formally introduced Oshikawa Shunro and his works to his fellow writers in China. He then took to translating the Japanese author's short story, *Katei Gunkan* (Submarine battleship), and renamed it *Xin wutai* (New stage) in Chinese.[43] The full phrase *wuxia xiaoshuo* first entered the Chinese language in 1915, when the famous turn-of-the-century translator Lin Shu (1852–1924) published a short story "Fumeishi" under that title in *Xiaoshuo daguan*. It was not until Lin Shu's 1915 short story, however, that a literary work in Chinese first advertised itself as "wuxia xiaoshuo," the full name by which this genre is known today.

The Origins of Bruce Lee:
Pingjiang Buxiaosheng, 1923

Zhang and Liang were early Chinese political reformers who took a strong interest in the relation between martial arts, language, and politics because of the crisis of authority engendered by the emergence of the modern martial arts novel. Zhang and Liang were right to point out the reciprocal relation between action and actor in the world of martial arts, and to characterize that relation as a problem in the philosophy of language. In 1923, these philosophical currents received a systematic treatment in the works of Pingjiang Buxiaosheng, the originator of the modern martial arts novel. Pingjiang Buxiaosheng was the penname of Xiang Kairan (1890–1957), a native of Hunan. In addition to authoring several works on kung fu practice, such as *Quanshu jiangyi* (Introduction to the art of boxing, 1911), Pingjiang was also a martial artist, an important fact that distinguishes him from later martial arts novelists such as Jin Yong and Gu Long, who were not trained in kung fu. In 1933 Pingjiang founded a martial arts training school in Hunan.

Pingjiang is commonly recognized as the "founding father" of the genre, and literary historians have used different metaphors to describe his role in the development of martial arts literature. Fan Boqun calls Pingjiang the "forefather" or "ancestral origin" (*wuxia bizhu*) of the martial arts novel.[44] Zhang Dachun, the prominent contemporary cultural critic and martial arts novelist, similarly describes Pingjiang as a father figure for the genre. Yang Zhao reiterates this assessment of Pingjiang in his important essay on the "genealogy" (*zhupu*) of modern martial arts fiction.[45] Cao Zhengwen, Chen Pingyuan, Chen Mo, Xu Sinian, Liu Xiang, Ye Hongsheng, Luo Liqun, Wang Hailin, and other literary historians of the genre observe that the early Republican period was dominated by the works of Pingjiang, which is why literary magazines and periods at the time frequently used the phrase, "nan xiang bei zhao" (in the south stands Xiang [Kairan, Pingjiang's real name], in the north stands Zhao [Huanting, 1877–1951]). Pingjiang, however, was the first person to write a modern *wuxia* novel.

In 1922, he began writing two novels simultaneously: *Jianghu qixia zhuan* (*Stateless Heroes of Marvels*) and *Jindai yinxiong zhuan* (*Modern Heroes*), and began serializing the stories in the following year. The first chapter of *Stateless Heroes* appeared in the January issue of *Hong* (Red) magazine in 1923. *Modern Hero* began to be serialized in *Zhentan Shijie* (The detective world) in the same year. While *Stateless Heroes* is distinctively *wuxia*, mixing in tales of Taoist magic with superhuman martial arts, *Modern Heroes* is a realistic novel with believable characters and plotlines. The fact that the novels were composed simultaneously eludes most scholars of Pingjiang, but Pingjiang's project suggests that a distinction was being formulated during the early stage of the development of the genre. In other words, Pingjiang was able to create the *wuxia* genre only by abstracting and distancing the aesthetic of *wuxia* from the realism of kung fu, the latter of which became the basis for the Bruce Lee films and similar works in the postwar period. While kung fu is physical, *wuxia* is linguistic. Despite modern critics' frequent confusion, this distinction remained central to Pingjiang's thought and served as the foundation for his critique of Chinese nationalists' teleological appropriation of the notion of history.

Of the two works, *Modern Heroes* is the true origin of the Bruce Lee phenomenon, namely the legend of Huo Yuanjia. Pingjiang Buxiaosheng twice recounts the legend of Huo Yuanjia and his *Jingwu* martial arts school: in his *Legends in the World of Chinese Martial Arts* (*Zhongguo wulin chuanqi*) and *Modern Heroes*. While the former work only mentions Huo briefly, *Modern Heroes* is an elaborate novel centered on a fictionalized account of the life of Huo Yuanjia. In the novel, Huo founds the Jingwu martial arts school after foreigners begin calling China the "Sick Man of Asia." Just as in the movies, Huo defends China's honor and restores pride to its people by defeating martial champions from Russia, Japan, Germany, and England. Several historical events are mentioned in the novel, including The Boxers and the Hundred Days' Reform. Eventually Huo falls victim to the trickery of the Japanese and dies at their hand. Huo and other protagonists in *Modern Heroes* are called *yingxiong*—great men in history, in deliberate contrast to the protagonists in *Stateless Heroes of Marvels* who are called *qixia*—enlightened swordsmen in myth.

The extraordinary swordsmen are sorcerers rather than martial artists. As in *Swordsmen of the Shu Mountains*—the magnum opus of his contemporary, Huanzhu Louzhu—Pingjiang's novel belongs more properly to the tradition of the "tale of the strange" in Chinese vernacular fiction. As in Ling Mengchu's and Pu Songlin's work, *Stateless Heroes of Marvels* presents a world populated by ghosts, demons, spirits in animal forms, familiars, Taoist priests, and Buddhist monks. The story is mystical, irrational, and antimimetic. The swordsmen wield flying swords and control the elements. They study the Way to improve in areas such as divination, healing, far-sight, communing with the dead, exorcism, blessings, seals, enchant-ments, transmogrification, and alchemy. In one story, a swordsman hurls a lightning bolt that kills a spirit fox miles away. In another, a sorcerer casts spells to strip young women of clothes in public. The novel, in short, is not concerned exclusively with kung fu. However, Pingjiang's text lays the foundation for the later martial arts novel as we know it by establishing three conventions: the Secret Scripture, the narrative of *jianghu* or statelessness, and the clans (*menpai*). In this sense, *Stateless Heroes of Marvels* is conceived in precise opposition to kung fu, tournaments, and physical performance.[46] The appearance of the first modern martial arts novel in Chinese literature entailed an act of translation, a systematic way of converting the descriptions of physical acts into the stuff of myth and literature.

Stateless Heroes of Marvels became China's first martial arts feature film, *The Burning of the Red Lotus Temple* (*Huoshao Honglianshi*). The film was the object of Mao Dun's wrath in his essay on the relation of martial arts and China's feudal petty urban-dwellers cited above. It was directed by Zhang Shichuan, produced by Mingxing Film Company, and adapted for the screen by Zheng Zhengqu. The first part of the film premiered on May 13, 1928, and became a phenomenal success. Additional parts of the story were filmed—eighteen films in total—until 1931, when *The Burning of the Red Lotus Temple* was banned by the Nanking government. The eighteen films depict events from chapters

73–81 of the original novel's one hundred and sixty chapters, which represent more than one million words. In world cinema, *The Burning of the Red Lotus Temple* is famous for being the longest studio release ever produced, running a total of twenty-seven hours.[47] The film continues to be an object of fascination and literary reference for later critics and writers. In Xia Yu's "Under Shanghai Eaves" (*Shanghai wuyan xia*), a famous 1937 "proletarian play" that is still frequently performed in China today, one of the most touching scenes deals with a member of the poor working-class who dies from poverty and illness before his last wish—a family outing to see *The Burning of the Red Temple*—can be fulfilled.[48] The film was a milestone in the history of Chinese cinema. It inaugurated a new movement of *wuxiashenguai* (magic and martial arts film). Countless films with the word "Burning" in their titles were produced in the wake of the film in the following years. By conservative estimates, over two hundred and fifty *wuxia* films were produced by the fifty major motion picture companies in Shanghai between 1929 and 1931, which took up more than sixty percent of the entire movie industry.[49]

The first film depicts the adventures of two swordsmen, Liu Chi and Lu Xiaoqing, who discover a secret cave underneath the sanctimonious Red Lotus Temple. The heroes realize that the Temple harbors many secrets and demonic figures. During their investigation they meet an official, Overseer Bu Wenzheng, who reveals many further surprising facts about the Temple. Eventually Bu falls prey to the traps set up by the monks, and Liu Chi and Lu Xiaoqing, leading their allies, invade the Temple. Upon victory, they burn the Temple down. Subsequent films narrate the escape and revenge plots of the head of the Temple, which lead to a feud between the Kongtong and the Kunlun clans. In 1994, another *The Burning of the Red Lotus Temple* film was produced by Ringo Lam, but this time as an allegory for the Tiananmen Incident.

Translating Martial Arts into a Nonteleological
Philosophy of Language

Stateless Heroes is a colossal work, containing one hundred and sixty chapters of interlinked stories revolving around roughly one hundred characters. Most of the stories depict people who leave their family behind to study the Way with enlightened Taoist priests and hermits in the mountains. Both the path to Enlightenment and the movement of time, however, are circular; history is represented as a process without a telos. Relations between the characters are built on both the diegetic level and the metafictional level. On the diegetic level, the travels, trials, and tribulations of one character might lead to an encounter with another. On the metafictional level, in the course of a story, the characters might become narrators themselves and begin telling stories about other characters. The text is reminiscent of a postmodern dictionary-novel, which has no definite beginnings or ends. Instead, each episode is a cross-referencing entry whose meaning is explained by some other episode within a symbolic whole. Time does not lead to the discovery of a higher order of Truth, a more advanced stage of evolution, or a more efficient mode of producing wealth and organizing society according to some kind of scripted principle. Instead, the experience of time is recursive and immanent, embodied in the practice of everyday life. The text is thus a radical rejection of teleological history. It finds in Taoism a model of holistic thinking and uses it to immunize itself against narratives of progress, modernity, and liberation that have dominated Chinese political philosophy since the May Fourth movement. The message and the structure of the novel mirror each other. The structure of the novel enacts the temporality its characters end up experiencing and preaching.

Stateless Heroes presents three types of strengths: physical, metaphysical, and ethical. The three types are interdependent, and the acquisition of one must necessarily lead to the study of another, or it will remain incomplete and inadequate. The novel begins with an episode that it will structurally repeat throughout the text: Liu Chi, a minor character, meets an extraordinary Taoist priest–

martial artist, who is traveling incognito as a layman. Liu Chi detects signs of extraordinariness in the priest and begs the priest to take him on as a disciple but the priest adamantly refuses. The refusal, however, is obviously a test, and the priest is eventually moved by the sincerity (*chengxin*) and determination of the prospective disciple, and decides to point him in the Way of martial arts—the path to Enlightenment. This basic exchange repeats throughout the novel in the form of different encounters and characters, but the significant problem is that the ability to spot an enlightened Taoist in a crowd of ordinary people is described as a sign of enlightenment, an extraordinary gift itself (*hui gen*), rather than the content of knowledge passed from teacher to disciple. The origin of knowledge lies within the recipient of knowledge. The beginning of the novel formulates the curious problem of the Way as follows:

> Liu Chi said, kowtowing: "Your humble student, I, have been seeking Master for three years, and today I have finally met Master! Master, please be merciful and admit me as a student." Liu Chi kept on kowtowing. Uninterested, the old Taoist kept his eyes closed. He seemed almost as if he were still asleep. Liu Chi kowtowed over ten more times, crawled closer to the Taoist on his knees, and repeated his request. (Vol. I, 7)

The initiative belongs to the student, who has been seeking the Master. When Liu Chi meets the Master, disguised as an ordinary-looking and somewhat repulsive old beggar, even though Liu is not yet initiated into the Way, the disciple somehow already possesses the ability to decipher the secret of the Way and recognize his Master. The Master is represented as the object of a quest and not the source of authority, although the guidance of the Master is required for the completion of Liu Chi's spiritual journey. After the Taoist accepts Liu as a disciple, he does not directly teach him martial arts. Instead, the Taoist instructs Liu in the arts of meditation and breathing (19) and helps him become a self-reflective subject.

The physical training of martial arts depends on awareness of one's position in the cosmos and one's metaphysical relation to the phenomena of the world, but discovering the metaphysical basis of one's existence will reestablish and reform one's ethical relation to other human beings as well. The martial arts that Liu Chi learns begin, then, as the ability to uncouple the physical appearance of an object from its presumed benefits. By disaggregating the physical properties of a thing from its spiritual essence, the student learns that no object exists without the mediation of thought, but the possibility of thought is grounded not in the self but in the species-being of mankind.

Liu Chi is described at the beginning of the book as a frail, scrawny boy who has suffered from chronic illnesses since birth. His parents are known throughout the village for their beauty, but Liu Chi is exceptionally ugly. However, he has a photographic memory, and he can recite the *Analects of Confucius* in their entirety after one reading. Despite his talents, Liu Chi shows no interest in formal learning, and prefers socializing with the elderly and listening to their stories. In fiction, Liu Chi discovers an ethical relation to other social entities whose existence precedes his and who remain unknowable but necessary for his metaphysical formation. The various episodes concerning this character highlight the chasm between physical appearance and metaphysical reality. Liu Chi is startled by the grandiose voices that come out of small-bodied people (21). An old woman in her eighties wields a steel staff as her weaponas easily as if she were holding "a bamboo stick" (27). "Like a dragonfly trying to shake a stone pillar" (I, 43), a manual laborer tries to push an old Taoist out of the door "with all the strength of his life," but the smiling Taoist will not budge an inch. The mysteries of the Way are more than meets the eye, and martial training promises to help reorient and decenter the subject from the perceptual field given by the subject's body. Literature and martial arts are identical in this sense. They reveal in their own potent ways how the self is formed and reformed by its obligations and relations to collective history.

While China's modernizers and critics charge Pingjiang and other martial arts novelists of failing to evolve past traditional

Chinese fiction, they fail to see that *Stateless Heroes of Marvels* is not the residue of traditional fiction, but a deliberate artistic *imitation* of traditional fiction, in particular the form of linked-chapter fiction (*zhanghui xiaoshuo*). Pingjiang ends every chapter with a set of rhetorical questions and a promise to answer them in the next chapter: "Who exactly is this old Taoist? What skills did he teach Liu Chi? Wait until Chapter Two to find out" (Chapter 1, 13). This formula was originally developed by the *huaben* tradition in the Song dynasty, when stories used to be narrated orally by a traveling storyteller as a public performance. The storyteller would collect donations at the end of each chapter and continue with the story only if sufficiently rewarded, which is why this novelistic form is called an "oral script" (*huaben*) and structured by a promise or impulse to "talk more" (*zaishuo*). By the time of Pingjiang's writing, the oral tradition and the organic face-to-face village have long ceased to exist, but Pingjiang seeks to reproduce the affect and pleasure of the traditional vernacular novel by adopting its form, addressing his reader as "viewer" (*kanguan*) instead of "reader" (*duzhe*) throughout the text. This organizational form of the linked-chapter novel creates an archaic aura that corresponds to the unnatural language spoken by the characters themselves, which mimics premodern vernacular usages in Chinese. The simulacrum of language retroactively invents and constructs a tradition, and *Stateless Heroes of Marvels*, at most, is a mock-traditionalist novel rather than a traditionalist one. It is not an unthinking replica or continuity of "tradition," "Old China," or "feudalism," but a self-conscious, artful, and indeed innovative construction of a relationship to tradition.

The novel describes a villain, Wan Qinghe, who is learning a form of magical swordplay that requires the sacrificial blood of virgin boys and girls. Pingjiang's narrator first describes the powers of the swordplay. The narrator then interrupts his own narrative in the following way:

> After one hundred days of training, the swords-
> man will be able to control the movement of the

sword with sheer will and make it fly across great
distances to assassinate people. This sword stance is
enormously more powerful than the one practiced by
the orthodox swordsmen. However, the virgin boys
and girls sacrificed this way must have enlightened
roots and a solid karmic foundation; otherwise
the sorcerer's sword will be clumsy and slow. These
stories are of course baseless idle talk (*wuji zhi tan*).
But previous chronicles of swordsmen have all been
written this way, and they contain stories that are by
far more absurd than these, so I cannot exclude these
stories from my writing just because they are absurd.
(Vol. I, 332)

This moment of "narratorial intrusion" (the omniscient narrator
breaking the realism of the novel by giving an external account of
the events at unexpected moments and thereby drawing attention
to the artificial status of the narrative) occurs several times later in
the book. The objective (external) omniscient narrator constantly
switches roles with a pseudo storyteller, creating the illusion of a
live storytelling performance at a teahouse or the marketplace
in a printed novel. Later, the narrator even inserts metafictional
comments that intentionally emphasize the artificiality of the text:
"Here is a perfect opportunity to apply a jaded expression from
the vernacular novels—'No book is written without coincidences.'
Just when Wan was in the middle of the preparations, the scouts
reported, 'The enemy has already arrived'!" (343). In such instances,
other classical Chinese novels are often named in an intertextual
framework: "What he does is just like the trick Dai Zong plays on
Li Kui in *Water Margin*" (360); "Tang's reactions to the woman
were just like the two sentences from *The Romance of the West
Chamber*: 'blinded and speechless, he feels half of his soul
has flown away from his body'" (370). While May Fourth reformers
and later critics dismiss the text as fantasy, it is crucial that this
wuxia novel actually parodies its own fantastic nature instead of
aiming at a realism effect.

Your humble storyteller here (*zaixia*) guesses that the average reader (*kanguan*) must think just like the Zhu family and assume that Zhu Fu has left with the monk to study the Way at this point. The reality is the opposite. In order to become the monk's student, Zhu Fu has to suffer many more near-fatal crises. This monk he has just met is Zhi Yuan whom we met in Chapter 19! The present chapter gives us an excuse to study the proper biography of Zhu Fu. (298)

And earlier in the novel:

Now that we mentioned this Sun Yaoting, he too can count as an extraordinary swordsman. … If you tell his story to a person of a scientific mind, that person will surely dismiss the story as pure nonsense (*wuji zhi tan*)! Even I, your humble storyteller here, thought of it as idle chatter when I heard it for the first time, and I was more prepared to believe the unbelievable than the average person. Only later, after I became more educated and well-read, did I understand that the story of Sun Yaoting is anything but nonsense. What is nonsense is the childish application of the so-called scientific mind to judge the validity of a story that is, even to the characters concerned, merely speculation, always beyond the reach of their own hearts and minds. (7)

The technique of metafiction not only constructs an organic relation between the modern martial arts novel and the lost tradition of linked-chapter fiction but also serves as a commentary on history as submission and transmission, a process that is signified and captured by the very idea of text itself—something that records the past. In so doing, Pingjiang formulates a nonteleological basis for imagining political community and participation. The literary idiom for political community in Pingjiang is the martial clan (*menpai*).

Characteristically, the novel does not begin with a single protagonist but features shifting conflicts and alliances between various political communities and social networks.

Consisting of such political communities, the operative word in the title of Pingjiang's novel, "jianghu," the Martial Order, is not the space of outlaws. It is a social world governed by the ethical relations between human subjects and forces of divine retribution. In this sense the subjects of the Martial Order are not lawless but stateless, answerable to a higher order of ethics than the laws of the state. Pingjiang's novel explains this distinction in detail and illustrates it through numerous episodes and dialogues, while later novelists simply take this definition of *jianghu* for granted:

> By merely willing it, I put an end to his life. In terms of pathos (*qing*), he deserved it. In terms of logos (*li*), the crime I committed is more severe than his. … I am only thirteen right now, and I have a long life ahead of me. There will be more arguments, unpleasant people, and heated moments in my life. … As a skilled sorcerer, I can kill at will, but while I am beyond the reach of the laws of the state (*guofa*), I am not beyond the mandate of heaven (*tianli*). (Vol. II, 88)

The distinction between what is understandable (*qing*) and what is reasonable (*li*) maps onto the distinction between the Martial Order and the ordinary world: "A criminal who has escaped *wangfa* (the laws of kings) is still subject to the stipulations of *jielü* [religious vows]" (Vol. II, 64).

Pingjiang's *jianghu* is therefore not a secret society or a world of outlaws. Rather, the idiom he invented is a theory of the subject that emphasizes the process of social subjectification. The martial arts aesthetics, invented by Pingjiang against the May Fourth paradigm, underscores the impossibility of becoming a *xia* without situating one in a social world. One becomes a subject only by virtue of one's social relations to the Other. This text provides a useful social theory against the personifying narratives of the twentieth century—

the proletariat, woman, the native Taiwanese—and a host of other political or politicizable subjects. The discourse of martial arts dramatizes this relationship, foregrounds it, and gives it a literary idiom for representation and reflection. It is impossible to invoke any preconceived notion of a presocial subject without acknowledg ing, and revaluating in some minimal way, the relation between the self and community. The formal structure of Pingjiang's text conveys a strong sense of being indebted to the community for what and who one is from the start. One becomes a "subject" by conforming to the norms and forces that define and sustain one's sense and boundaries of being. *Wuxia* is, in this sense, another word for our radical and primary dependency on these norms. In the years following Ping-jiang's work, this social theory would receive even more sophisticated, elaborate, and multifaceted treatment in the hands of Wang Dulu, Jin Yong, Gu Long, and other talented martial arts novelists in a variety of political situations.

NOTES

1. Leon Hunt, *Kung Fu Cult Masters: From Bruce Lee to Crouching Tiger,* 2.
2. Mao Dun, "Fengjian de xiaoshiming wenyi."
3. Qu Qiubai, "Jihede de shidai."
4. Cao Zhengwen, *Xia Wenhua,* 99–100.
5. Ye Hongsheng, *Wuxia xiaoshuo tan yi lu,* 33–34.
6. Chen Pingyuan, *Qiangu wenren xiake meng,* 102.
7. Siu-leung Li, "The Myth Continues," 55.
8. Larissa Heinrich's "Handmaids to the Gospel: Lam Qua's Medical Portraiture" analyzes the ways in which China's military weakness was pathologized and literalized. Medical and cultural discourses represented the Chinese as the "Sick Men of Asia" in order to justify Western imperialism as a logical response to a declining civilization.
9. In his *Racial Castration: Managing Masculinity in Asian America,* David Eng provides a detailed account of literary and cinematic configurations of the emasculated Asian male within a psychoanalytic framework.

10. The United States Chinese Exclusion Act, legislated in 1882, was repealed in 1943. In 1952, the prohibition on naturalization for other Asian nationalities was removed with the passing of the McCarran-Walter Act, but more strict quotas on immigration from Asian countries remained effective until 1965. For an account of the relation between the legal status of Asian Americans and literary naturalism, see Lye, *America's Asia*, esp. 141–203.

11. Stephen Teo points out that while the appeal of the earlier kung fu films (such as the Wong Fei-hung series) was based on regionalism and local flavor, "Lee's significance as a martial arts icon has relied on his charismatic ability to cross over from East to West," an ability that combines what the film critic Tony Rayns calls "narcissism and nationalism." Teo, *Chinese Martial Arts Cinema*, 75–76.

12. This recurring theme subtends most of Jet Li's works through the 1990s, including other legendary martial artists he portrays. Song Weijie insightfully argues that in Li's *Once Upon a Time in China* series, "the confrontation between China and the West is sometimes reduced to the spectacles of fighting scenes between Wong Feihong and Western forces," but Song reminds us that this metonymic figure of China's encounter with the West encodes a "crisis of modern consciousness" that cannot be so easily generalized. Song, "The Reproduction of a Popular Hero," 187–188.

13. In a famous article that advocates action cinema as a pedagogical tool for postcolonial resistance, Meaghan Morris begins with an autobiographical note on her own confusion of *kung fu* and *wuxia* in her own exposure to the genre(s): "I'm embarrassed because I remember what it was like to see a 'Hong Kong film', any Hong Kong film, in that blankly Orientalist way—unable to distinguish one film from another let alone kung fu from swordplay (or, indeed, from karate and then from chambara), wholly ignorant of Chinese genres, and believing in response to the famously bad English dubbing that the films were uniformly so terrible they were funny—a camp reception of Hong Kong films that survives in some Western fan subcultures today." "Transnational Imagination in Action Cinema: Hong Kong and the Making of a Global Popular Culture," 182.

14. Chang Hsiao-hung correlates these traditions with two different bodily ideals. The *wuxia* tradition narrates a soft, plump, saggy body overflowing with "haptic *qi*," which is informed by traditional Chinese medicine and cosmology. For Chang, this physical ideal explains Ang Lee's choice of Chow Yun-fat over younger actors as the main actor in *Crouching Tiger, Hidden Dragon*. By contrast, the kung-fu tradition makes use of a muscular body that is more compatible with the Western imagination of the male ideal, which is epitomized by Bruce Lee. "'Globall' Flight," Center for Chinese Studies,

Berkeley, March 6, 2005. On Bruce Lee's muscular physique as the main reason for his transnational appeal, see Chris Berry, "Stellar Transit."

15. The trope of "Enlightenment" is immensely influential. Studies of specific topics in Chinese culture, such as Zheng Wang's (1999) and Yuxin Ma's (2006) work on Chinese women's lives, suffrage, and labor movements (*Women in the Chinese Enlightenment* [1999] and "Women Journalists in the Chinese Enlightenment" [2006], respectively), for example, take as their starting point the discourse of China's 1919 "Enlightenment." Zhang Xudong's work on contemporary, postsocialist Modernist literary movements (such as Misty poetry) employ a similar vocabulary and characterize them as the "restoration of the spirit of the Chinese enlightenment of the May Fourth era."

16. See Jing Tsu, *Failure, Nationalism, and Literature.*

17. On the production of the means of destruction, see Mandel, *Late Capitalism.* On the treadmill effect, see Postone, *Time, Labor, and Social Domination,* 286–306.

18. See Paul Cohen, *History in Three Keys: The Boxers as Event, Experience, and Myth.*

19. In the early Republican period, Zheng Yimei argued that martial arts fiction posed a threat to China's social order because young readers, unable to distinguish between fact and fiction, might actually abandon their families and go into the mountains to practice martial arts ("Wuxia xiaoshuo de tongbing"). The idea that martial arts fiction is particular to children and family values found contemporary expression in a special issue of *The Humanistic Education Foundation* magazine (No. 113, 1998), which was devoted to a discussion between parents, educators, and legislators on the growing influence of martial arts fiction on young children's behavior.

20. See Andrew Morris, "From Martial Arts to National Skills," and Ruth Rogaski, *Hygienic Modernity.*

21. Lin Baochun, ed., *Aoshi Guicai.*

22. Yu Yingshi, "Neither Renaissance nor Enlightenment," 300–301.

23. Lee, "Incomplete Modernity: Rethinking the May Fourth Intellectual Project," and Wang, *Fin-de-siècle Splendor.*

24. Wagner, "The Canonization of May Fourth"; Ng, *The Russian Hero in Modern Chinese Fiction.*

25. Wang Hui, *Xiandai Zhongguo sixiang de xingqi.*

26. See Chang-Tai Hung, *Going to the People.*

27. In *Chinese Modern: The Heroic and the Quotidian*, Xiaobing Tang offers a critical reassessment of Chinese modernism as the installment of a modernist politics instead of a periodizing concept. Tang reminds us that "[t]

he point [of evoking modernism] … is not to lament the loss of an indigenous language" but to call into question "a Eurocentric historical paradigm" (51–52).

28. Marston Anderson's *The Limits of Realism* argues that the cultural authority of Lu Xun and other May Fourth authors was largely dependent on the claim to represent European culture correctly for the Chinese—namely, the real representational object of May Fourth "realism" is its own relationship to the West. At the same time, Anderson also argues that the Chinese "lack" a Western notion of mimesis, which makes realism an intellectually incoherent enterprise in China. Yi-Tsi Mei Feuerwerker argues more specifically that May Fourth literature invented, through the use of realism, the category of the "downtrodden people" as an object of political action as the strategy for its own legitimation. Feuerwerker discusses Lu Xun's repeated invention of the scene of an encounter between a returning writing self (from Japan, Europe, or America) and the illiterate, victimized peasant ready to be radicalized and enlightened by Western knowledge.

29. Rey Chow, *Woman and Chinese Modernity*, 37, 39. Chow suggests that a reading of mandarin ducks and butterflies literature by way of "woman" as the locus of social change might be a strategy to recover the internal complexity of this literature.

30. For details, see John DeFrancis, *Nationalism and Language Reform in China.*

31. Dirlik, *Revolution and History,* 48.

32. Dirlik, 100.

33. Chen Duxiu, "Wenxue geming lun," 47.

34. Zheng Zhenduo, "Lun wuxia xiaoshuo," 838.

35. Qu Qiubai, "Jihede de shidai," 82–83.

36. Su Min, "Huoshao guopian."

37. Mao Dun [Shen Yanbing], "Fengjian de xiao shimin wenyi" (The literature of the feudal petty bourgeoisie).

38. On the conflation of these two senses of value, see John Guillory, *Cultural Capital*, 19–38.

39. *Congshu*, collected works, 792.

40. Liang Qichao, *Zhongguo zhi wushidao*, 17.

41. On the history of these linguistic exchanges, see Lydia H. Liu, *Translingual Practice*, Appendix C (299–300).

42. Ye, Hongsheng, *Ye Hongsheng lun jian—wuxia xiaoshuo tanyi lu* (Ye Hongsheng on the sword—martial arts fiction and aesthetics), 11–12.

43. *Xiaoshuo Lin* 9 (Jan. 1909), Shanghai, 7–10.

44. Fan Boqun, *Zhongguo xian dai tong su wen xue shi.*

45. Yang Zhao, "Xipu de pohuai yu chong jian," 113.

46. The introduction chapter of Chris Hamm's *Paper Swordsmen* (parts of which consist of a verbatim paraphrasing of Cao Zhengwen's work) restates Cao's claims that the origins of the modern martial arts novel lie in a martial (kung fu) tournament in Macau. Hamm, 3–10.

47. According to film historian Zhang Zhen's research, after the first *Burning of the Red Lotus Temple* film was made in 1928, three more were released in the same year, and the other fourteen were made over the following three years. Zhang Zhen, *An Amorous History of the Silver Screen*, 208. A detailed history of the film's production is provided by Chen Mo, *Zhongguo wuxia dianying shi* (History of the Chinese martial arts film), 48–66.

48. Xia Yu, Act II, 48.

49. Jia Leilei, *Zhongguo wuxia dianying shi*, 50.

Chapter 2

WOMEN AND MARTIAL ARTS
Crouching Tiger, Hidden Dragon's Marital, Martial, and Marxian Problems

> "Marriage is long-term prostitution."
> —Eileen Chang, "Love in a Fallen City"

Feminist criticism of martial arts fiction as the expression of patriarchy is not new. Recently, however, the representation of women in martial arts fiction also became an object of postcolonial and globalization studies, a development that owes much to the phenomenal international box-office success of Ang Lee's *Crouching Tiger, Hidden Dragon* (2000). Postcolonial critics are surprised and delighted by the film's novel focus on strong, independent women in a genre known for its masculine and muscular images: finally, a film from China that does not represent the subordination of women as natural and inevitable. Accordingly, the appearance of the film has invited critical commentary on the current state of feminist consciousness in China and speculations on whether China is becoming increasingly similar to the West. In other words, in *Crouching Tiger, Hidden Dragon* criticism, the analysis of gender has become inextricably tied to the interpretations of China's colonial and postcolonial relations to the West.

Another connection critics have made between the film and postcolonial studies is the fact that the film, produced by a Taiwanese director and an American scriptwriter, is set in an idealized, mythical China. Lee's representation of China has led various critics to view the film as a reflection of the degree to which China has psychologically colonized Taiwan—or vice versa. Indeed, since *Crouching Tiger,*

Hidden Dragon, tomes of articles and books have been published on Ang Lee's "China complex." Because of the film's unprecedented visibility and prestige in international circles, the controversy surrounding the geopolitical origins of *Crouching Tiger, Hidden Dragon* has produced one of the most vibrant intersections of the scholarship on postcolonialism, feminism, and globalization for China studies in the past ten years.

This chapter offers an intervention in these theoretical debates first by attending to the film's correct historical origins: *Crouching Tiger, Hidden Dragon* was invented by neither Zhang Yimou, nor Ang Lee, nor James Schamus, but by an early twentieth-century Chinese martial arts novelist named Wang Dulu (1909–1977) in the late 1930s. It is therefore a historical error to read the story of *Crouching Tiger, Hidden Dragon* and its putatively "radical" representation of women as a reflection of the state of feminism in China today. Instead, I argue that *Crouching Tiger, Hidden Dragon* is a historically determinate response to the project of Chinese May Fourth feminism, which is specifically invested in the abolition of foot-binding and the promotion of women's literacy. Placing *Crouching Tiger, Hidden Dragon* in the proper context of Chinese martial arts novels in the 1930s has important implications for contemporary debates. Such historicization reveals that, contrary to the common perception of the film as a postmodern feminist manifesto, in the literary contexts of the 1930s it was standard for martial arts novelists to represent a woman as the protagonist. This fact necessarily changes critical claims about the relation between gender and postcoloniality, neither of which can be comprehended in transhistorical terms.

The highest-grossing foreign-language film in U.S. history, *Crouching Tiger, Hidden Dragon* was nominated for ten Academy Awards. It won four, in addition to three from BAFTA (British Academy of Film and Television Arts) and two Golden Globes. The surprising box-office success of a nondubbed, subtitled Chinese-language film naturally leads people to ask: What exactly distinguishes this film from the multitude of previous martial arts movies coming out of Hong Kong, Taiwan, and Shanghai? The answer most critics find lies in the film's novel treatment of the topic of women's oppression, which is assumed to be a radical departure from the masculinist tradition defined and monopolized by the immortal icon of Bruce Lee. Since its international release, the film was perceived as a groundbreaking, defiant feminist manifesto designed to revolutionize a genre that has hitherto subordinated women to men.

Feminist interpretations of *Crouching Tiger, Hidden Dragon* tend to treat the film as a belated Chinese version of Western liberal-pluralism and feminism. John Eperjesi points out that promoting the film's "feminist values" was an important marketing strategy during the prescreening phase for the film's U.S. release, which is why "the queen of neo-conservative feminism," Naomi Wolf, was drafted to host U.S. screenings that targeted "women, teens, karate fans, action aficionados and foreign film aesthetes."[1] Sheldon Lu compares *Crouching Tiger, Hidden Dragon* to another 2000 success story in Hollywood about "women who kick ass": *Charlie's Angels*. While the original 1970s series *Charlie's Angels* employed three Caucasian actresses in the lead roles, Lu observes that the casting of the Asian American Lucy Liu in the 2000 movie remake was a strategic move on the part of the filmmakers, designed to take advantage of a resurgence of interest in Hong Kong action cinema in America at the beginning of the new century that may be termed the "Hong Kongization, Sinification, and Asianization of Hollywood." Lu argues that the confluence of globalization and feminism turned *Crouching Tiger, Hidden Dragon* into a "trans-Chinese talent show" starring actors from mainland China (Zhang Ziyi), Taiwan (Chang Cheh), Hong Kong (Chow Yun-Fat, Cheng Pei Pei), and Malaysia (Michelle Yeoh), with music by the Asian American Coco Lee and Yo-Yo Ma.[2] For Sheldon Lu, the film's achievement amounts to nothing less than rendering the analytical usefulness of the entire category of national cinema obsolete. With *Crouching Tiger, Hidden Dragon*, film studies has entered a new chapter called "transnational cinema."[3] Like *Charlie's Angels*, Lu argues, *Crouching Tiger, Hidden Dragon* indicates the newfound importance and strategic value of the image of the (Asian) "woman warrior" in an age where it is no longer possible to speak of "national cinemas" because Hollywood and Asian cinemas have become one.

The presumed novelty of *Crouching Tiger, Hidden Dragon* formed the basis of the film's international acclaim, yet the film's divided reception history points out dangers implicit in international critics' assumption of its radical feminism. Popular international criticism has emphasized the film's extreme, even radical, newness. *Newsweek*'s David Ansen calls the film "a rousing action film and an epic love story."[4] Echoing Ansen's apparent lack of knowledge of the long history of *wuxia* film in Chinese, *New York Post*'s Jonathan Foreman promoted its novelty in an even more forceful language: "You have never seen a movie like *Crouching Tiger, Hidden Dragon* because there has never been a movie like it."[5] These observations often assume a political edge, mystifying the movie as a heroic struggle of Chinese women against oppressive traditional customs. Writing for *Entertainment Weekly*, Lisa Schwarzbaum commends director Ang Lee for "advanc[ing] a revolutionary agenda of female equality, in a country that tradition-ally—officially—undervalues females."[6]

To its original Chinese audience, however, the film was a com-mercial flop. Most Chinese critical reviews found it to be unimaginative and lackluster compared to earlier works like Tsui Hark's *Swordsmen* series. *Wuxia* film has been a staple in Chinese-language cinema since King Hu and Chang Cheh, and Ang Lee has neither Tsui Hark's bold exuberance nor Wong Kar-wai's poignant lyricism. Whereas previous *wuxia* films by King Hu, Chang Cheh, Tsui Hark, and Ching Siu-tung (in contrast to non-*wuxia* kung-fu films popularized by Bruce Lee, Jackie Chan, Sammo Hung, and Jet Li) consistently failed to break into the American market, *Crouching Tiger, Hidden Dragon* achieved this unimaginable feat precisely by foregrounding what Chinese May Fourth feminist thinkers would call "the woman question." The presumption of *Crouching Tiger, Hidden Dragon*'s feminist novelty in the film's global reception history suggests the dangerous possibility of reading white paternalism as progressive feminism. Interpretations like Lisa Schwarzbaum's present the film as a belated copy and validation of American feminist values set against an oppressive, traditional, and backward country of origin, which in turn allow international viewers to feel casually superior to the film's original audience.

And yet, exactly what country is being represented in and by the film's putatively feminist agenda is far from clear. The film's feminist commentators cannot decide if *Crouching Tiger, Hidden Dragon* is an American, Chinese, or Taiwanese film, or simply transnational—evidence of cinema's ability to create a borderless world. The film entered the Academy Award competition as a Taiwanese film in the category of foreign language picture. However, some critics, including the influential film theorist David Bordwell, have mistaken *Crouching Tiger, Hidden Dragon* for a "Hong Kong film" simply because it is a martial arts film.[7] Other critics have characterized *Crouching Tiger, Hidden Dragon* as a diasporic film.[8] Much of the political controversy and critical commentary on the film has indeed focused on the question of why a Taiwanese director would choose to produce a story that seems to glorify China.[9]

The two main interpretive paradigms employed for the film's criticism, feminism and globalization, are closely related. The assumption is that *Crouching Tiger, Hidden Dragon* is a late twentieth-century feminist intervention in a field (or country) that knew no such values, and that this newfound feminist discourse came into being as a result of globalization. The latter assumption logically depends on the former, which can be addressed from a different angle if we raise the more fundamental question of whether the film can be unproblematically viewed as feminist. Both assumptions, however, vitally depend on the perception of the film's originality, a perception that knowledge of Chinese film history can help dismiss. In light of the industry's longstanding interest in female *wuxia*, the interpretation of *Crouching Tiger, Hidden Dragon* as an original feminist work and a result of globalization appears particularly absurd.

Critics who work with the original Chinese-language material emphasize the significance of intracinematic relations, raising more complicated questions about colonialism and globalization. Some of the most dynamic conversations in the field have come to focus on the mutual charges of imitation, derivativeness, neocolonialism, and ethnocentrism. Shih Shu-mei's eloquent critique of Zhang Yimou is an instructive example. As part of a larger argument for how cinema facilitates a "feminist transnationality," Shih Shu-mei delivers a trenchant critique of Zhang Yimou's China-centrism and the "minoritization" of Taiwan.[10] As Shih points out, Zhang Yimou, a prominent mainland Chinese filmmaker, began making martial arts films (*Hero* [2002] and *House of Flying Daggers* [2004]) only after witnessing Ang Lee's enviable international success. Zhang realized after Lee that the *wuxia* genre—which had always been locally successful within Asia—could open the American market to Chinese cinema. Zhang, however, claimed that both of his own martial arts films were conceived and developed long before the Taiwan director's 2000 *Crouching Tiger, Hidden Dragon*. In an interview, Zhang went so far as to say that he made martial arts films to show the Taiwanese how a "martial arts film is really done."[11] Shih's intervention demonstrates that the political rivalry between Taiwan and the PRC is configured as a "compulsion to claim temporal precedence." The controversy further allows Shih to show that coloniality is produced through the allochronism of racial time—that is, racial domination is produced by claims to temporal originality.

More attentive to the history of martial arts film outside Hong Kong such as 1920s Shanghai, film historian Zhang Zhen emphasizes that Michelle Yeoh is not a "miracle woman with a 'pair of lethal legs' born in a postmodern vacuum" but a "descendant of the pantheon of female knight-errant stars" from Wu Lizhu to Xia Peizhen.[12] Their divergent explanations of the origins notwithstanding, both Bordwell and Zhang argue against the perceived novelty of Ang Lee's feminist intervention by invoking historical precedents in cinema. Critics have also noted the intertextual borrowings between the "bamboo scenes" in Ang Lee's work and King Hu's 1971 legendary "female knight-errant" film, *A Touch of Zen* (*Xia-nü*), which is featured in Zhang Yimou's 2004 *House of Flying Daggers*. *Crouching Tiger, Hidden Dragon* is in this regard a self-conscious heir of, and an homage to, a longstanding tradition of female *wuxia* on the silver screen. The intercinematic analysis, however, is insufficient because the literary influence on the prototype is not yet properly contextualized.

Feminist and postcolonial readings of the film both risk making the unhistorical error of reducing the film to a product of Ang Lee's directorial intention. Instead of seeing *Crouching Tiger, Hidden*

Dragon as a result of a confluence of historical and institutional forces dating back to the beginning of the twentieth century in China, critics who regard the film as a novelty often produce psychologizing and decontextualizing readings. Given that the story of *Crouching Tiger, Hidden Dragon* was actually invented by Wang Dulu in the 1930s, the invention of the "woman warrior" has little to do with the infantilizing and fetishistic gaze of the West, patriarchal society in rural Taiwan, or the jingoistic attitude and imperialist ambitions of the People's Republic of China. Rather, the female martial figure was constructed more than half a century ago, and the story embodies a historically determinate literary interest in the category of women in the 1930s and 1940s vocabulary of anticolonial nationalism. *Xia-nü*, which is variously translated in English as swordswoman, female knight-errant, lady knight, or simply the "woman warrior," is a stock character developed by martial arts novels during the Republican era. A historicist reading of this cultural artifact would situate it in the antinomies of nationalist thought in the May Fourth period, and recover its relation to the historical trajectory of feminist thought in China. The story of a woman's martial rebellion against patriarchy cannot be viewed as a textual accident, the whims of a filmmaker, or interfilmic intertextuality and borrowings. Instead, it is a product of the concrete historical events, circumstances, and lived experiences that made the original story—feminist or not—intelligible and meaningful to Wang Dulu's anticolonial readers in the 1930s and 1940s.

Understood as a product of and a participant in late Republican Chinese literary culture (1937–1949) rather than late twentieth-century globalization, the story of *Crouching Tiger, Hidden Dragon* elaborates on a relationship to official Chinese feminism that began with the May Fourth period. This relationship is far more complex than the film's customary interpretation as a simple celebration of women's independence would allow. Comprehended historically, *Crouching Tiger, Hidden Dragon* advances a pointed critique of Chinese feminism's failure to understand gender as a multifarious, heterogeneous, and often internally contradictory social formation. Written in a moment when the category of "woman" was being formalized as a political subject in various anticolonial and nationalist discourses, *Crouching Tiger, Hidden Dragon* emphasizes that subjects who are interpellated into the category of women do not always live, desire, and self-identify in accordance with the norms and prescriptions implied by that name. The novel's chief interventionist tactic is a narrative of desire that exposes May Fourth feminism as an empty political formalism founded on a conception of gender that is evacuated of sexuality. By emphasizing instead the mutually constitutive character of sex and gender as discursive forces that shape characters' experience of female identity, the novel offers an alternative to May Fourth feminism, resisting dominant culture's attempt to appropriate the sign of womanhood for state-building purposes. Rather than appealing to the masses through "the heroic and the erotic," *Crouching Tiger, Hidden Dragon* achieves the opposite of what critics have commonly taken as the main goal of martial arts fiction. Here gender is a historicity, presented through heterogeneous relations and modes of intersubjectivity, and diffused through networks of desire.

Historicizing *Crouching Tiger, Hidden Dragon*

In the late Republican period it was entirely conventional, even banal, for a martial arts novelist to feature a *xia-nü* or *nüxia* as the protagonist or a major character. As Roland Altenburger demonstrates in a detailed study, the figure of the female *xia*, already well illustrated in a variety of classical tales since the Tang dynasty, became a stable and fixed convention in the 1930s and gave rise to famous works like Zhang Henshui's *Tiexiao yinyuan* and Xu Zhuodai's *Nüxia Hongkuzi*. The idea of "female knight-errantry" represents either a practice of "social policing" outside the boundaries of law and custom under a weak state, or "a longstanding pattern of sanctioned violence based on a radical concept of reciprocity as an archaic notion of justice."[13] Martial arts novels in Republican-period were dominated by the figure of the female *xia*, and it was not until the postwar period that it became conventional for martial arts novels to center on the adventures of a male protagonist. Wang Dulu's own contemporaries include Gu Mingdao's influential martial arts novel *Huangjiang nü-xia* (A female knight-errant from Huangjiang, 1928) and Hu Jichen's *Luoxiao nü-xia* (A female knight-errant of Luoxiao, 1926). The "female knight-errant" figure in *Crouching Tiger, Hidden Dragon* was therefore not an invention, but a contribution to the construction of a prototype that was already well underway with these normative precedents, which were themselves part of a broader emergent discourse of women warriors in mainstream literary trends of the 1930s and 1940s. This period witnessed a renewed interest in the ancient legend of Mulan, and a host of literary works began transforming this famous story of a female soldier and patriot legend into a modern rallying point during the War of Resistance, such as Ouyang Yuqian's popular war-time play *Mulan Joins the Army* (*Mulan congjun*, 1937), Zhou Yibai's 1941 dramatic rendition of the same theme, *Hua Mulan*, and Guo Morou's *Three Rebellious Women* (*Sange panni de nüxing*, 1926). Xie Bingying's account of her experience as a war correspondent and a soldier in the National Revolutionary Army, *Autobiography of a Woman Soldier* (*Nübing zizhuan*, 1936), includes stories about her escape from an arranged marriage in order to become educated and to pursue a career in writing. Xie's work stands as the defining statement of the "New Woman" from this period.

The use of the figure of the new woman as a symbol of patriotism and resistance, in short, was anything but new.[14] Wang's text was embedded in and indebted to the New Woman discourse of his time. Importantly, Wang's protagonist is not just a martial woman: like Xie in her account as a New Woman, Jiaolong is also a literate woman. In this sense, Wang's text is not the representation of a transhistorical feminist framework but the sedimentation of a historically determinate mode of conjoining the pillars of May Fourth feminism—the promotion of women's education, the abolition of arranged marriages, and women's martial participation in anticolonialist efforts. As a participant in this dialogue, Wang's text defends the historical connection between women's literacy and women's freedom from the traditional family, but resists the state's co-option of this figure as a symbol of national resistance. *Crouching*

Tiger, Hidden Dragon radically challenges the appropriation of the category of women by male elite nation-building reformers and the nationalist mobilization of women as a political subject. In order to accomplish this end, Wang interprets gender as a productive constraint that defines a field of political possibilities under objective conditions. He develops a literary model for the deconstruction of gender that recasts it as an alternative mode of thinking about political responsibility, historical necessity, and social transformation.

In 1938, soon after the city of Qingdao fell under Japanese occupation, Wang Dulu (1909–1977) began publishing in the local newspaper *Qingdao xinmin bao* (Qingdao new citizens' news) the first part of five interlinked martial arts novels, one of which would eventually become *Crouching Tiger, Hidden Dragon*.[15] Collectively known today in Chinese as the Crane-Iron Pentalogy (*he-tie wubuqu*),[16] the five novels chronicle the rise and fall of four generations of male and female martial arts fighters caught in a series of moral dilemmas between the pursuit of individualistic "free love" (*ziyou lian'ai*) and the rites (*lijiao*)—the Confucian order of social relations and propriety. In both Ang Lee's film version and Wang Dulu's original 1940 novel, Yu Jiaolong ("Jen" in the English subtitle) is the daughter of a high-ranking Manchu official who promises her to an unattractive son of another wealthy, aristocratic family. Jen's parents are not aware that since a young age their daughter has been secretly studying the martial arts of the Wudang school under the tutelage of a female household servant, Jade Fox, who is actually a criminal in disguise. For generations, the Wudang school has admitted only male disciples, and the Wudang techniques are known exclusively to men. Jiaolong meets Xiulian, a renowned woman warrior who "openly roams the Martial Order" (6) but during their meeting Jiaolong pretends to be ignorant of martial arts and expresses her envy for Xiulian's lifestyle. Jiaolong reveals her true identity when she steals a legendary sword under Xiulian's watch, but later shows repentance and returns the sword. On her wedding day, Jiaolong steals the sword again and escapes. The back story reveals that Jiaolong is passionately in love with Tiger, a bandit she has previously met in the western deserts. Subsequent narrative centers on Jiaolong's adventures as she encounters and battles other martial arts masters, often disguised and cross-dressed as a man. In the novel, Jiaolong is a morally ambiguous character, frequently switching sides between friends and foes. Unable to find her true self, Jiaolong makes surprising decisions that alternate between altruism and self-indulgence. She develops a complicated relationship with the mannish Xiulian and Xiulian's lover, Li Mubai. Mubai is the proper owner of the sword (the novel's main phallic symbol) Jiaolong has stolen and the true heir of Wudang. In other words, Mubai embodies the patriarchal rule of Wudang. Several episodes in the original novel deal with Mubai and Jiaolong's protracted battles over the sword, which passes back and forth between the two characters, although Mubai defeats Jiaolong and reclaims the sword effortlessly in every honest duel, defending the patriarchal rule of Wudang. The movie version changes the story slightly and has Mubai experience a change of heart, at which he offers to take on Jiaolong as the first female disciple of Wudang, but she declines.

Jiaolong and Xiulian are both represented as oppressed victims of the institution of arranged marriage but are characterized with opposing choices and outcomes. Mubai and Xiulian are tragic lovers who are each other's soulmate, but they have maintained a platonic relationship throughout their lives out of respect for Xiulian's deceased fiancé, who was Mubai's best friend before his untimely death. Although their marriage was never consummated, Xiulian honors the deceased as her rightful husband in accordance with the Confucian code of propriety, and never remarries. While Mubai and Xiulian are victims of the Confucian rites, they project their feelings onto Jiaolong and encourage her to pursue her individualistic love with Tiger in defiance of tradition. Seeing that Jiaolong has a chance to live out the life they never had, Mubai and Xiulian repeatedly spare Jiaolong's life after catching her in acts of wrongdoing and defeating her. In the end, Jiaolong jumps off the cliff (to escape society by faking her own death, although the movie version leaves her motivation unexplained).

The feminist thrust of the tale—to the extent that it is feminist at all—is derived from a historically instituted moral difference between "free love" (*ziyou lian'ai*) and tradition. The notion of free love entered Chinese political discourse and gained wide currency in the early twentieth century.[17] A special issue of *New Youth* in 1928 was devoted to the discussion of Henrik Ibsen's play, *A Doll's House*, after which Nora became a symbol of the New Woman in China. Ibsen's play inspired Lu Xun's famous 1923 speech at the Peking Women's Normal College, "What Happens After Nora Leaves Home." In this lecture, Lu Xun suggested that the Chinese could become modern only if they were willing to overthrow the shackles of marriage, leave home, and become productive citizens. Feminism, in Lu Xun's thinking, was quite narrowly construed as the abolition of arranged marriages. In his short story "Mourning for the Dead" ("Shangshi"), Lu Xun depicts a woman's heroic decision to cohabit with a man out of wedlock in a conservative society. She describes her choice as an act of feminism, a result of the realization that "I belong to myself! None of them has any right to interfere in my life!" Her lover, however, loses his job after their relationship becomes exposed as a scandal. The couple falls out of love, the female protagonist dies, and the story ends on a tragic note that satirically emphasizes society's intolerance. Lu Xun's social realism, lacking in subtlety and complexity, uses women's plight as a means to caricature China's lack of modernity. These works reinforced the equation between marriage reform, Chinese modernity, and human freedom as such.

It is therefore no coincidence that Wang Dulu's story represents freedom specifically as the rebellion against the institution of arranged marriage. Instead of being an example of a globally uniform feminist consciousness, Wang Dulu's text is a product of early twentieth-century China's revolutionary culture, from which it inherits a specific understanding of feminism. May Fourth advocacy for the emancipation of women from arranged marriages was part of a developmental discourse that presented itself as an iconoclasm based on principles of science and democracy, the critique of the hierarchical structure of the Confucian family, narratives of progress and modernity, racial improvement, and the assertion of individuality. The image of the New Woman was mostly a vehicle for mass mobilization invented by nationalist intellectuals. Indeed, the reduction of feminism to the moral difference between arranged marriages and free love exchanges one form of heteronormative union for another, restricting the scope of feminist politics to competing routes to procreative sexuality.

It must be emphasized from the start that the specific form of feminism articulated by May Fourth intellectuals was only one of many historical feminisms, and that the idea of free love is not freedom as such: free love does not refer to a woman's freedom to engage in premarital sex, take on multiple sexual and romantic partners, defend her bodily autonomy and reproductive choices, or distance herself from compulsory heterosexuality. Rather, free love in the May Fourth context meant specifically a woman's freedom to choose her husband in a monogamous heterosexual relationship. Although Wang Dulu writes in relation to the specific culture and vocabulary of feminist thought defined by Lu Xun and other mainstream May Fourth intellectuals, his work maintains a critical distance from that tradition in that it offers a critical analysis of the limits of human freedom with philosophical insight, aesthetic complexity, and narrative power. On the surface, Lu Xun and Wang Dulu express a similar set of ethical concerns that we may describe, using Gayle Rubin's classic phrase, as the "traffic in women": the social mechanisms by which women are consigned to a secondary position in the economy of needs and their means of satisfaction. Unlike Lu Xun, however, Wang emphasizes gender as a discursive production. Whereas Lu Xun begins with women and their social oppression, Wang presents the category of women itself as a social construct that is internally fraught with tension and often produced in the service of oppressive aims. Seeing gender as a set of social relations rather than the properties of a person, Wang presents an account of gender that shows the difficulty of abstracting the gendered body from the larger field of human productive activities.

In *Crouching Tiger, Hidden Dragon*, Wang represents gender not as an identity but as a differential. In *wuxia* novels, martial arts are not so much a set of physical skills that a person can acquire to different degrees; rather, they represent a concept of martial arts used to divide the fictional universe of *jianghu* into two distinct classes of human beings: those who are (openly or secretly) capable of quasi-superhuman martial abilities (*wugong*), and those who do not know *wugong* and are represented as ordinary human beings, exempt from the social rules of *jianghu*. The non-*xia* characters are typically identified by their occupations—peasants, merchants, butchers, ironsmiths—but the *xia* are removed from the economic sphere of production and conventionally represented as a class of social agents whose sole purposeful and productive activity is the study and practice of martial arts. The martial clans (*menpai*) are self-sufficient units of economic reproduction whose means of subsistence is simply suspended from view by the generic logic of this narrative tradition. Wang Dulu uses this dichotomous representation of the material foundation of the world afforded by this specific concept of martial arts to examine the exterior appearance and interior essence of gender, or the form and content of womanhood.

The title of the story, *Crouching Tiger, Hidden Dragon* (*wohu canglong*), is a common Chinese idiom, meaning that true talents are often hidden beneath false appearances of weakness, which is derived from the character Zhuge Liang (Kong Ming) the Hidden Dragon. Wang's choice of the title suggests the high significance he attached to the narrative device of thwarted expectations, or the disjuncture between appearance and reality, which is borne out by a transgendering narrative structure whereby a feminine-looking character turns out to be a member of the Martial Order. The "hidden dragon" in the novel refers to Jiaolong (her name means "dragon"), a delicate, aristocratic woman whose hidden martial skills are a surprise for the reader and other characters. Much of the novel's opening section is devoted to an emphatic and repetitive description of Jiaolong's femininity, which is connected to her feigned ignorance of martial arts. The novel describes her initial appearance as a lady of extraordinary beauty, as if she has just "descended from the moon" (4–5). Elsewhere she is also compared to "blooming peonies" (47) and other images in nature that connect her femininity to the biological and the natural. In the novel's opening scene, a minor female martial artist arrives at her mansion and, per the request of the crowd, performs a demonstration of martial arts wielding her pole arm with a "handsome aura" (*yingqi*). At this point in the novel, Wang represents Jiaolong as a passive object of desire and a passive object of narration as well, using a limited third-person omniscient narrative to hold her actual knowledge of martial arts in reserve as a surprise for his reader. The demonstration appears to frighten Jiao-long, who quickly hides behind a servant (6). But this "properly feminine" behavior—hiding behind a servant at the sight of martial arts display—denotes not just a chasm between the two worlds created by the concept of martial arts. It also casts a sharp light on the social norms that differentiate women from men. Jiaolong's femininity is consistently constructed against the masculinity of another woman, the open woman warrior Xiulian. In the opening scene, Jiao-long's properly feminine reactions invite comments from another spectator in the room, who compares the female martial artist to the legendary Xiulian and emphasizes the latter's lack of femininity.

> She roams freely around the world of *jianghu* on horseback. No bandits—no matter how many standing together—could be her match! She is rather handsome, but there's nothing in the way she talks and acts that is like a woman. (6)

When the narrative shifts to the perspective of Xiulian in a later part of the novel, a similar description occurs. Xiulian arrives from Beijing to assist the inspectors in their investigation of Jade Fox. She is described as a woman of "dashing and handsome looks" (*qiaoba*, 124) who speaks in a "strong, heavy voice" while "her eyes glow with a fierce, handsome spark" (125). Upon meeting Xiulian, one of the female inspectors comments on her appearance by a gendered comparison to Jiaolong.

> "I have often heard of your honorable names before and I just assumed you must be tall, and dark-faced like Brother Sun. Now that I have finally met you in person … you are really handsome!! There is a lady in the Yu family. She is quite good-looking too. I have thought of infiltrating the Yu mansion by working as a maid for her, but that plan failed. No words can describe Lady Yu Jiaolong's beauty. I really love her. But she pales in comparison to you! Your face is really handsome." (126)

To the compliments from the female inspector, Xiulian answers:

> "Rich women are often good-looking and followed by an entourage of homely maids everywhere they go. … I can't compare to those people. I have been on my own since the age of sixteen. Life is hard for a woman who travels on her own. Even finding an inn is difficult. My own regret in life is that I was born in the body of a woman, that I am not strong and masculine enough!" (126)

Before Wang Dulu allows these two women, Jiaolong and Xiulian, to meet in person and forge a personal friendship in a later chapter, the author first begins with a semiotic comparison of their functions in the text as opposing signifying elements. Although given diametrically opposed gender characteristics, Jiaolong and Xiulian serve a single purpose, which is to highlight the dissonance between the form and content of gender. Since the narrative is focalized through gossiping minor characters at this point, Jiaolong's interiority is inaccessible to the reader, and her gender appears to be a social construct grounded in her actions. The exterior form of Xiulian's gender is itself only reported as a "rumor" and hence belongs to the order of unreliable narration, since Xiulian's masculine attributes are reported only as the omniscient narrator's citation of a minor character's opinion without further commentary. That the novel begins with a contrastive relationship between these two women through the speech act of a third person is crucial because neither Jiaolong's supposed fear of martial arts nor Xiulian's lack of femininity turns out to be quite true. As the story progresses, both Jiaolong and Xiulian evolve into properly feminized, and properly desired, female characters in a heterosexual romance, and both turn out to be skilled in martial arts. The novel's narrative structure hinges on the forced convergence of two kinds of comparisons—a comparison of martial arts and a comparison of gender attributes—but in terms of the narrative functions these characters perform for the text, the true difference lies between an open woman martial artist and a closeted one. The performance (in the sense of "success") of one's masculine, heroic deeds while roaming on horseback is contrasted with the performance (in the sense of social mask or "disguise") of one's lack of knowledge about such matters. The contrast between these two kinds of performances is furthermore represented as a difference between normative and failed gender development—Jiaolong's "beauty" and Xiulian's "regret."

While *Crouching Tiger, Hidden Dragon* is commonly read as a celebratory depiction of women's rebellion against patriarchy, the question that is never raised in the vast body of writings on *Crouching Tiger, Hidden Dragon* is: Why does Jiaolong have to be a literate woman? The subtle logic of the story links martial arts, women's freedom, and cultural capital in a causal manner and suggests that the true force that emancipates Jiaolong from the shackles of traditional or arranged marriage is not her strong personality or willpower, but her privilege as an aristocratic woman who has access to literacy. Writing in accordance with the idiom of Chinese martial arts novels, Wang employs the device of the Secret Scripture, the *miji*, as a source of Jiaolong's superhuman martial abilities. Jiaolong is able to escape the arranged marriage by virtue of her martial arts, but her martial arts are not the Western kinds in the novel. Rather, these are mystical skills one learns from reading a book, *The Book of Jiuhua* of Wudang. The novel explains clearly that Jade Fox, by contrast, is a low-class woman who is unable to access the secrets of *The Book of Jiuhua,* so that despite her role as Jiaolong's mentor the young aristocratic woman's martial arts surpass those of her own, and in one critical scene, the disciple arrives just in time to rescue the master by using the secret techniques of Wudang she has learned from the book. The apparently radical and feminist freedom Jiaolong evinces and endorse is only accessible to women of a certain class and not a universal condition everyone is free to choose as a lifestyle. What appears to be a subjective mindset turns out to be an objective social condition. Through its emphasis on class as the true determinant of women's freedom, the text displaces the question of free love from the realm of personal choice and subjectivity to its material conditions.

Women and Chinese Marxism

Wang Dulu was China's first fulltime professional martial arts novelist. Born to an impoverished Manchu family in Beijing in 1909, Wang's real name was Wang Baoxiang. He wrote thirty-three major works during his lifetime using two different pen names, Wang Dulu and Wang Xiaoyu. The novels he wrote under the name of Wang Xiaoyu belong largely to the category of romance or sentimental fiction, while Wang Dulu was his chosen name for his *wuxia* novels. Among early Republican martial arts novelists, Wang Dulu was unique in introducing the conventions and motifs of social romance into the martial arts genre. The result of the combination of love and martial arts was that, in contradistinction to the styles of his contemporary martial arts novelists such as Huanzhu Louzhu, Wang "humanized" *wuxia*: "A martial arts novel is unimaginable without a hero, but in Wang Dulu's novel, the hero is not a superhero, but a human being with human flaws."[18] Wang's literary project was to inject a narrative of desire into the genre in order to represent the category of the human in a more complex way than traditional martial arts novels would allow. And yet, in the literary history produced by official Marxism in China, Wang's interest in the productivity of desire has been persistently misrepresented. During his own lifetime, Wang's martial arts novels were dismissed by Marxist and other leftist critics as "mandarin ducks and butterflies" fiction, traditional Chinese novels depicting idealistic or tragic relationships between lovers (symbolized by mandarin ducks and butterflies), although the fact that Wang used two different pseudonyms indicated a conscious and calculated distance from such stories in at least his martial arts novels. In the post–Cultural Revolution era, Wang Dulu was vindicated as one of China's greatest authors from the Republican era, although now his stories tend to be interpreted as allegories of women's struggle under China's traditionally feudal, Confucian society in anticipation of their liberation by the Communist Party. Wang's thematization of the tension between "free love" and the institution of arranged marriage is now interpreted between feminism and feudalism.

In Marxist-inflected criticism of Wang Dulu, his novels are consistently linked to a *mode of production*—feudalism. *Fengjian lijiao*, "feudal customs of Confucianism," is the object of Lu Xun's 1918 satire, "Diary of a Madman." Seeing themselves as liberators of China and its women, May Fourth intellectuals developed a superficial use of Marxist vocabulary that collapsed the entirety of four thousand years of Chinese history into feudalism, which Lu Xun also called "cannibalism" in his story.[19] Influenced by May Fourth stagist theory, critics of Wang Dulu commonly describe his literary project as the thematization of the irresolvable tension between individual desires and obstacles of feudalism. According to Wang's widow, Li Danquan, Wang created his female warrior characters to encourage women to rebel against the "feudal system" (*fengjian zhidu*).[20] Wang's depictions of "tragic romance under feudalism" have become his signature style, and he is famously unique among martial arts novelists for his sustained interest in tropes of love. Gu Long, the most influential postwar martial arts novelist from Taiwan, praises Wang as "a unique, *sui generis* stylist" (*fengge qingxi, zicheng yipai*) for his textured portrayal of human emotions (*xie qing xini*).[21] The historian of martial arts literature Ye Hongsheng calls him "the founding father of a tragic and chivalrous kind of romance" (*beju xiaqing zhizu*).[22] Wang Dulu's student and biographer, Xu Sinian, characterizes Wang's work as a "social romance" (*shehui yanqing*) grounded in an explicit critique of "feudal customs" (*fengjian lijiao*). Neither the word nor the concept of "feudalism" is found in Wang's own texts, which represent the forces of Confucian social hierarchy and rites merely to highlight the complexity of human nature, morality, and emotions when the subject is torn between the demands of social norms and individualistic desire.

The uncritical use of Marxist-Leninist stagist theory in early Chinese leftist thought has unfortunate consequences for the development of feminist thought. "Woman" is transformed from the signifier of a set of social relations—which Wang's texts set out to explore through the thematization of desire and sexuality—into a concrete person. As many critics have pointed out, China's own feminist discourse before the importation of Western stagist theory was actually more radical than the May Fourth version that has become the official doctrine in the People's Republic. Xia Xiaohong points out that the early stage of late Qing feminism was founded on the notion of "equality between men and women" (*nannü pingdeng*) before that ideal was gradually replaced by the discourse of "women's rights" around the turn of the century.[23] Liu Jen-peng similarly argues that while Chinese feminism in the late Qing period understood gender as a relation and promoted equality *between* men and women, by the May Fourth period feminism was taken over by a liberal discourse of "women's rights" (*nüquan*) and "New Woman."[24] Angela Zito and Tani Barlow characterize China's indigenous feminist movement as a relational model rather than a possessive model. Unlike the Western discourse of possessive individualism and political subjects of rights, which portray men and women as ontologically and anatomically distinct bodies, premodern Chinese medicinal, literary, and political writings are founded on a yin-yang cosmology that is radically different from the Western conception of bodies.[25] Indeed, prior to the emergence of "funü" and "nüxing" in the Republican period, the Chinese language had no vocabulary that would correspond to the English category of "women."[26] A fluid, relational model of gender grounded in social relationships was suppressed by the possessive or substantive one. As a result, gender was reified as the attributes of a distinct person—in fact, as the very foundation of modern personhood. The emergence of women as political subjects was therefore not simply the historical telos of a human essence or the natural unfolding of "woman" as manifest destiny, but the effect of a process of formalization. It transformed the signifier of woman from a nexus of social and psychological relations, which Wang's texts set out to explore through the thematization of desire and sexuality, into a clearly delineated person.

The reduction of feminism into a critique of feudalism occurred in tandem with the introduction of British liberal thought. As Hu Ying argues, the figure of the Chinese New Woman was constructed as much through the printing, reading, and translating of Western thought as it was through indigenous materials.[27] While the rhetorical presentation of feudalism as the root of the problem with Chinese women professes Marxist allegiance, in actuality this discourse is more liberal and Social Darwinian than Marxist.[28] In the late nineteenth and early twentieth century, Herbert Spencer became one of the most ardently translated Western thinkers in China. In 1890, preliminary translations of Spencer's thought were already used by the missionary-founded *Yizhi* Book Society as part of the ninety-eight standard textbooks for modern education. Beginning in 1898, Zhang Taiyan, collaborating with translator Zeng Guan, published a series of translations of *Mr. Herbert Spencer's Works* in the newspaper *Chang Yan*. Spencer's writings on the rights of women and his application of Darwinian theories to explain the development of human societies were translated as one coherent idea. Between 1902 and 1903, under the auspices of Liang Qichao, Ma Junwu began a systematic translation of various western writings on the subject of women's rights and women's liberation, including J.S. Mill's "The Subjugation of Women" and Spencer's "The Rights of Women." "The Rights of Women" proved to have an enduring and profound influence on modern Chinese political culture. Its most widely cited line was: "That a people's condition may be judged by the treatment which women receive under it, is a remark that has become almost trite," which Ma translated as "If one wishes to know how civilized a country's people are, one must judge it on the basis of the condition of that country's treatment of women. This is a principle that never changes."[29] This view apparently prompted Liang Qichao to advocate in 1902 that "A New China needs a New Woman" in *Xinmin Congbao*.[30]

The transformation of women into anticolonial political subjects has even earlier roots in the Social Darwinian discourse on natural selection that gave rise to May Fourth thinking. In the 1890s and early 1900s, Liang Qichao and other reformers started advocating that the Chinese could strengthen their race in the struggle for survival by having their women engage in more physical exercise and bear better sons. "All countries that wish to have strong soldiers insure that all their women engage in calisthenics, for they believe that only thus will the sons they bear be full in body and strong of muscle."[31] Mao's essay on the fate of women in China, "On the Suicide of Miss Zhou" (1919), was written soon after his essay on the importance of physical education, "A Study of Physical Education," in which he argues that

China was weak because the Chinese have focused on the mind and neglected strengthening the body.[32] Recent scholarship has further emphasized that May Fourth reformers' efforts to promote free love was not the agenda of a grassroots feminism, but part of a larger project that sought to regulate and control women's bodies, one that used love and revolution as interchangeable tropes in a new technology of governmentality.[33] A radical view of this situation holds that "the woman question" was reduced to a "political strategem for advancing China's nation-building program."[34]

Contemporary critics seem divided on the authenticity of May Fourth feminism. Some believe that the trajectory of feminist thought retained a certain degree of autonomy even as it was articulated by male intellectuals.[35] Most critics, however, conclude that May Fourth intellectuals took an interest in gender only because the emancipation of women was considered a necessary *step* in China's evolution from feudalism into a strong and prosperous modern nation. Li Xiaojiang, for example, argues that the May Fourth movement merely produced a "patriarchal feminism" that substituted the state for the father for women."[36] As Lydia Liu points out, the woman question was ubiquitous in May Fourth discourse of modernity. "In fact, no self-styled progressive thinker ever let an opportunity to offer an opinion on the so-called woman question slip by."[37] Patricia Sieber makes a pertinent remark: "Insofar as the 'woman question' was thought to reflect on China's standing as a nation both inside and outside China, the New Woman also was a touchstone for China's national progress."[38]

The idea that gender can be said at once to be a form of property (in the sense of private property) and a property of a person (in the sense of characteristics) resonates uncannily with other ideologies of acquisitiveness, rationalization, and accumulation underlying the modern possessive individualism that C.B. Macpherson has analyzed.[39] As reified by May Fourth feminism's discourse of the "New Woman," gender ceases to be a mode of inscribing selfhood in the large field of social responsibilities in the service of a politically progressive agenda, and instead becomes an account of individual rights and entitlement. This form of feminism's ideological foundation in the competitive personality of the *homo economicus* in civil society, produced by China's incorporation into the world economy, is a standpoint that Wang's novels call into question. May Fourth feminism posits a naturalistic "person" preexisting its subjection in the matrix of the social. By making gender a consequence of anatomy and then the basis of rights-claims, this feminism effectively erases the social character of gender from view.

May Fourth feminism's ideological foundation in the competitive personality of the *homo economicus* in civil society, produced by China's incorporation into the world economy, is a standpoint that Wang's novels call into question. Though he shares with Lu Xun a diagnostic interest in the problem of woman and modernity, what sets Wang apart from Lu Xun and other May Fourth feminists is his deep recognition and understanding of the dynamics of sexual transgression and the mutually constitutive character of gender and sexuality. Womanhood in Wang Dulu is not simply a biological sex. It is a set of socially differentiated positions, personal qualities, and styles of inhabiting and relating to the world. Gender is represented as something that is thinkable only in the context of sexuality and Others, and desire is what moves and transforms these subjects of gender. Unlike Lu Xun, Wang is gifted with the capacity to render this dynamic in a literary narrative that departs from Lu Xun's clinical, satirical vision of Chinese women's lack of modernity. By contrast, gender in Lu Xun's writings is embodied and personified as the illiterate woman, the peasant woman, the female victim who suffers from the stigma of free love. These women are invariably represented as the male intellectual's burden, or a "problem" that China must solve in order to progress beyond "feudalism."

In May Fourth literature, the relation between men and women is hypostatized into a stable object of intellectual contemplation, which is further satirized as a failure of nationalist consciousness. Lu Xun's vision of womanhood is founded on a feminism devoid of all sexuality. Women are not desiring subjects, but objects exchanged between men within systems that Lu Xun and his contemporaries reductively understand as feudalism and patriarchy. In addition to "Mourning the Dead" discussed above, Lu Xun's major feminist stories are "New Year's Sacrifice" and "Medicine."[40] "New Year's Sacrifice" portrays the possibility and the failure of a feminist consciousness. The story begins with a nameless first-person narrator returning to a place called "Lu Town"—a name that evokes Lu Xun's self-identity—where the narrator's clansmen are preparing for a traditional ceremony known as the "New Year's Sacrifice." The narrator aimlessly wanders into his uncle's study, which is filled with "an incomplete set of the *Kang Xi Dictionary*, a copy of *Collected Commentaries to 'Reflections on Things at Hand*,' and a copy of *A Lining to the Garment of the 'Four Books'*"—the symbols of the "traditional learning" that Lu Xun's feminist story seeks to dismantle. The narrator then meets Sister Xianglin, a female house servant who later dies ("ages away") from hard work, mistreatment that includes gendered violence, and poverty. The exact cause of Sister Xianglin's death is dismissed by the other characters in the story as an insignificant detail. At this point the narrative becomes a *mise-en-abyme* that consists of fragments of the narrator's reminiscences about Sister Xianglin, other stories within stories, and stories about storytelling. The other women characters become narrators, setting up a narrative frame that portrays Sister Xianglin as the dual victim of male patriarchy and female gossip. It is revealed that, after her first husband dies, Sister Xianglin's mother-in-law sells her to a rich man for money. As a widow, Sister Xianglin is shunned by society and has no employment opportunities other than reselling her labor-power into slavery under Fourth Uncle's family, where the products of her labor are appropriated by means fair or foul. The emotional crux of the story is formed by the force of superstitions that persist in modern China. Sister Xianglin attempts to commit suicide to avoid remarriage after hearing a story from another woman that, in hell, a woman who has married twice will be split into two. As a widow, she is considered "bad luck" and prohibited by the family she works for to touch the sacrificial foods for the ceremony. The conclusion of the story indicates that its title, "New Year's Sacrifice," refers not to the ceremony but to Sister Xianglin—the real object that is sacrificed and exchanged as a result of China's inability to evolve past superstition. In telling the story, the male narrator feels "an occasional pang of guilt" (225), but he, too, is unable to awaken from the hypnosis of tradition.

Wrapped in this comforting symphonic embrace, I too was filled with a deep sense of well-being and felt wholly free of worldly cares. All the worries and concerns that had plagued me from morning till night the day before had been totally swept away by the happy atmosphere of the New Year. I was conscious of nothing except that the various gods of heaven and earth were enjoying the ritual offerings and all the incense that burned in their honor. Comfortably tipsy by now, they staggered through the sky and prepared to shower the people of Lu Town with infinite blessings. (241)

Lu Xun's intention is to use the gap between the narrative frame—the anger at the persistence of China's superstition the reader should arrive at by the end of the tale, and the narrator's own antipathy—to tell a story about "failed consciousness." The male intellectual who narrates the story is moved by the plight of Sister Xiangliang and has a chance to transcend his class privilege and form solidarity with the peasant woman but at the end of the story he too becomes intoxicated by the "infinite blessings" the gods showered down from the sky. "Swept away by the happy atmosphere of the New Year," the narrator forgets about his duty to rescue Chinese women from the shackles of feudalism. As it turns out, the male intellectual who narrates the story is the true object of the satire, and Lu Xun is more interested in the failed consciousness of the prospective revolutionary than in the plight of women, which merely serves as a vehicle for the dramatic caricature of China as a feudal society in need of change. The framework of this self-proclaimed feminist story goes hand in hand with Lu Xun's famous metaphor that the people of China are suffocating in an Iron House, slowly dying to its own tradition while the only conscious intellectual wrestles with the question of whether to wake up the masses to their impending death, or let them pass away in their sleep.

The themes of superstition and traditional folk beliefs as the cause of Chinese women's oppression are repeated in "Medicine," another story by Lu Xun. "Medicine" tells of a superstitious father who believes that his son's tuberculosis can be cured by a blood-soaked *mantou* (steamed bun) instead of Western medicine. The story rests on a contrast between Western "science" and Chinese "superstition" and develops an allegory that is also a call to arms for China's (female) revolutionaries. The blood on the *mantou* comes from the remains of an executed revolutionary whose name is said to be Xia Yu in the story. Xia Yu is clearly an allusion to the famous female revolutionary in the Qing dynasty, Qiu Jin, since Xia means "summer" and Qiu means "autumn," and Jin and Yu are two different words for "jade." The two families in the story, the Hua family and the Xia family, have surnames that together form an ancient designation for China, "Huaxia." The stories launch a systematic attack on the teachings of Confucius and classical Chinese literature in general, which are confused with feudalism and metonymically represented through the institution of arranged marriage, but Lu Xun's works merely delineate the social effects of misogyny through a reified category of women. The characters are not individuals but fixed social types. Ultimately, they fail to offer a problematization of gender itself, which Wang Dulu's work explores in a more sophisticated fashion.

Wang's Radical Feminism as Counter-discourse: Sex as the Foundation of Feminism

While Lu Xun's women are represented as a mode of production, China's feudal past, Wang's feminist agenda is accomplished through the concept of "sex-negativity." Most notably, the female heroines in Wang's texts are referred to as *liangjia funü*, "women from respectable families," while the villains in Wang's oeuvre are not thieves, nor criminals, nor outlaws, but *jianfu yinfu*, "licentious men and adulterous women." The opening scene of the first novel in the pentalogy, *Crane Startles Kunlun*, is a clan master's "rightful execution" of disciples who have committed the sin of adultery. We must first understand Wang's feminism, then, as a historically specific understanding of the notion of women, which contemporary "anti-essentialist" critics have demonstrated and problematized as an internally dissonant, and historically shifting, category.[41] The historical question posed by Wang's novels is therefore the precise relation and relevance of what Gayle Rubin calls "sex-negativity" (the assumption that sex is inherently immoral except when it takes the form of the insertion of a penis into a vagina in the context of legal marriage) to a "martial arts" story.[42]

How are we to understand the connection and compatibility between the celebration of women as *nü-xia* and the conservative sexual ideology of the texts? In part, this contradiction derives from the formalization of women as political subjects and of the limitations of a liberal model of personhood. Furthermore, the formalism of the gendered self is connected to the formalism of literature in important ways. Republican martial arts literature contributed to the stigmatization of certain gender-based elements of Confucian philosophy (the social codes of a feminine propriety, relationships between husband, wife, and son, "rites" [*li*]) as an obstacle to modernization. Significantly, this modernization program was understood as a cultural reform, a transitive act rather than an unfolding historical moment, and "women" became precisely the "object" to be reformed and reeducated by this program. In the May Fourth anti-imperialist protests and the New Culture movement that followed, literature was both the means and the object of modernization, and the trope of women emerged as a type of formalist discourse. The formalism of women explains the asymmetry of gender and sexuality in martial arts fiction, a distinction on which the construction of *xianü* relies for its intelligibility. The figure of *xianü* is therefore a contradictory explanation of gender as an instrument of modernity and a fear of sexuality as a degenerative disease of civilization.

Wang's texts do not depart from these traditional themes. To tell an original and compelling story without frustrating his readers' horizon of expectations, Wang Dulu tries to take advantage of a new cultural interest in women's literacy at the time of the stories' genesis, and he relies on gender differences as his main element of surprise. In so doing, he naturalizes the formalism and visibility of women as a newly available and emotionally charged category of political discourse.

In order to make the generic conventions of martial arts fiction and those of romance novels compatible, Wang introduces a formula that would logically solve the problem: the Secret Scripture as a training manual. Unlike earlier single-hero martial arts stories, Wang's novels typically feature two protagonists, a man and a woman, and the romantic entanglement between the two takes precedence over the usual emphasis on features made famous by martial arts films: "trials of the Shaolin monks," the transformation of the inner self, or graphic descriptions of combat. However, the requirements of romance, now incorporated by the martial arts novel, contradict a central tenet in Confucian moral philosophy and the narrative convention of this genre itself: that superior martial skills have to be *learned* in conjunction with the transmission of a specific kind of ethics. Conventionally, the *wuxia* of the martial arts novel can never be acquired independently from solitary reading. Rather, the aspiring disciples have to be part of an institution (a martial clan [*bang pai*] or a martial school [Shaolin or Wudang]) and undergo a series of (moral) trials and spiritual practice. Therefore, martial arts stories invariably emphasize that a person's martial powers correspond to that person's age and experience, and the powerful martial artists are naturally the older characters. By constructing this power differential, martial arts fiction defends and naturalizes a kinship structure that is essential to its conservative sexual ideology. But while older men and women are the "natural superiors" according to this kinship structure, beginning with Wang, the cross-fertilization between martial arts fiction and romance dictates that the novel needs to focus on a *younger* couple. The rhetoric of development and respect for the social hierarchy (which rewards time and effort) and the ideology of romance (which requires a young couple) thus came into conflict at the time of Wang's writing, but this contradiction is resolved through the convention of the secret scroll, which allows the young martial artist to acquire supernatural skills *fortuitously*, often without a master. A sexually active protagonist then can also become the subject of exciting adventure stories and marvelous martial feats, and his or her achievement in martial arts is saved by the Secret Scripture from appearing as a logical contradiction. Two modes of development are thus recorded in these stories: one either learns under the tutelage of a renowned martial master or one may experience accelerated growth by being culturally immersed in a book. The symbolic resolution of this contradiction reveals, finally, the most powerful core of the ideology of an East Asian developmental paradigm: the notion of acceleration. The figure of the young martial artist who manages to escape the constraints of the normal course of development by virtue of his access to Chinese literary culture testifies to a causal relation between the "stage" of national progress and the transformative power of literature.

Although apparently endowed with an unprecedented kind of psychological depth, women in Wang's stories invariably serve in the conclusion of the text as either the male protagonist's beautiful reward or tragic loss; in this way, their gender comes to mark the relation between the male protagonist and different types of martial arts rather than signify greater equality between men and women. In *Crane Startles Kunlun* (*Hejing Kunlun*), Ji is said to be able to win over the beautiful Phoenix from the bandits by virtue of his superior martial arts, while the suicide of the beautiful Cuixian in *Precious Sword, Golden Hairpin* is a narrative punishment Wang metes out for Li Mubai's obsession with martial arts. Either a loss or as reward, the women are always conveniently beautiful, and they allow for a comprehension of gender relations as a question of moral and historical significance. It is through men's relation to women, therefore, that Wang's novels are able to inscribe an economic logic of reward and exchange derived from the rise of bourgeois society and generalized exchange. By making men's romantic possibilities with women dependent on different types and different degrees of martial training, these novels ask us to read martial arts as a moral choice. The contrast between "women"—good, bad, mannish, feminine, beautiful, lost or earned—are the outcomes that allow the novel to develop a taxonomic discourse that divides men's relation to martial arts into proper and improper kinds.

The use of women as a narrative device to define men's pursuits and virtues is not new in Chinese literature. What distinguishes Wang Dulu's model from the standard formula in classical Chinese narrative fiction and drama, *caizi jiaren* (talented scholar meets beautiful woman), is the theme of "free love." For the first time, a female character becomes a notionally "free and equal" partner in a contractual relationship, represented both as the subject of "free love" and an independent social actor whose mobility derives from her "martial arts."[43] A *xianü*, however, only assumes a false subjectivity and independence in a novel that says her ultimate desire is her union with a man. Crucially, in writing stories about women who are skilled in martial arts, Wang Dulu is not striving to promote equality between the sexes or to dismantle dominant beliefs that martial arts should be practiced by only men. Rather, the stories record an imagination of a transgendered person—a woman trapped in the body and in the accoutrements, skills, weapons, and social meanings of a male—and her final submission to a "real man" who will restore her to her proper place as a wife (and, in the case of Jiaolong, as a mother as well).

Crane Startles Kunlun

In the story of *Crane Startles Kunlun*, composed between 1940 and 1941 but set chronologically prior to *Crouching Tiger, Hidden Dragon*, the formalism of women is represented as a hypervisibility of bodies standing in sharp contrast to the invisible cosmic forces of sexuality and sexual relations. Like *Crouching Tiger, Hidden Dragon*, the story is concerned with women and unrequited love under the social constraints of China's Confucian past. The story's use of women as a literary device, as a principle of narrative organization, is similar to that of *Crouching Tiger, Hidden Dragon*. The advantage of reinterpreting *Crouching Tiger, Hidden Dragon* as part of the pentalogy and instead of an independent, free-floating text is that this framework allows us to comprehend the significance of sexuality in Wang's construction of gender. Unlike the nationalist conception of the category of women, gender in Wang's texts is not devoid of sexuality, as the overlap between *Crane Startles Kunlun* and *Crouching Tiger, Hidden Dragon* demonstrates.

This reciprocal relation between the visible and the invisible facets of sexuality instituted in *Crane Startles Kunlun* a specific matrix of social relations in which subjects of martial development emerge. The connection between privatized sexuality and allegorical national development is ideologically veiled by the novel's inheritance and elaboration of a grid of intelligibility that foregrounds the formal attributes of gender at the expense of sexuality. The novel begins with a narrative summary that explains the brief background of the patriarch, Master Bao, who has founded the Kunlun martial school after killing some twenty or thirty "sexually licentious men and adulterous women" (*jianfu yinfu*) and now teaches martial arts for the dual purpose of physical fitness and producing a lineage of morally principled disciples. The narrative structure of the novel switches between what narratologists call "scene" and "summary," and after a long summary of sixty-four years of Master Bao's life, his past concerns and future hopes, the very first "scene" (in which the reading time or narrative time roughly approximates narrated time) concerns not martial arts action but how sexual pleasures would ruin a masculine martial artist.

> It was a typical day in the second lunar month of spring. The village is surrounded by green willows and young grass sprouts. Crops are fully grown and birds are chirping loudly. Neighing sounds of horses are heard all day and all night, as if they were in heat. Early in the morning Master Bao woke up. The sky has already turned purple, but his second son Bao Zhilin still had his door closed, a sight that greatly infuriated Master Bao. His second son just got married. This daughter-in-law has not even been in his family for two months, and she has already ruined a masculine man. It was already past dawn and his son was still in bed. Did he want to abandon all the martial skills he had spent three, four long years developing? Master Bao thought angrily, and he coughed loudly to send a warning to his second son. (3)

What kind of sexual ideology is presented here? What is in reality a depiction of a father who is intensely interested *in* his son's sex life is transformed—by rules stipulated by the incest taboo and male social bonding—into an emphatic prohibition *against* sex. The text, however, does not directly represent sexuality as a visible social relation. Rather, sexuality is only understood as a linguistic and psychological displacement. Making liberal use of traditional Chinese metaphors ("spring" [*chun*] is a code word for sex) and modernist narrative techniques (free indirect discourse), this passage allows for a pornographic effect—the reader never really "hears" or "sees" the sex scene (or the morning after sex scene), but the text is filled with a proliferation of silences. The novel provides the reader with an excessive number of details about animal sounds instead of orgasmic moans; at the same time, it also insists that the horses are hissing only *as if* they were in heat. This mode of circumlocution sustains and amplifies a voyeurism that is situated squarely at the intersection of moral edification and sexual policing. Through its narrative mechanism, sexuality in this novel is inversely inscribed in the developmental paradigm as its constitutive foreclosure. The objects that "grow" and "prosper" are not the male genitals, but the spring grass sprouts. The excitement of the horses implies an inverse correlation between the son's sexual stimulation and his lack of martial progress.

After an opening scene that connects sexuality to productivity, it is perhaps unsurprising that the very next narrative scene available in Wang's text—an encounter between Jiang and a married woman— addresses the causal relation between literary education and martial skills. The scene is prefaced, not incidentally, by an interior monologue in which Jiang laments his choice to study martial arts under the stern, morally austere master instead of pursuing a career in literary studies (10). As he is entertaining these thoughts, Jiang meets a "young and restless wife," whose husband is a traveling merchant who is "rarely home." A scene of seduction ensues, but the seduction line is spoken by a man rather than the young woman. Another man compliments Jiang on his excellence in both letters (*wen*) and martial arts (*wu*), concluding that "no wonder Mrs. Jiang looks so happy all day long." The narrator continues to describe Jiang's response: "Jiang was extremely flattered by Mr. Zhu's compliments, and fixating his gaze on the young Mrs. Lu, said, 'She [my wife] is happy, but I am yet not quite happy!'" (10). As in the earlier scene where Master Bao eavesdrops on his son's sexual activity, the reference to sex can only be made obliquely, through a euphemistic description ("happy"). The merchant's wife is silent in this scene, while the seduction is discursively initiated by and exchanged between two men. However, the true ideological force of this rhetorical substitution derives from a discourse of literacy as human developmental capital, which allows for Jiang's achievements in literary scholarship ("*wen*") to be interpreted as *evidence* of his sexual prowess in this passage ("no wonder"), despite his apparently subpar martial arts.

The emphasis on literature and the transmission of national culture explains in part the novel's contradictory investment in the project of freeing women from the institution of arranged marriage, and in the defense of the importance of kinship. The development of martial arts is represented in Wang Dulu's stories strictly in *kinship* terms, where the transmission of martial knowledge between master and disciple follows rules that determine the control, access to, and transfer of resources between clans and sects (*menpai*). Each clan functions as a kin-based income-pooling unit, whose boundaries are policed by kinship metaphors such as one's "filial" obligations to one's martial master, kin terms and symbolic titles (one's "martial brother," also translated as brothers-in-arm [*shi xiong, shi di*] or "martial sister" [*shi jie* and *shi mei*]), or rules of marriage and inheritance (*nei chuan*). Knowledge of the martial arts specific to one's own clan in these novels is considered to be a form of property and the most valuable of all resources, and the protection or pursuit of these secrets is the narrative foundation for virtually every novel in the genre. Animated by this understanding of martial arts knowledge as private property, the competition between different martial masters and their disciples invokes notions of pre-state societies, where the organization of labor and the distribution of its products are not determined by competitive logic of the individual as *homo economicus* but by kin relationships and patriarchal authority. The constellation of kin-based metaphors in martial arts fiction then attests to the mixed nature of its production: its historical mission to reconcile the concerns of a kin-based society that is being destroyed with the logic of generalized economic exchange in civil society.

Wang Dulu's *Crane Startles Kunlun* invents an exemplary narrative apparatus that dissolves these contradictions. More than his other novels, *Crane Startles Kunlun* displays an unprecedented concern with the turn of cultural logic that made productive time indispensable for collective national struggle. If kin-units rather than "the nation" serve as the fundamental sociological category in martial arts fiction, the invisible presence of the nation or questions of national development can only be restored to view if we remain sensitive to the fact that what is being described is irreducibly an allegory of how *identity* comes to be formed by the inexorable force of culture. The operative notion of cultural determinism serves to produce— in depicting and imagining kin-based networks unshaken by forces of world capitalism—the discourse of Oriental exceptionalism or the illusion of cultural insulation. It also legitimizes "genealogy"— the transmission of cultural ideals through the reproduction of male heirs—as the basis of collective struggle. The capacity of male filiation for inscribing individuals in a common racial identity crucially depends on a historically instituted differentiation between male homosexuality and male homosociality. In this context, then, it becomes particularly urgent to understand how sexuality, far from being a "merely cultural" question, is profoundly implicated in the structures of colonial domination and resistance.

The language of male bonding (fictive kinship, community-building, and secret societies) that has become the signature of martial arts fiction since Wang Dulu's time was derived from a specific form of male sociality where excessive display of men's physique was conducive rather than disruptive to male bonding. Written in the early twentieth century but set in the Qing period, the story of *Crane Startles Kunlun* employs a language of sexuality that is recognizably rooted in the Qing codes of gender (Qing sodomy legislation, late Qing feminist thought). Like other martial arts novels, *Crane Startles Kunlun* makes ample use of kinship metaphors to describe the factional conflicts between different martial schools or pseudokin units. But

Crane Startles Kunlun is revelatory of a different historical rhythm in that the distinction between kin and nonkin in the novel is made by the procreative sexuality of the heirs rather than the patriarch. Speaking of his disciples, Master Bao explains, "They're all like my sons, unless they have broken the commandment against lust" (190). In other words, the ideal of fictive kinship in the community is conditional upon the sons' sexual conduct. The absence of nonprocreative sexuality in the younger generation then is said to encode and enable a certain kind of kinship relation between the two generations. The ideal equation between discipleship and kinship, or male bonding as the basis of the transmission of culture, then depends on what constitutes "lust" or what counts as "sexual."

As the Qing legal scholar Matt Sommer has shown, homosexuality in late imperial and early Republican times was defined as an act rather than a social identity,[44] and this distinction explains why the absence of genital contact allows a number of scenes to be interpreted as instances of homosociality rather than homosexuality. What is then permitted by the cultural foreclosure of homosexual possibilities is a distinct mode of male socialization. The men in the novel are constantly undressing themselves and each other, and we find detailed, almost graphic, descriptions of their naked torsos throughout the text; often the language describes a penetrative or invasive desire. In Crane's encounters with older males, the men who take on the role of martial mentors often ask him to "open up" (*jie kai, ban kai*) his shirt and pants (rather than undress) so that they can inspect his wounds (169).

The main story plot hinges on the competition between Crane and Ji for the martial heroine Phoenix. Although the two men constantly assert their own masculinity in relation to their shared object of desire—in particular by vying to be the man who can deprive her of her virginity—the novel does not convey a sense of contradiction in filling the scene of the two men's first encounter with much homoeroticism. After a near-death experience, Ji is saved by Crane, a young man who appears to be exceedingly "masculine and strong" (*xiong zhuang*) to him. Crane then takes Ji back to his inn, where Ji's friends are appalled by the sharp contrast between the gentleman who left in the morning all prettied up (*piao liang*) and the wounded naked boy (*lian shenshang de yifu ye mei chuan*) now returning to them in the arms of another man. While Ji retires to his room "to change into something more respectable," Crane chats with Ji's friend about the weather and, commenting on the heat, takes his shirt off to reveal his "masculine, healthy, iron-hard body" (368). In their original context, these details were neither viewed as nor intended to be homoerotic. But the point is that their irrelevance to the ostensible movement of the main story plot was not questioned. There is no indication how such details were required by the novel's plot, and their usefulness, from a narrative point of view, can only be attributed to the novel's interest in gender and the ways male sexuality help the novel formalize gender.

It is precisely through male homoeroticism that women in the novel are produced as women—by distancing themselves from nonprocreative male desire. In other words, the novel relies on the demarcation between properly sexualized and putatively platonic desires to differentiate between women and men, whose genders are given and marked by the form of desire they sustain. Phoenix, although married to Ji, remains a virgin for (and thus faithful to) Crane, and within the story she offers no evidence that she is in fact biologically a woman. She does not disrobe, and there is no narrative description of her body that sufficiently feminizes her. While her gender is unintelligible according to the type of martial arts she practices, she does not need to be sexually active in order to prove to other characters or the reader that she is a woman, for her sex life is dissociated from her gender by the same mechanism that male social relations become cemented, rather than stigmatized, by their intimacy.

The discourse through bodies—the fictional display of men's naked bodies—narrates processes of male bonding. It is precisely through touching, watching, healing, feeling, emulating, and enjoying each other's bodies that teachers are able to pass on their martial knowledge to the disciples. It is also through observations of each other's physiques that the "heroes of the martial world" can identify each other. Insofar as *Crane Startles Kunlun* serves as a didactic story about the various ways in which men bond with each other through the exchange of women, it is not heterosexual desire as much as homosocial desire that is being defined by the plot of the novel. *Crane Startles Kunlun* then must be read as a cultural document testifying to the conditions before the advent of the "radical disruption" between sexuality and sociality (in Sedgwick's celebrated phrase) that has come to mark contemporary culture.

Furthermore, the cultural consensus on what counts as sexual is historically gendered, for the continuum between homosociality and homosexuality, as Sedgwick points out, is radically disrupted only in the social regulations and interpretations of male behavior, while for women, these two forms of desire are not nearly as sharply dichotomized. Foregrounding the asymmetry of power between the two genders does not lead Sedgwick to a gender-separatist model; rather, this asymmetry enables her to demonstrate that patriarchy logically and structurally depends on a prohibition against same-sex desire, and that male-male desire, immanent rather than exterior to the institution of heterosexuality, is refracted through a cultural prism as male-female bonds and for that reason remains "intelligible only through triangular relations involving a woman."[45] Sexuality in this view acquires the status of a structuring patriarchy that is capable of *defining* and producing social relations rather than passively reflecting biologically demarcated bodies. The culturally maintained separability between male homosexuality and male homosociality, moreover, derives from a conceptual framework within which certain acts are authorized to have this structuring and defining power and others do not. This cultural logic is most dramatically realized in the story of Crane's father, Jiang. After his affair with the married woman is exposed, Jiang is executed by Master Bao for breaking the "codes of martial arts," which then leads to Crane's vow to avenge his father's death, the main motor of the rest of the narrative. Before he becomes a "licentious man," however, Jiang is said to be Master Bao's favorite disciple, but not by virtue of his diligence or superior martial skills. Quite to the contrary, he is more favored than the Master's biological sons because of his exceptional looks. Watching him practice, Bao thinks to himself, "If I had a son like Jiang, wouldn't I be greatly honored? Then I would have a son to pass on my fourteen secret *Kunlun* moves to so that they wouldn't be lost." The narrator continues to describe Jiang's appearance: "His jet-black hair, a queue that's tied on top of his head three times, complements his snow-white face. Endowed with exquisite eyebrows and crystal-clear eyes, he looks almost like a beautiful woman." However, Jiang's beauty, described by a gendered language ("like a woman"), is also the cause for his master's suspicion. To Master Bao, men who are "so beautiful that they look like women" must also be excessively lustful. The distinction made between effeminate and masculine males here is clearly not one between heterosexuality and homosexuality, or heterosexual men and homosexual men, but between sexuality and nonsexuality—that is, between men who are easily aroused sexually and spread their seeds wastefully, and adherents of the Confucian order of procreative monogamy. Although Jiang protests and resents his master's accusation, his supposedly natural penchant for extramarital affairs, suggested by his "exquisite eyebrows and crystal-clear eyes," turns out to be a self-fulfilling prophecy. In order for his son's revenge to take place, there must be a mortal enemy, but Wang also wants the death of Jiang to be justified in some sense in order for there to be a genuine conflict. Since Jiang does have an affair with a woman, Master Bao feels he is enacting the will of heaven in punishing his disciple by death.

Marking certain sites—such as male-bonding—the absence, silence, and erasure of eroticism, *Crane Startles Kunlun* expands the apparatus of sexuality instead of reducing it. This distinction between what is sexual and what is nonsexual is always culturally contingent, and made in the service of classifications that augment and legitimize the interest of certain groups. Crucially, however, the text is able to present the male gender as a gender anchored in a physical body by constraining the meanings of homosexuality to an act rather than a desire. If the legal, political, and medical texts at the time indicate that late Qing Chinese culture viewed homosexuality as an act rather than a species, an orientation, or a minority group, then this distinction was further predicated on the naturalization of women as an anatomically distinct species of human being, the politicization of women as rights-bearing individuals, and the objectification of women as the state's pastoral concerns. This text, in other words, is informed by a historical system of gender and sexuality that began to read woman as a rights-bearing individual whose gender is predefined, and man as a desiring subject whose gender is acquired through processes of homosocial bonding. The fact that this late Republican text could be written in this language without being read as sexualized text suggests a historically contingent mode of differentiating between act and desire. This interpretation identifies gender in the domain of the visible, while containing sexuality in the invisible interstices of society. Through Wang's radical intervention, however, we might come to a more precise understanding of the gendered meaning of the body, one that perhaps has useful implications for contemporary uses of feminism as well.

NOTES

1. "Crouching Tiger and the Dream of Cultural China," 25.

2. "Crouching Tiger, Hidden Dragon, Bouncing Angels: Hollywood, Taiwan, Hong Kong, and Transnational Cinema," 223.

3. Stephen Teo makes a similar argument in his "*Wuxia* Redux: Crouching Tiger, Hidden Dragon as a Model of Late Transnational Production."

4. David Ansen, *Newsweek*, April 18, 2005.

5. Jonathan Foreman. "From China With Love" *New York Post*, Dec. 8, 2000.

6. Lisa Schwarzbaum, *Entertainment Weekly*, November 29, 2000.

7. Bordwell describes Lee's film as the "millennial synthesis" of the entirety of the *wuxia* cinema created by "Hong Kong directors" in "Hong Kong Martial Arts Cinema." *Planet Hong Kong*, 20.

8. Christina Klein identifies Ang Lee's Chinese cultural identity, his position in the Chinese diaspora, and the influence of Hollywood as three overdetermining sources that shaped the film. "*Crouching Tiger, Hidden Dragon*: A Diasporic Reading."

9. Kenneth Chan's "The Global Return of the Wu Xia Pian (Chinese Sword-Fighting Movie): Ang Lee's *Crouching Tiger, Hidden Dragon*" reads the film as a tortured critique of China-centrism that nevertheless inculcates a false sense of Chineseness in the Chinese diaspora.

10. *Visuality and Identity: Sinophone Articulations across the Pacific* (University of California Press, 2007).

11. Shih, 37.

12. Zhang Zhen, "Bodies in the Air," 53. See also her *An Amorous History of the Silver Screen*, 199–243.

13. Altenburger, *The Sword or the Needle*, 364.

14. See Hung Chang-tai, *War and Popular Culture: Resistance in Modern China, 1937–1945*, 72–78, for a detailed analysis of the influence of these works and the common use of women as a symbol of resistance during this time.

15. The city of Qingdao has occupied a unique emotional place in the Chinese nationalist imagination. Between 1897 and 1918, Qingdao was Germany's prized, sole colonial possession in China, which served as a naval base, industrial center, and terminus of railways for the German Far East Squadron. China entered the war on the side of the Triple Entente in 1917 with Britain's promise that the Province of Shandong, in which the city Qingdao was located, would be restored to Chinese sovereignty after the defeat of Germany. However, at the conclusion of the First World War, Article 156 of the Treaty of Versailles transferred all German concessions in Shandong to the Empire of Japan instead. The "Shandong Problem" of 1919 is often compared to the Munich agreement with Hitler of 1938 in Chinese nationalist writings, and historians have commonly identified the Shandong Problem as the catalyst for the May Fourth Movement in China, which in turn has been exalted and reified as the beginning of Chinese modernity. In 1922 Qingdao reverted to Chinese rule, only to fall to Japan again in 1938. For a detailed analysis of German Orientalism and German colonial operations in China, see David Goodman and Yixu Lu, *Germany in China: Colonial Interactions, Qingdao 1897–1914*.

16. Wang Dulu did not publish the novels in the order of their internal chronology. Wang's first story in the series, *Baojian jinchai ji* (Precious Sword, Golden Hairpin), was followed by the sequel to the story, *Jianqi zhuguang lu* (Sword Energy, Pearl Shine, 1939–1940), and a prequel, *Hejing Kunlun* (Crane Startles Kunlun) (originally *Wu he ming luan ji* (Dancing Crane, Singing Phoenix, 1940–1941). The fourth and fifth novels are *Wohu canglong* (Crouching Tiger, Hidden Dragon, 1941–1942) and *Tieji yinping* (Iron Steed, Silver Vase, 1942–1944).

17. For a useful cultural history of the changing relationships between love and politics, see Lee Haiyan, *Revolution of the Heart*.

18. Xu Sinian, *Xia de zongji*, 127–132.

19. On feudalism, see Chapter One.

20. Cited in Sang, "The Transgender Body in Wang Dulu's Crouching Tiger, Hidden Dragon."

21. Gu Long, "Wo kan wuxia."

22. See Ye Hongsheng, *"Beiju xiaqing zhizu"* (The founding father of a tragic, chivalrous kind of love), *Minsheng bao*, June 1982.

23. Xia Xiaohong, "Cong nannü pingdeng dao nüquan yishi—wan qing de funü sichao" (From equality between men and women to the consciousness of women's rights—women's movement in the Late Qing period), *Beijing daoxue xuebao* no. 4, 1995, and *Wan qing funü wenren guan* (Late Qing women literati's view).

24. Liu Jen-peng, *Jindai zhongguo nuquan lunshu.*

25. See Tani Barlow and Angela Zito, eds., *Body, Subject, and Power in China.*

26. Tani Barlow, *The Question of Women in Chinese Feminism*, 37–59.

27. Hu Ying, *Tales of Translation: Composing the New Woman in China, 1898–1918.*

28. Lu Xun's own intellectual debt to Darwinism is a widely published secret. See James Pusey, *Lu Xun and Darwinism.*

29. See Liu, Ibid. 109.

30. Liang Qichao, *Xinmin Congbao*, 2/8/1902, quoted in Peng Hsiao-yen, 2.

31. James Pusey, *China and Charles Darwin*, 101–103. Charlotte Furth delivers a trenchant critique of May Fourth feminism as a nationalist ideology of "producing strong mothers to bear healthy sons," in *Gender Politics in Modern China.*

32. Mao, *New Youth*, April 1917.

33. Haiyan Lee, "Governmentality and the Aesthetic State: A Chinese Fantasia"; Hiroko Sakamoto, "The Cult of 'Love and Eugenics' in May Fourth Movement Discourse."

34. See Peng Hsiao-yen, "*Wusi de xin xingdaode: nüxing qingyu lunshu yu jian'gou minzuguojia*" (May Fourth "new sexual ethics": The discourse of female desire and nation-building), in *Haishang shuo qingyu*, 1–26.

35. Focusing on the oral histories of women, Wang Zheng's *Women in the Chinese Enlightenment* positions itself as a critique of the official Chinese Communist Party's stories of women's liberation. Wang concludes that the "new woman" as an ideal was both instrumentalized by male nationalists and conducive to progressive social change for women.

36. See Li Xiaojiang, *Xingbie yu Zhongguo.*

37. Lydia Liu, *Translingual Practice*, 194.

38. Sieber, *Red Is Not the Only Color*, 11. For a lucid analysis of the limits of recuperative feminist history and ways to "cultivate alternative habits of mind in thinking about gender," see Gail Hershatter, *Women in China's Long Twentieth Century.*

39. Macpherson distinguishes between an "ethical" imperative and a "moral" imperative of possessive individualism. In his view, the development of world capitalism logically preceded the rise of liberal philosophy, which came into being only because competitive society first created an ethical "pressure for democracy" that sought to include the disenfranchised in the

system. An economic restructuring of society then became misunderstood as the ethical requirement to extend individual rights to the masses. This ethical imperative, however, then gave rise to a somewhat different moralizing discourse, which conjured up an image of the "new society" for both the liberal thinkers and the now enlightened masses to distance themselves, once and for all, from the older system (utilitarianism, etc.). C.B. Macpherson, *The Political Theory of Possessive Individualism: Hobbes to Locke*; see also, Carole Pateman, *The Sexual Contract*, 154–188.

40. All citations here refer to William Lyell's standard translation of Lu Xun.

41. In response to the influential work of Judith Butler's problematization of the category of women as the basis of feminism, critics in China studies have begun to historicize the various forms of Chinese feminist thought without abandoning the feminist project itself. Ding Naifei's *Obscene Things*, Josephine Chuen-rui Ho's *Haoshuang Nüren* (*The Gallant Woman*), Tani Barlow's *The Question of Woman in Chinese Feminism*, and Lisa Rofel's *Other Modernities: Gendered Yearnings in China after Socialism* represent a concerted effort in this direction.

42. Gayle Rubin, "Thinking Sex."

43. On the relation between sexual autonomy and "conversation," see Denise Riley, "The Right to be Lonely."

44. Marinus Meijer suggests that male anal intercourse was not banned until the mid-Qing, but only then "as part of a consistent effort to ban all sexual intercourse outside marriage" (Meijer, Marinus, "Homosexual Offenses in Ch'ing Law," *T'oung pao* 71[1985], 109, quoted in Sommer, 115). Here Matthew Sommer raises the pertinent question—why among "all sexual intercourse outside marriage," Qing lawmakers singled out male anal intercourse "over other possible scenarios." "For example, they never banned sex between women—indeed, I find not a single mention, let alone prohibition, of female homosexual acts in any Qing or earlier legal source (not to mention other extramarital practices familiar from the Western legal tradition, such as masturbation and bestiality)." Sommer finds an explanation in the "penetration hierarchy" that anal intercourse creates; in other words, in the fact that anal intercourse between men (or, more accurately, by men to men) is uniquely capable of posing itself as *analogous* to heterosexual vaginal intercourse, an analogy that is not culturally available to other "scenarios" or social offenses "outside marriage" such as masturbation. Sommer's findings suggest that Qing legal culture made a distinction between "gender" and "sexuality," where genders were retroactively derived from by sexual acts, and for that reason only a finite number of sexual acts that were generative of meanings of gender received a legal definition.

45. Eve Sedgwick, *Between Men*; and *The Epistemology of the Closet*, 15.

Chapter 3

THE PERMANENT ARMS ECONOMY
Jin Yong's Historical Fiction and the Cold War in Asia

> "It is clear that the arm of criticism cannot replace the criticism of arms."
> —Marx, "Contribution to the Critique of Hegel's Philosophy of Right"

The best way to characterize Jin Yong, the only living Chinese author still using the idiom of traditional Chinese narrative fiction, is as the last organic intellectual of China. In the popular imaginary, Jin Yong's name is synonymous with *wuxia* fiction. No other author in twentieth-century Chinese letters has been nearly as successful at creating an aesthetic paradigm—the New School martial arts novel—from China's own indigenous resources. Since the May Fourth period, the concept of literary modernity in China has been equated with the translation, introduction, and emulation of Western fiction.[1] Although certain literary movements in the post–Cultural Revolution phase, such as root-seeking literature (*xungen wenxue*), have questioned the May Fourth iconoclastic belief that modernity could only be attained through the radical negation of one's own past, the idea that Europeanization equals modernization prevailed. Over the course of the twentieth century, the Chinese language was Europeanized and simplified, and its classical usage abandoned. The only historically successful alternative to the Europeanization of Chinese letters has been the indigenous aesthetic form of martial arts literature. Instead of turning to Western modernism for inspiration, Jin Yong finds intellectual sustenance for modern literary creativity in the discarded and demonized aesthetics of traditional Chinese vernacular fiction.

Jin Yong's project converts stigmatized nodes of local knowledge and practice into a modernist movement that can serve at once as a tool for the critique of contemporary politics and as a restorative agent, allowing his readers to recover and reestablish meaningful relations with a cultural heritage that had been violently severed and destroyed by Chinese intellectuals themselves. Jin Yong's efforts have not been in vain. The best-selling Chinese author alive, he has penned fifteen martial arts novels in addition to a multitude of essays and commentaries on current events. As a prominent public intellectual, he has also participated in a number of pivotal political events: among other things, he served on the drafting committee for the transfer of Hong Kong's sovereignty to China. Jin Yong's passion for contemporary politics joins with his belief in a creative, almost mythical, energy that emanates from China's history to produce an oeuvre that is full of brilliance, surprises, and insight into the human character. His works are justly loved not only for their ingeniously described martial actions, but for the complex array of memorable characters and cultural personalities he has crafted. Jin Yong's characters represent the arduous but necessary struggles of human life in emotional, social, and political frameworks. By exploring "character" as the total effect of social and political processes involved in the formation of culture, Jin Yong develops a unique theory of the subject in the beginning years of the Cold War when Mao's China descends into a permanent arms economy.

Jin Yong was a product of a unique historical moment, and his fiction was a conscious response to the political conditions of that moment. Much like his writing style, which is firmly grounded in classical motifs, Jin Yong's career as a writer signifies a condition of literary production that was no longer possible in China after classical Chinese education was replaced in the curriculum by the instrumental, technical knowledge geared toward the professional needs of bureaucratic and managerial elites. Unlike the Confucian literati in China before the abolition of the Civil Examination system, the modern dominant bourgeoisie no longer needed the cultural capital of classical Chinese literature for cultural distinction, social benefits, and upward class mobility. This context makes Jin Yong's writing particularly significant. Born in Zhejiang, China, Jin Yong was able to receive a classical education (and, later, a university education in international law at Dongwu University) before emigrating to Hong Kong in 1948. Jin Yong's life experience and literary career bear witness to the great transformation in China's literary market and education system—a transformation that quantified knowledge production and intellectual labor. Jin Yong has found great success since the publication of his first martial arts novel, *Book and Sword*, in 1955. No other living novelist has been able to support himself or herself over half a century—and fund further study overseas, a large personal library, a newspaper, and other self-improvement projects—on fame and revenues derived from fifteen novels alone. On the strength of his fictional works, composed in a language that the committee could not even read, Jin Yong received the Order of the British Empire from the British government in 1981 and has been made an honorary doctor and an honorary professor by over twenty prestigious universities in China and abroad, including Peking University and the University of Cambridge. Yet the unprecedented success of Jin Yong's career is the product of unique and transitional circumstances that were not reproduced since the advent of universal capitalism.

Jin Yong's literary career represents the successful transcendence of the requirements of industrial capitalism. It is fitting that a mythical sense of man's preindustrial history forms the thematic nexus of his fiction, while his characters constitute a distinctively precapitalist, antisystemic ensemble of social relations. Jin Yong is famous for using fictional anecdotes to concoct logically satisfactory explanations of well-known gaps and holes in the official dynastic records of the Chinese historians. These gaps include the mysterious disappearance of an official, the coincidence of historical events, and unexpected failures of armies and leaders. The novels are squarely grounded in both historical research and literary erudition: one of his characters, for example, claims to be the object of an enigmatic allusion in a famous Chinese poem. Jin Yong's blending of fact and fiction—are we reading a historical novel, or fictionalized historiography?—has always been an object of scholarly fascination and debate. Jin Yong deftly converts a mountain of historical facts into exquisite etiological myth, and the result is a tour de force that astonishes as much as it seduces the reader. A dense interweaving of classical artifacts and contemporary politics, Jin Yong's oeuvre compels and enables its readers to reflect on their relation to history. In Jin Yong's early martial arts novels, this reflection takes place through a genealogy of selfhood, an investigation of the historicity of the self.

The panorama of imperial Chinese history, combined with the intellectual landscape of contemporary politics, serves as the foundation of Jin Yong's aesthetic practice. It provides the last bastion against the reification, mechanization, and fragmentation of modernity. Jin Yong's martial arts characters live in a unified, holistic community where mankind is one with the natural world. The community, *jianghu*, exists in a suspended space of statelessness, devoid of any vestiges of capitalism, rationalized governance, or clamors for economic growth. The persistent thematization of the prelapsarian innocence of martial arts culture in a late twentieth-century modernist novel embodies a critical consciousness of the loss and pain that attend the universal advent of industrialization. Jin Yong's works are not an escapist fantasy; they offer concrete critique of industrialization grounded in contemporary politics. What appears to be an advocate of violence—the genre of martial arts fiction—in Jin Yong becomes a pacifist objection to war, one that uses the theme of martial violence to highlight the vulnerability of the human body and the precariousness of human life. Jin Yong conducts this critique through a dialectical movement between self and history that I call "ethical alterity." This chapter provides a reinterpretation of the theme of ethical alterity in two of Jin Yong's early martial arts novels in relation to his little known political writings on Mao's concept of revolutionary violence. I argue that Jin Yong's New School martial arts fiction should not be viewed as a reactionary piece of traditional culture; rather, Jin Yong's novels present a critique of "necropolitics," the regime during the Great Leap Forward and the

Cultural Revolution that channels the fruits of human labor, not into the production of the means of production, but into the production of the means of destruction.[2]

A journalist by training, Jin Yong composed only fifteen fictional works in his life, all martial arts novels published between 1955 and 1972. Aside from one novella, the fourteen major novels use titles that form an elegant seven-character couplet (*qiyan shi*) that Jin Yong composed himself. His vast erudition and grandiloquent language incurred the wrath of his critics and competitors in Beijing, whose own formal education was interrupted by the Cultural Revolution. In a particularly notorious incident in 1995, Wang Shuo, a prominent writer in Beijing, attacked Jin Yong's novels as "poisonous weeds from Old China." Wang dismissed Jin Yong's kaleidoscopic display of traditional Chinese cultural knowledge as "a big show-off," and Wang's statement quickly angered many academics and fans of Jin Yong.[3] The Wang Shuo incident is illustrative of the perception that Jin Yong's novels appear utterly out of sync with the contemporary realities of modern China in the People's Republic, where the Chinese language has been simplified, a "New China" and "Liberation" proclaimed, and Western literary models heralded as the standards of modernity.

The reception of Jin Yong reveals much about his aesthetics and the political interventions he seeks to make through his fiction. Since the 1990s, Jin Yong has become canonized in the People's Republic of China. If Confucianism and other relics of "feudal" culture once served as the imaginary Other and principal antagonist in the stories leftist intellectuals told about China's need for Westernization and revolutions, today the same cultural references are being reclaimed by the People's Republic of China as a significant component of its modern self-identity. Just as Germany's Goethe Institute and France's Alliance Française were created to promote their nations' cultural history, the Confucius Institute in Beijing was created by China's Ministry of Education in 2004 to teach and promote Chinese culture worldwide. In a similar reclamation process, the authorities in Beijing who once saw martial arts fiction in general and Jin Yong in particular as a cause for embarrassment now consider the Hong

Kong-based author to be the gem of the culture of the People's Republic of China—a transformation that certainly complicates the nationalist–antinationalist debate that marked his early reception.

Controversies surrounding Jin Yong's rehabilitation erupted in 2004 when an excerpt of his martial arts novel, *Tianlong Babu*, appeared in the revised high school textbook published by the People's Education Press, and then again, more violently, in 2007 when another excerpt of his work replaced a short story by Lu Xun—the figure lionized as "the father of modern literature" by the Chinese Communist Party—in the official high school textbook for Beijing high school students.[4] Heated debates, furious diatribes, and pseudo-scientific polls mushroomed in newspapers and on the Internet. The controversy soon led to the internationally notorious "Kubin Incident." Wolfgang Kubin, a German sinologist at Bonn University, was appalled by the replacement of Lu Xun by Jin Yong, which he considered to be a telling sign of the degeneration of Chinese culture. In an interview with Deutsche Welle (Germany's international broadcaster) and several highly publicized exchanges with prominent Chinese scholars such as Li Jingze, Kubin described contemporary Chinese fiction as "trash" and "prostitution." Kubin argued that by world standards Chinese writers are inferior, backward, and uneducated, and the reason is simple: they write in Chinese instead of English or German. "After 1949, you basically cannot find a Chinese writer who can speak a foreign language. Therefore, he cannot use another language system to examine his own work. ... When Chinese writers go overseas, they have to rely on the Sino-logists because they can't even speak a word of foreign language. They rely on us completely."[5] In a later article published after the interviews, Kubin states that Jin Yong belongs to the ranks of "female writers specialized in the description of private parts, who sell ten thousands of copies of whatever they can get published in German or English. This is a sales figure Lu Xun—even in times when his works were a hot item—could have only dreamt of."[6] Kubin's remarks naturally angered the Chinese public, but the backlashes against Kubin often only replaced his Orientalism with nationalism. The "Kubin Incident" catapulted Jin Yong and the "Jin Yong phenomenon"—the surprising fin-de-siècle canonization of martial arts fiction in mainland China after decades of official censorship and opposition—to the forefront of media attention. Instead of adjudicating between nationalist and Orientalist interpretations of Jin Yong, I would argue that such frameworks are wholly inadequate for responding to the historical questions raised by his fiction.

In Jin Yong's own words, "Lu Xun and Ba Jin did not create a modern Chinese literature. They merely wrote Western literature in the Chinese language."[7] Jin Yong's novels, by contrast, have gone largely untranslated, mainly due to their extraordinary length, the unprecedented density of their historical allusions, and the lexical complexity of their prose.[8] When the ambitious project of translating Jin Yong's major novels was first proposed, it was taken up by John Minford, the learned British translator of Chinese classics that include *The Story of the Stone* (*Dream of the Red Chamber*) and *The Art of War*.[9] Minford spent eleven years on *The Deer and the Cauldron* alone, beginning the project in 1991. Although he was able to finish translating only one-third of the novel after several years, from the publication of that fragment by Hong Kong University Press in October 1997 he "learned at first hand to what extent [he] was enmeshed in a public event."[10] Translating Jin Yong into English was a politicized event that attracted much media attention. The last installment of the translation appeared more than a decade after the project began. Yet Jin Yong himself is an even more rigorous wordsmith than Minford. At the peak of his career in 1972 he announced, to the consternation of his fans, that he would "seal off his pen" (*fengbi*) and never write another martial arts novel. Instead, he would spend his remaining life refining and revising the fifteen novels he had already published, further confounding would-be translators. As a result, Jin Yong's novels today exist in three official editions (not counting the original serialized versions in newspapers),[11] and since 1979 there has been at least one TV series adaptation of one of the fifteen novels produced by Hong Kong, Taiwan, or (since 2001) mainland Chinese stations per year. In recent years, Jin Yong's novels have also been adapted into theatrical performances, including productions in the United States, such as Yangtze Repertory Theatre of America's "Laughing in the Wind: A Cautionary Tale in Martial Arts." Perpetually readapted and consumed by contemporary Chinese-language communities, these fifteen novels contain an emotional depth and richness that seem inexhaustible.

Despite the intense interest in Jin Yong's literary works, his early journalism has received little scholarly attention. Critics who hold Jin Yong to be a nationalist writer might be surprised by the fact that he was a steadfast pacifist in the debates about China's nuclear experiments in the early Cold War era. Before he elaborated on his theory of ethical alterity in his novels, Jin Yong had already delivered a critique of the political concepts of "just war" and "ethical violence" in the wake of the destruction of Hiroshima and Nagasaki. We should not therefore reduce his novels to either a "nationalist" or an "antinationalist" framework of understanding. Rather, they express a pacifist resistance movement to the Cold War political culture and its rhetoric of "permanent emergency." Jin Yong's writings, especially his martial arts fiction, explore the precariousness of human life and the vulnerability of the body in order to highlight the constitutive sociality of the self. This philosophical exploration of the subject as radically dependent on Others allows Jin Yong to contest the notions of sovereignty and freedom in the nationalist imagination.

Jin Yong's journalistic work responded to Mao's insistence that the acquisition of the nuclear bomb would be the only path to national independence from the hegemony of the Soviet Union and the United States. Jin Yong's critique revealed Mao's brand of Marxism to be a form of voluntarism, a discourse of Oriental exceptionalism founded on the premise that a Great Leap Forward program would allow China to skip certain stages in the materialist conception of history and directly advance to socialism. It is well known that while China followed the Soviet model in the 1950s and prioritized the development of heavy industry funded by surpluses extracted from the peasantry, the Great Leap Forward was a distinctively indigenous idea of Maoism. Mao argued that China could advance directly to Communism through a mobilization of its massive labor force. Jin Yong's journalistic and fictional writings constitute an intellectual critique of voluntarism. Jin Yong consistently emphasizes that a person's identity is never decided or authored by that person; rather, a subject is produced in and by a field of norms that exceed the self. To be a socially viable being means to consign oneself to the social norms that constitute one's existence—norms which do not originate with an individual personhood and may indeed threaten and imperil one's livability. The point is not a masochistic call to accept and surrender oneself to an oppressive external power that encroaches on one's livelihood; rather, the point is to take stock of the limits of social autonomy and to recognize that there is no "I" that is not in some way constituted by unwelcome constraints, norms, and regulations. Jin Yong's early Cold War novels are devoted to the development of this ethical perspective on the primary sociality and vulnerability of the self. These philosophical ruminations, in turn, offer a critique of the nationalist response to violence through the radical assertion of autonomy.

The standard interpretation of Jin Yong today is that he is a nationalist writer who routinely depicts the virtues and superiority of Han Chinese civilization in the face of foreign invasions. Critics in the Anglophone scholarly community have commonly accepted the assumption that Jin Yong's works represent scenarios of national crisis and cultural identity, which have become appealing to the Chinese audience (in particular the Chinese diaspora) as a result of the political weaknesses of the Chinese states and the problems of "modernity." This presupposition dominates Chinese-language scholarship as well. It is certainly true that Jin Yong's fiction repeatedly represents scenes of a China under foreign invasion. Whether these themes immediately serve the purpose of the promotion of patriotic values, however, deserves a careful consideration. If we study Jin Yong's development of martial arts aesthetics against the historical trajectory of Chinese nationalism, the representation of nationalist struggle might appear less a defense of China's sovereignty and need for modernization, and more a martial arts idiom serving as an aesthetic mode of narrating the relationality of the self, which sets the author precisely apart from the nationalist rhetoric of territorial integrity, political autonomy, and economic independence.

As I argued in Chapter One, the project of rewriting the idiom of classics such as *The Romance of the Three Kingdoms*, *Three Gallants and Five Knights*, and *The Water Margin* into the modern *wuxia* novel became stigmatized as "popular fiction" precisely because it was historically incompatible with the aims of Chinese nationalism when Confucianism came under attack. In Jin Yong's literary imagination, China's own indigenous history is a potentiality, not a liability. The turn to martial arts—a preindustrial use of the body and obsolete mode of combat—as the defining idiom of a new aesthetic practice resists the effects of mechanization and automatization in industrial capitalism, including industrial state capitalism in nominally socialist countries. In Wang Dulu's pre-1949 novels, characters still have nameable occupations that allow the reader to situate them in the concrete world of labor, and they often practice martial arts as a "pastime" in contrast to their real jobs as peasants, merchants, or ironsmiths. By the time we get to Jin Yong's works, martial arts takes on the phantasmagoric character of a pseudo-occupation. More accurately, the question of productive labor—what constitutes and reproduces a human being materially—is simply suspended in Jin Yong's works, and *wuxia* presents itself tautologically as both the source and the reward of all human productive activity, standing in for all concrete labors. Martial arts, in this case, masquerade not as the universal equivalent of concrete and real labors, but as the only imaginable form of human productive activity.

Because Jin Yong's fiction deliberately occludes the need for industrialization, martial arts are abstracted from real kung fu and represented instead as a mode of social mediation, grounded in the principles of classical poetry rather than action. Jin Yong's greatest contribution to the genre is indeed the invention of an imitable, idiomatic apparatus for the representation of martial arts as elegant "four-character phrases" (*chengyu*). The martial arts of his characters are given names created in accordance with the poetic principles of parallelism and symmetry, which serve as organic links between the pre-statist intellectual resources such as Buddhist scriptures and Confucian exegeses before the "Literary Revolution" of the May Fourth era. Jin Yong's immersion in neo-Confucianism, Buddhism,

Taoism, and classical Chinese poetics produced an aesthetic apparatus that feels *sui generis*. His erudite martial arts novels blur the distinction between historical scholarship and creative writing. Combining the density of poetry with the versatility of prose, Jin Yong's narratives construct complex, dazzling verbal labyrinths with materials gleaned from years of rumination and archival research in Chinese historiography, medicine, astrology, mathematics, botany, divination, and philosophy.

By today's standards, these novels belong to obsolete conditions of cultural production where the right to write a work with a long shelf life, fictional or nonfictional, could be earned only by hours of labor in the library. No other contemporary trend—experimental fiction, avant-garde literature, root-seeking literature, scar literature, rural literature—places a similar emphasis on historical research. Crammed with fascinating lore, Jin Yong's novels often read more like cultural encyclopedias than traditional novels. This is true of his plots as well. The "martial" development of his characters is more typically concerned with historical knowledge than with real martial arts. For example, an adventure undertaken by the characters in *The Eagle-Shooting Heroes* (*Shediao yingxiong zhuan*, 1957) focuses on a mathematical puzzle first formulated by ancient Chinese philosophers, with which modern readers would likely be unfamiliar. This gives Jin Yong's novels an additional function as a reintroduction to the intellectual heritage of Chinese antiquity. A protracted "battle" in the same novel describes not martial arts but the deployment of stones and combatants in formations according to the hexagrams in the *Book of Changes* (*Yijing*), one of the oldest texts in the classical Chinese canon. The "martial arts" acquired by his characters are not limited to kung fu narrowly conceived in terms of combat. They take the form of the mastery of musical instruments; poetry composition contests; chess-play; proper identification and use of herbs and other medicinal remedies; and culinary knowledge of the ingredients of real or fantastic dishes in historical China. Jin Yong's martial arts novels, in short, are brimming with cultural lore that is invariably rendered with detail, infused with vividness, and bursting with arcane brilliance. At his best moments, Jin Yong moves effortlessly between the microscopic detail of ancient everyday life and the telescopic grandeur of dynastic change and revolutions, creating novels of unprecedented emotional import and richness that restore the organicity of ancient China to the contemporary reading public.

The Permanent Arms Economy of *Tianlong Babu*

In the immediate postwar period, Jin Yong confronted the political and ethical question of an oppressed people's right to armed response as a path to liberation. China's answer to this problem took shape as Mao's Third Worldism, which demonstrated characteristics of Frantz Fanon's radical revolutionary violence and conservative "just war" theories. To some extent, the conservative character of third-world revolutionary movements is obscured by the very logic of power that they oppose. In the era of state-based colonialism, domination appeared to be a relation between states, as an act of intrusion, as one nation's conquest and subjugation of another nation's subjects and territories. In the Cold War era where both the oppressors and the oppressed turned to technology as a source of empowerment, domination took on a novel meaning. It became an internal and internalized relation between the spheres of production, circulation, consumption, and distribution within the third-world country itself. In hindsight, we might conclude that the most deleterious and insidious effect of the Cold War era was the creation of a "treadmill effect" to which Chinese revolutionary politics willingly or unwillingly subscribed. Resources were funneled into war mobilization efforts in the name of peace, security, sovereignty, and survival; civil liberties were suspended for the greater cause of national independence. Power was no longer external. It became the political logic of the oppressed. The colonized country's unfreedom from power was also its unfreedom from the determinations of real or perceived foreign threat, even in times of peace.

The logic of the Cold War transformed communism from a social justice program into a recipe for national development. China's "power struggle" with the advanced capitalist countries replaced domestic redistributive economic justice as the aim of collectivization. Instead of solving the problem of egoism and self-interest in civil society, the Great Leap Forward transformed socialism into the endless accumulation of capital on the global scale. China's enmeshment in the global arms race rendered the idea of "socialism in one country" a mockery of itself. Responding to American imperialism with a policy of increased productivity and military modernization meant, ironically, that accumulating industrial capital became the main national objective of a socialist country. In 1957 Mao declared that China's industrial output and steel production would overtake that of Great Britain and the United States in fifteen years (*chaoying ganmei*). That the Great Leap Forward had to be accomplished through forced collectivization— the expropriation of the peasantry—reveals capitalism's uglier face.

The force of capitalist power no longer merely pressed China from the outside. It also shaped China's internal responses to imperialism; its priorities, policies, and commitments; and its self-identity. The mainstream discourses of the Great Leap Forward and the Cultural Revolution offered only one solution to the American strategy of containment: modernizing China's military. By extension, China could become sovereign, independent, and free from American blackmail only by acquiring nuclear powers. The burden of an intellectual during the Cold War was to devise an effective means to counter the simplistic dichotomy of domination and resistance, which was a particularly appealing discourse when the threat of U.S.-led global crusade against Communism was real enough, and destructive enough, but the idea of national independence and memory of colonial dismemberment was already too easily and too frequently abused by nationalist writers and policymakers.

Tianlong babu (1963) is Jin Yong's most ambitious exploration of the problem of "permanent emergency." It draws on the Buddhist concepts of the transience or impermanence of life, suffering, and attachment, to critique the contemporary rhetoric of preemptive war mobilization. Above all, the novel builds on a secularized idea of the Buddhist notion that one can only exit the cycle of suffering and reincarnation inherent in life by coming to realize that the self is an illusion. Jin Yong reformulates the Buddhist concept of compassion here, in a secular context, as a philosophy of ethical alterity, a demand placed by an Other. In the context of the political culture of the early Cold War era, the novel's deconstruction of the category of the self provides a series of powerful reflections on the structure and conditions of permanent war.

This lengthy novel, published in either five or ten separate volumes in mainland Chinese, Hong Kong, and Taiwanese editions, contains four overlapping parts. The first three parts of the novel are focalized omniscient narrations, each filtered through the consciousness of a different protagonist. In the fourth part, the three major characters meet again, and a unified perspective is offered as the novel reaches its climax and denouement. Thematically, the novel is explicitly concerned with interstate, interethnic, and geopolitical conflicts, and for this reason it has been interpreted by numerous critics as a nationalist text.[12] Its narrative organization, however, shows that the novel does not endorse any one particular set of cultural values; rather, it enacts and represents a multiplicity of political perspectives. In this sense, it construes the human subject as contingent and decentered, and relativizes it by emphasizing its radical dependency on sources and agencies that will always remain incomplete and unknown to the erroneous self that claims to be the center of its own being.

The three protagonists: Duan Yu, Xiao Feng, and Xu Zhu, represent a diverse range of national identifications, life experiences, birth-accidents, and cultural values; their martial adventures form a web of causations that takes the narrative to different regions both within and outside China's national borders during the Song dynasty. The first protagonist, Duan Yu, is the prince of the Buddhist Kingdom of Dali. The bulk of this section of the novel takes place in China's southern provinces—famous for their lakes, rivers, canals, and beautiful wo-men. The second protagonist, Xiao Feng, is the martial leader of the Beggar Clan in Song China who spends the latter half of his time in the novel living with the nomadic Khitan people in the northern steppes. The third protagonist, Xu Zhu, begins as an ordinary, talentless novice monk in the enclosed Shaolin monastery. Driven by circumstances beyond his will and control, Xu Zhu travels to the remote mountains of the West. He eventually becomes the leader of a powerful and mysterious martial clan made up of exclusively female acolytes, and marries the princess of the empire of Western Xia, another political rival/ally of China during this historical period. The novel is thus set in an extremely complex geopolitical map of the Northern Song that, as Carlos Rojas points out in a brilliant study, itself relies on the visual objects in the text to construct "social and psychic processes of identification with 'imaginary' communities of various sorts."[13]

By design, the three characters are extremely mobile in their physical location and emotional identification. The idiom of statelessness here, however, is not the same as utopian cosmopolitanism; the novel does not represent these characters as unbounded beings who freely choose their own political allegiance, cultural identification, or personal subjectivity. Rather, their movement across political boundaries and through competing modes of political jurisdiction forms the historical context that allows Jin Yong to elaborate a theory of the stateless subject. Philosophically grounded in the novel's Buddhist intertexts, this subject is the product of social constraints and only appears to be autonomous and voluntary. Each character's life story appears to be independent at first, in either the geographical or logical sense of the word. The characters are separate; in fact, the unity of the novel is not understood by the three characters themselves. Although they are bound by fate, all three together neither meet nor know each other. In an episode reminiscent of the famous Oath of the Peach Garden in *The Romance of the Three Kingdoms*, Duan Yu and Xiao Feng meet at an inn and become sworn brothers. Later, Duan Yu also meets Xu Zhu and becomes brothers with him, although Xiao Feng and Xu Zhu never learn of each other's existence until the final part of the novel. In contrast to the classical novel, where Liu Bei's value of the bonds of brotherhood alters the course of history and brings about the downfall of his nation and the eventual triumph of the Wei state, the sworn brotherhood in *Tianlong babu* takes place on a whim and has very little bearing on the novel's plot development.

The tenuous and misrecognized connection between the protagonists is part of the novel's design and symbolism. The reader's
knowledge of the events is consistently greater than that of the
characters, and the novel's narrative structure highlights the
limitations of individual consciousness, the fact that the human
subject is always opaque to itself. The three characters, who live
seemingly independent lives and values, turn out to be connected
to each other through a complex web of interpersonal relations
and prior histories, to which the reader alone is privy. Through a
story based on these characters, cosmopolitan in their movement
but limited in their consciousness, Jin Yong represents and
captures the tragedy of our atomized existence. The appearance
of an autonomous self turns out to be an illusion. This novelistic
irony provides the basis of Jin Yong's ethical critique of nationalist
responses to the problem of Western imperialism in the Maoist era,
such as the rhetoric of delinking from the world economy, self-
reliance, mass labor mobilization, the Great Leap Forward, and
above all, the idea that nuclear weapons are the only way to ensure
China's sovereignty against the imperialist West.

The illusory belief that the "I" is the author of one's social identity
is a continuous theme that connects the three protagonists. Each
of the three characters initially believes himself to be the center of
his social practice and the origin of his present life, and feels that
he has fashioned himself in accordance with values he himself has
chosen. Each character then discovers in the course of the novel
that being a subject depends on one's compliance with social norms
that are neither a matter of choice nor immediately intelligible to the
person who becomes a subject by virtue of these norms. The social
field's epistemological and ontological priority over voluntarism
produces drastically different but structurally parallel results in the
novel's three substories. The first story, that of Xiao Feng, concerns
the extent to which "race" is a matter of personal choice or social
construction. Xiao Feng is a character who believes, for most of the
novel, that he is a Han Chinese person. Despite compelling evidence
that suggests his non-Chinese origins, Xiao Feng endeavors through
a series of heroic deeds to prove to himself and his comrades that

race is not a biological determinant. At the end, however, he comes to see himself as an impossible subject, and commits suicide. The story of Xu Zhu, by contrast, comes to a happy ending. Xu Zhu grows up as an orphan and a humble monk committed to the Buddhist vows of chastity, simplicity, and obedience. By accident, he solves a chess puzzle invented by ancient sages and becomes the rightful heir of the Care-free Clan. The fate of Xu Zhu himself is comparable to a chess piece. He resists indoctrination into the Martial Order, but somehow always finds himself implicated in the affairs of others, and receives martial power, prestige, and social companions that he neither desires nor identifies with. In the end, he inadvertently breaks every Buddhist vow he has taken and is expelled from the monastery, but he also discovers parents he never knew he had, and finds fulfillment in the mundane, secular world. Xu Zhu's reluctant journey from orphan to ruler, from detachment to worldly entanglement is mirrored by Duan Yu's descent from prince to illegitimate child. In the course of the novel, Duan Yu becomes involved with a multitude of attractive women who all turn out, one after another, to be his half-sisters. As he discovers, his father, the Duke of Dali, is a philanderer with countless lovers outside the Kingdom. The revelation of his father's previous deeds continues to haunt and determine Duan Yu's present identity. After the biological kinship between himself and his present object of affection comes to light, he is again and again torn between desire and the incest taboo. By the end of the story, however, it is revealed that his mother, too, has been unfaithful, and Duan Yu is not his father's child, but that of his father's arch nemesis. The conflict between desire and the prohibition against incest is resolved, and Duan Yu is free to marry as he pleases, but at the same time his self-perception as a child of a loving family and as prince disintegrates.

By decentering the moral authority typically vested in a single protagonist, Jin Yong creates an order of unreliable narration that disperses the reader's sympathy and presents the juxtaposition of competing viewpoints, rather than any particular moral value, as its object of novelistic discourse. The narrative mimics and formally enacts the theme of the book: the human subject is always opaque to itself, constituted by forces and norms beyond its choosing and knowledge. Philosophically and politically, Jin Yong's text refutes a voluntarist view of the subject as a creation of an attending consciousness without social constraints. Jin Yong takes the view that an "I" comes into being only by virtue of others—only in accordance with norms and conventions established by a world we did not choose—to argue along Buddhist lines that the autonomous self is only an illusion.

Jin Yong's chosen title for the story, *Tianlong babu*, is a Chinese translation of the Sanskrit *deva-nāga*. In Mahayana Buddhism, *devas* and *nāgas* are the two highest categories of the eight entities that protect the Dharma. In his preface to the novel, Jin Yong states that the phrase is commonly found in Buddhist scriptures and commentaries such as *The Lotus Sutra* (*Fahua jing*). He explains the characteristics of all eight entities but attributes a special affective significance to the story of the Asuras, entities that at once signify the idea of perpetual war itself and participate as agents in ceaseless combats. As wrath, greed, discord, and belligerence, the Asuras are celestial beings who are unable to transcend the permanent, cyclical nature of violence. Jin Yong then mentions that the Chinese expression *xiuluo chang*, "killing fields," is etymologically derived from the Buddhist concept of Asura (*axiuluo*) (Vol I, 6). In the novel proper, a character named Xiuluo Dao, Asura's Blade, is a vindictive jilted lover who raises her daughter to be a cold-blooded, man-hating assassin. Xiuluo Dao trains her daughter in deadly martial skills to assist her in her revenge plot. Unfortunately, her plans turn out to be disastrous, and her daughter ends up falling in love with her half-brother Duan Yu, one of the three protagonists. Xiuluo Dao's fruitless attempt to extract revenge only pushes her own daughter into further pain and suffering, now in an impossible and tortured relationship with her own half-brother, an event that serves as another example of the cyclical nature of pain and violence engendered by desire.

Jin Yong explains his chosen title for the novel in the context of Buddhist philosophy:

> Tian is short for *tiansheng* [*devas*]. In Buddhism,
> the *devas* are not supreme beings above mankind.
> They are simply beings who have earned greater,
> and longer, karmic blessings (*fu bao*). According to
> Buddhist belief, there is no constancy in the world
> (*shi wu wu chang*), and once the *devas* have exhausted
> their blessings, they will perish as well. (5)

What Jin Yong is trying to emphasize here is the difference between transcendental and immanent religious systems. His novel rejects the philosophical systems derived from or inflected by the Judeo-Christian traditions that posit a transcendental telos, such as salvation, or a divine authority external to the world. For Jin Yong, Buddhist teachings serve as an immanent cosmology that provides an alternative to the Judeo-Christian, Hegelian, and Marxist visions of worldly matters as episodes in a single unfinished plot.

The devas are not gods; rather, they are subject to karma and not above or beyond mankind, while the Buddha is solely a teacher (who helps the individual discover a path to spiritual awakening) and not a prophet who reveals a divine truth. *Tianlong babu*, the eight categories of beings guarding the Dharma, are not "deities" or "gods" in the Western sense, but forces, categories, or enlightened modes of existence that are coextensive with the mankind they oversee. The fact that they are given human attributes, genders, and images makes it possible for human beings to relate to them, but they are not external beings in which human beings place their faith, and from which salvation is expected to be delivered.

Xiao Feng and the Interpellation of the Racial Subject

The identity crisis produced by the realization of one's primary dependence on others in the story of Xiao Feng is race, or more accurately, racialization—the process whereby one becomes interpellated into a culturally recognizable subject of race. The novel stages an ethical struggle with the problem of racialization by showing Xiao Feng claiming to be the author of his race but faltering in that endeavor. He discovers, painfully, that one can never choose the social signifiers that make one's body intelligible to others. Rather, one is compelled by one's material dependency on others to assume a symbolic position in a preconstituted social field of power in order to qualify as a viable being.

In Jin Yong's works—and in the martial arts genre in general— Xiao Feng is a unique character in that his story radically departs from the conventional formula of initiation into the world of martial arts (*lian wu*), followed by treasure hunt (*miji*), revenge (*fuchou*), and rise to leadership in the Martial Order (*wulin mengzhu*).[14] Most protagonists in the genre begin as ordinary men and women whose character development and martial development are isomorphic— that is, the narrative arc that fleshes out a character's substance, dimension, and personality typically coincides with that character's acquisition of superhuman martial skills. Contrary to convention, Xiao Feng makes his first appearance in the novel, *in medias res*, as a developed and accomplished martial artist. Indeed, the story of Xiao Feng begins where most characters end: he is introduced as the ruler of the Beggar Clan, the most prestigious and powerful martial school in China. Xiao Feng does not acquire new martial abilities in the course of the novel. Instead, his adventures in the martial world uncover hidden facts pertaining to his past, which, however, continue to elude his efforts to systematize and categorize his identity into a coherent name. In fact, Xiao Feng is known as Qiao Feng throughout most of the novel until he comes to terms with an identity he dreads. For reasons of clarity, I refer to him by his preferred name in this analysis.

The novel starts in the year 1094, when China in the Song dynasty—like the time of Jin Yong's own writing—was under threat of foreign encirclement. Song China at the time was at war with the Liao Empire (907–1125) of the Khitan, a federation of seminomadic tribes who ruled over large parts of present-day Manchuria and Mongolia. To China's northwest stood a potential ally or foe, the powerful Tangut Empire of the Western Xia (1038–

1227), which controlled the upper course of the Yellow River and the Gansu corridor. Southwest of China's border was the Kingdom of Dali, a state that maintained warm but tenuous diplomatic relations with China. In the northeast, the Jurchen tribes were also rising to power; soon after the end of the events recounted in *Tianlong babu*, the Jurchen would destroy the Liao Empire, conquer all of north China, send the Song court fleeing to the south, and establish their own empire called the Jin dynasty of China.

Xiao Feng's Beggar Clan is a fictional organization of martial arts masters that participates in Song China's war of resistance against the invading Khitan army. As leader of the Beggar Clan and the only true heir of the powerful martial techniques of the Shaolin Temple, Xiao Feng is an exalted hero in all of China. However, a dark secret is carefully kept away from him: he is actually a Khitan orphan whose parents, innocent civilians, were killed by the former leader of the Beggar Clan. Filled with remorse and moral anguish after this incident, the Chinese heroes brought the week-old Xiao Feng back to China, and a debate broke out over the proper way to raise the orphan and right their wrong. One enlightened monk suggested that they should place Xiao Feng in the care of a simple Chinese peasant family, who would raise him to be an honest, hardworking commoner. This way, Xiao Feng would remain ordinary and poor all his life, but he would be blessed with inner peace and freed from the perpetual pain and violence of the Martial Order (*juanru jianghu enchou*, Vol. II, 671). Another enlightened monk disagreed. He argued that their past misdeeds had to be rectified by a different kind of gift to Xiao Feng. They had to educate Xiao Feng in the Way of martial arts and raise him to be a great hero. They owed it the child's murdered parents to inspire greatness in Xiao Feng. The dissenting monk's argument prevailed, and Xiao Feng indeed grew up to be a man of unmatched martial abilities and personal virtue. After the old leader's death, Xiao Feng became the undisputed master of the Beggar Clan. However, the leader left behind a letter relating Xiao Feng's origins. This letter falls into the hands of Xiao Feng's political enemies and becomes their most powerful weapon in the political coup that begins the Xiao Feng section of the novel.

The letter from the old leader is filled with racist prejudice. With it, Jin Yong begins to explore racialization as a complex social process that accrues different meanings and associations in the course of the novel. Schematically, the novel presents at least three different viewpoints on what makes a person a racial subject. In the beginning, the story of race is told as a story of racism. Xiao Feng is introduced as a benevolent hero and a victim of a political conspiracy. Since the weapon used against Xiao Feng is the letter, and the letter represents the force of racism, Xiao Feng is depicted at this point as a victim of racism. The letter states that since Xiao Feng is actually biologically Khitan, he was born with the barbaric instincts of an alien race that even the strongest martial and moral education could not fully eradicate. The Chinese heroes must prepare themselves for the possibility that one day these instincts might reveal themselves and turn their leader against the Chinese. The letter implicitly describes the situation of the Clan and the Chinese war on barbarism as a state of permanent emergency, a world filled with invisible enemies from within that justifies a preemptive war: should Xiao Feng begin to evince any such Khitan racial characteristics, the vice leader is instructed to rally the rest of the Clan to dispose of him, by fair means or foul. A preemptive strike is necessary to prevent not just a disastrous battle with the most powerful martial arts master but, what is worse, the leakage of secret Chinese martial techniques into the hands of the Khitan.

Xiao Feng treats the letter as forged evidence and the entire story as a shameless ploy of political conspiracy, expressing shock and disbelief at this feeble attempt to dislodge him from power by undermining his credibility.

> "No!! You are lying! You made up this speech to destroy my reputation. I am an honorable Chinese. How can I be a barbaric Khitan? Sir Sankui is my dear father … If you … you good fellows want to remove my title as chief of the Clan, I … I'll voluntarily resign. You did not have to make up these lies to smear my reputation. What have I done to deserve this, to make you all hate me this much?" His voice was getting

choked up with these last few words, and even his political opponents began to feel pity for him. (Vol. II, 669–670)

Playing on the mutually exclusive binary of Chinese and Khitan, the letter from the former clan leader derives its rhetorical force from the binary between nature and nurture as well, where nature is represented by the determinations of racial and genetic makeup, and nurture or culture by the force of social mores, as well as by the individual's capacity for moral reasoning. If the racial traits implanted in Xiao Feng's blood, like a time bomb or a virus, mature and manifest themselves, they are predicted to be able to override the existing ties and loyalties between Xiao Feng and his cohorts, family, and teachers, making him unable to distinguish between friend and foe. Thus, the opposition the letter invokes is not between the warring states of China and the Empire of Liao, but between two different aspects of martial arts—as brute force and moral edification. Xiao Feng's innate penchant for violence, his "barbaric instincts," are precisely the opposite of martial arts, precisely what a martial education is presumably unable to stamp out.

The debate that ensues within the clan continues to question the point as being racist or antiracist and is characterized by a dichotomous mode of thinking.

> Elder Song said, "I don't think Chief Qiao [Xiao Feng] is Khitan. Khitans are cruel and savage, but he just showed us mercy when we rebelled against him. How could a Khitan act like this?"
>
> Elder Xu said, "He was raised by the enlightened monks of the Shaolin Temple and the late Chief Wang, and has already got rid the savage habits of the Khitan."
>
> "You sound ninety-percent like a Khitan just now."
>
> "We are all loyal patriots of China. Is there anyone here who is willing to be a slave to an alien race (*yizu de nuli zougou*)?" Once he said these, several people

who had already moved to the other side [in support
of Xiao Feng] moved back to the side of the loyalists.
(Vol. II, 682–683)

This passage contains an example of the nationalist argument
that accepting foreigners in China is tantamount to accepting China's
status as a colonized and enslaved state, a form of anti-imperialist
rhetoric that permeates Chinese public debates on the U.S.-led
crusade against Communist China during the years Jin Yong was
composing this novel. In a later section, I will discuss this point in the
exchange between Jin Yong and one of his critics, who writes under the
pseudonym Zhang Hennu ("I hate being a slave").

Jin Yong emphasizes the bigotry of this position by foregrounding
it again in the oral testimony given by the eye witnesses of the
original tragedy:

> Zhiguang said, "That Khitan ran to the corpse of
> his wife, and started bellowing with sorrow. His cries
> were sad indeed. I heard his cries and I couldn't help
> but feel bad for him. I was surprised to see that this
> Khitan dog, who murdered us Chinese like a vicious
> beast, like a demon, also had human emotions, and
> the pain he felt at the loss of his wife does not seem any
> less shallow than that of the Chinese." Zhao counters
> chilly, "What exactly is so surprising about that? Beasts
> have feelings for their young too. The Khitan are
> also humans. Why do you expect any less of them?"
> Several members of the Clan started clamoring, "The
> cruelty of those Khitan dogs surpasses the venom of
> serpents and the savagery of beasts. They cannot be
> compared to us Chinese." (Vol II, 663–664)

Immediately after the truth of his birth is revealed to him, Xiao
Feng reacts to the disclosure and the political coup with "benevolence"
(the Confucian concept of *ren*): he defeats his political enemies but
shows them clemency and forgiveness, and even mutilates his own

body in order to atone for the crimes committed by the traitors, in accordance with the laws of the Beggar Clan. The construction of Xiao Feng as a benevolent Confucian subject preemptively establishes the point that his tragic fate in the end does not result from failure to take stock of one's responsibility to others in the social field. The operative dichotomy here is therefore not concerned with race as such (as an opposition between Chinese and Khitan), but with racism and its opposite: "benevolence," the ability to think and act beyond injury.

Jin Yong's interest at this point lies less in exposing and caricaturing the hubris of the Han Chinese than in highlighting the extent to which a person's identity depends on the very social power that oppresses that person. Jin Yong paints Xiao Feng as a subject inhabiting an unlivable world. His desire for recognition and acceptance from the people who sustain his existence in cultural and material ways is countered by a different power that shapes his identity as an abject subject who does not quite qualify as a human being according to the terms and norms of his social world. To reclaim or accept his Khitan identity in a hostile climax defined by deep-seated prejudice would be tantamount to social or literal death. Xiao Feng, like many children of first-generation immigrants who do not speak the language of their parents, seeks assimilation and defines racism as biological determinism, the assumption that the truth of one's national identity must be visible in bodily identifiers like skin color. The letter about Xiao Feng attributes his biological roots to an alien race, a race that he does not recognize, and has indeed spent his lifetime fighting. The allegation not only threatens to destroy his reputation as the tireless champion of the Chinese cause, which will put an end to his political career in the Martial Order, but also throws into crisis everything he has cherished and believed in as the basis of personal identity—his memories of his parents, his love for his martial arts teachers, his trust in his friends. The care he received from his (foster) parents turns out to be the product of a political arrangement (or, more precisely, the product of one hundred taels of silver), and his martial education the result of his teachers' moral guilt. The letter links his identity to an unspeakable stigma, to an uninhabitable world that he neither recognizes nor identifies with.

The narrative rests on an important assumption: there are no phenotypical differences between the Khitan and the Chinese. Whether this lack of observable physical differences is anthropologically accurate is not important; the novel's presuppositions allow Jin Yong to represent race emphatically as a cultural construction, one of social power's ways of producing, demarcating, and forming the body. As long as race is culturally constructed, fluid, and even arbitrary, it is a matter Xiao Feng can accept or disavow, even as subsequent plot development produces a host of witnesses, testimonies, documents, and new arguments that confirm his Khitan roots. In the second phase of the story, Xiao Feng refuses the cultural inscription of race and seeks to refashion his personal identity by extricating himself from the Martial Order—from its web of social conflicts and responsibilities. He meets a romantic companion, Ah Zhu, and the two decide to go into self-exile and live a solitary life. Ah Zhu's character performs the important function in the novel of convincing Xiao Feng that one's race is a matter of choice.

> Ah Zhu tries to comfort him by quoting an enlightened Buddhist monk's words of wisdom: "'Han Chinese or Khitan, what appears real is an illusion. Debt, revenge, honor, and disgrace, everything turns into dust eventually.' What difference does it make if you are Han Chinese or Khitan? As for this bloody world of martial arts we are living in, you must have had just enough of it. Why don't we go out of the gate of Yenmen [northern border of Song China] and live as free-spirited hunters and shepherds? We can leave the conflicts in the Central Plains behind."
>
> Qiao Feng says, "Ah Zhu, you don't look down to me because I am a lowly Khitan bastard?" Ah Zhu says, "Khitans and Han Chinese are both human. What sense does it make to speak of one as high and the other as low? I … I like being Khitan" [her coy way of saying she is willing to marry Qiao Feng]. (Vol. III, 892)

Ah Zhu's words persuade Xiao Feng to go into exile and to live a new life unmarked by his race. At this point, he believes that race is an exterior artifact to be donned on or taken off at will. Xiao Feng and Ah Zhu's plan, however, quickly fails as they come to realize that there is no such thing as a self-invented or self-chosen "race"; one becomes a racial subject only when one enters an ensemble of social relations with others, and race is only meaningful in the social context. To be in that social context means in part to surrender some of one's claim to agency. Before Xiao Feng and Ah Zhu can make it to the nomadic steppes and become self-sufficient shepherds, Ah Zhu's own past surfaces with haunting echoes and disastrous consequences. She turns out to be a daughter of the Duke of Dali (Duan Yu's father), who Xiao Feng erroneously assumes to be responsible for the deaths of his parents and teachers. Ah Zhu disguises herself as her father, challenges Xiao Feng to a duel, and dies at his hands in order to sacrifice herself to prevent a blood feud between Xiao Feng and her father. Ah Zhu's discovery of her own birth identity entails a sense of filial obligation to a father she has, in fact, never known, in a fashion parallel to Xiao Feng's discovery that the meaning of race is embedded in the social fabric instead of the individual genetic makeup. At this point, the problem of racialization shifts its meaning from racism to a problem of voluntarism—that is, the ontological problem that race appears to be authored by the subject, who may choose to identify or dis-identify with a given community, set of beliefs, or cultural norms. The tragedy once again places Xiao Feng in a web of social responsibilities and debts, and enmeshes him in the Martial Order from which he is desperate to escape; but the loss of Ah Zhu also has the strange effect of demonstrating to him that this vision of self-made man is folly, and Xiao Feng comes to embrace his Khitan identity in the third phase of the story.

In Xiao Feng's mind, what dispels the last shadow of doubt is not an encounter with another eyewitness, the discovery of a new piece of physical evidence for his Khitan origins, or rational argument of any kind, but the reactivation or recontextualization of a psychic scene. It is not the surfacing of a lost or repressed memory but the discovery of a proper language for comprehending the emotional import of what Freud calls a "trace," something that one has known all along but eludes language. Ah Zhu's first meeting with Xiao Feng inaugurates this process and begins to alter the sense of racialization. When Xiao Feng first meets Ah Zhu, he fatally injures her by accident. Unsure of her own chance of survival, Ah Zhu begs Xiao Feng to tell her a story to entertain her (II, 790–795). Unable to refuse her dying wish but too uneducated to come up with an interesting story, Xiao Feng first flusters and stutters, then tells a true story from his childhood in the third-person as if it were fictional.

A father of a seven-year-old boy in the poor countryside falls sick and the family has to liquidate their sole capital and source of income—six chickens—for some cash so that the mother can take their son to the city to find a doctor. Repelled by the family's clothes and the paltry sum of money offered, the doctor turns them away. The woman pleads with the doctor and injures herself, unknowingly dropping her money in his house in the tussle. On their way home, the child steals a knife from a butcher shop. When the mother sees the shiny knife, she assumes that her son bought it with the money that has gone missing; but instead of demanding a confession or threatening punishment, she merely begs her son to give her back whatever change was left over from the purchase of the knife so that she can buy some meat soup for the sick father. The boy, of course, has neither the money nor a feasible story to cover up the source of the knife so he simply takes the blame for stealing from his own mother in a time of great need. When they reach home, the father reprimands the mother for chastising their son, saying that it is natural for boys to want toys, and it is their own fault that they could never afford to buy him any. In this touching scene, love becomes a burden and an excess, suffocating and confounding. The emotional weight of the misunderstanding, coming from a father who is deathly ill and exceedingly tolerant, is too much to bear, but still the boy refuses to explain himself and simply takes the blame for the theft. Later that night, the reason for the theft and his inarticulateness reveals itself when the boy creeps into the doctor's house and kills him in his sleep with the stolen knife. Explaining the source of his "toy" would exculpate him and recoup the lost love or respect from his parents, but it would also foil his plan of revenge.

In a way, the child takes the blame for a crime he never committed in order to execute another one. To kill the doctor would avenge his father, who he thinks at this point has no chance of surviving the disease without medical care; but the revenge takes the form of an internal debate, a kind of sacrifice or symbolic and emotional exchange. This impasse further illustrates the forces that simultaneously construct Xiao Feng as a "good Confucian subject" and an "impossible Khitan subject" the text delineates later. The love the boy Xiao Feng exchanges with his foster parents indicates the social force that instantiates the racial subject.

This emotionally unsettling and morally complex story serves as an important turning point in Xiao Feng's own racial identification. Not realizing that the story is real and autobiographical, Ah Zhu responds to the surprising ending of the tale with an offhand remark, "A seven-year-old capable of murder? That is so 'Khitan' of him" (Vol. II, 795), at which point Xiao Feng jumps in horror, lifeless, as all color drains from his face. Ah Zhu's inadvertent comment on a story that she believes to be merely fictional, based on stereotypes rather than observable events, turns out to carry a greater truth for Xiao Feng than all of the compelling evidence the heroes of the Martial Order have gathered against Xiao Feng.

On the surface, the story dramatizes the pain of material privation for those who have been denied access to the bare necessities of life—food, health care, human dignity, shelter, protection from violence. The lack of distributive justice becomes a matter of life and death in the story. But the pain it narrates is deeper and greater than that. It is a complex story about an unspeakable love, and a loving deed that is at the same time a crime and never investigated.

If Xiao Feng initially understands race to be a choice—an identity to be decided by the subject—then after Ah Zhu's death he comes to understand that race is in part what decides the subject, but the literary representation of that earlier misunderstanding of how subject construction works is as crucial to the text as the undoing of that assumption. He leaves China and becomes a subject of the Khitan Empire. Whereas initially Xiao Feng understands the accusation of him as Khitan as the politically motivated use of a racial slur to smear his reputation, now he sees his own rejection of the accusation as racist. He comes to see, in the course of the novel, that he has internalized the violence of race by assuming that it is an insult. The meaning of racialization changes from the assumption that one must be of a given race to be entitled to the protection and privileges of the nation, to the disciplinary functions of race itself. Race is no longer racism, the power of one group over another that oppresses and subordinates the subject from without. Rather, race is given a new definition as the power that produces the cultural boundaries of the body.

Xiao Feng's first rediscovery of his identity is physical: while traveling near the borders of Liao, he sees a tattoo on several Khitan tribesmen that is identical to the one on his own chest, which he has had since birth. Here the social markings of race are made literal, and dramatized as the inscription on the body. Xiao Feng changes his last name from the given Qiao, the Chinese family name of his foster parents, to Xiao, his Khitan last name, and starts living among the Khitan (Vol. III, 888). While the earlier "Qiao Feng" is portrayed as the wronged victim of racism who seeks to disarticulate the biological from the cultural, the meaning of racism changes in the story, and Xiao Feng comes to realize that his own fear of being marked as Khitan issues from his own internalized racism, which is the combined effect of the stigma attached to the Khitan name and his desire for acceptance, respect, and safety among those he was brought to recognize as his own kind.

Xiao Feng's commitment to his newfound Khitan identity is emphasized in dramatic ways. One example is the surprising loyalty Xiao Feng shows to his Khitan father after the latter, long believed to be dead, turns out to be not only safe and sound but the mastermind behind the schemes and murders of which Xiao Feng has been wrongly accused. Instead of blaming his father for murdering his friends and teachers, Xiao Feng embraces and defends his father. The surprising change in Xiao Feng's character appears to underscore the determinism of race over other cultural priorities, but the reader will be forced to change this interpretation of the effect and nature of race again later.

The undecidability of Xiao Feng's race necessitates a rethinking of the notion of "self-defense" in the novel. Before the final battle between the Khitan and the Chinese, Xiao Feng asks the Reverend of the Shaolin Temple what one should do if the Shaolin Temple is under attack from the Liao Empire. The monk answers that one should rise to arms (*fenqi shadi*) and come to self-defense (*husi hufa*), asserting that this principle is natural and infallible (*gengyou he yi?*). Xiao Feng, however, presents a different view.

> "Reverend, you are Han Chinese, and you are only capable of seeing the Chinese as good and the Khitan as evil. We Khitan are only capable of seeing the Liao Empire as good and Song China as evil. ... During the Tang dynasty, you Chinese were more accomplished in martial arts, and you murdered countless Khitan soldiers and raped countless Khitan women. Now that your martial arts have declined and we are on the offensive, how do we possibly imagine an exit out of this cycle of revenge?" (Vol. V, 2106)

At this point, Xiao Feng and Duan Yu recite two literary works. The first one is "Zhan Cheng Nan" (Nefarious war), composed by the famous Chinese poet, Li Po; the other is a folksong of the Xiongnu, a nomadic people residing in the steppes north of China, composed after their civilization was destroyed by the expanding Chinese empire of the Han dynasty. The verse of the soulful, beautifully composed Xiongnu song captures the everlasting anguish and sorrow of pillaged villages, lost livelihood, and fragile culture of a defeated people. The Chinese poem conveys the horrors of war through naturalistic images, ending with the haunting couplet, "Only after [lives have been sacrificed on the alter of pride] did we understand that war is an instrument of evil. The sage does not use it" (Vol. V, 2106, my translation).[15] Both the Xiongnu and the Khitan are commonly described in Chinese sources as "barbarians" on the peripheries. The use of a Xiongnu folksong to describe the plight of the Khitan is already an act of cross-identification, but the chiasmus of good and evil, presented in Xiao Feng's speech and in the poetry-exchange, highlights the need for self-reflexivity and empathy between the "we" and the "they."

Contrary to popular conceptions of the genre as an advocacy of violence, Jin Yong's martial arts novel stakes a strong claim to pacifism. Literature is invoked as one of the means by which cross-cultural understanding and nonviolent solutions to war, can be achieved.

The Novel and Its Intertext

Named after the Buddhist philosophy of "tianlong babu," Jin Yong's novel draws upon numerous Buddhist themes, scriptures, and teachings to develop his motifs. The Buddhist concept of *anicca*, that all things are impermanent, is particularly prominent in this work. *Anicca* is the belief that suffering is an inherent part of existence and that only with the cessation of attachment and craving can the cycle of reincarnation come to an end. This idea provides the philosophical basis for Jin Yong's critique of China's descent into the "permanent war economy" that I will discuss later. The novel's Buddhist sources and philosophical precepts are amply acknowledged by the characters and their dialogues, a narrative situation facilitated by Jin Yong's deliberate choice to set the first part of the story in the Kingdom of Dali during the Northern Song dynasty. As Jin Yong explains in the preface:

> Dali was a Buddhist country. All of their emperors were devout Buddhists, and the country was famous for having many emperors who abdicated the throne to become ordinary monks. According to historical records, among the emperors of Dali, Emperors Shende, Xiaode, Baoding, Xuanren, Zhenglian, Shenzong and several others all did this. (7)

The theme of the abdication of political power is both enacted by various characters in the text (such as the Dali emperor) and reinforced by the ironic resignation of the authorial tone toward the worldly, less enlightened characters; central to Jin Yong is the idea that the cessation of worldly attachment is specifically a stateless cessation.

Tianlong babu is an exceedingly elaborate, multilayered palimpsest. The intertext for this novel is thick. Structurally, the novel may be seen as a cross between *Romance of the Three Kingdoms* and *Dream of the Red Chamber*. While the oath of the three brothers pays homage to the former, the character of Duan Yu serves as a metacommentary on the latter. The name Duan Yu 段譽 is a clear allusion to Jia Baoyu 賈寶玉, the protagonist of *Dream of the Red Chamber*. The eighteenth-century novel begins with the birth of Baoyu (literally, "precious stone"), who is named so because he is born with a piece of jade (*yu* 玉) in his mouth. The event literalizes and ironizes a common Chinese expression, "han yu er sheng" (every man is born with desire [*yu* 慾]) through the homophonic substitution of *yu* 玉 (jade) for *yu* 慾 (desire). Baoyu's surname, Jia 賈, is homophonous with another Chinese character *jia* 假, meaning "fake." This linguistic pun is clearly intentional, since the story centers on the relations between two families, the Jias and the Zhens 甄, where the surname Zhen 甄 is also homophonous with a different character, *zhen* 真, meaning "real." Jin Yong is aware of the linguistic wordplay in the *Dream of the Red Chamber*. In his own final novel, *The Deer and the Cauldron*, Jin Yong names his main character Wei Xiaobao 韋小寶. Wei 韋, like Jia, is another common Chinese family name that is homophonic with a word that means "fake," *wei* 偽. The word *bao* in "*Xiaobao* 小寶," "small treasure" (translated as "Trinket" in Minford's edition) is an unmistakable reference to or parody of the word *bao* in *Bao*yu 寶玉.

In *Tianlong babu*, Jin Yong develops the intertextual relations between his own work and *Dream of the Red Chamber* in a similar fashion. *Dream of the Red Chamber* is famous for being a commentary on the futility of human desire. As soon as he comes of age, Baoyu's character becomes a self-fulfilling prophecy of the destructive nature of desire inscribed in his name. Jia Baoyu is surrounded, and his life defined, by a multitude of desires and desirable objects. Embodying the concept of desire itself, Baoyu finds himself perpetually entangled with lovers who include both men and women, lower-class maids and virtuous maidens, transient and lasting, licit and illicit ones. The love triangle between Bao Yu and his two cousins, set against the family's declining fortunes, forms the bulk of the novel. In the end, Baoyu realizes that desire is nothing but a dream of "red dust" (the Buddhist term for the mundane world) and becomes a celibate monk who lives a solitary life. His surname, Jia ("fake"), and his fate suggest that human desire is illusory, ephemeral, and dreamlike.

In *Dream of the Red Chamber*, Baoyu gives up on his worldly desires, detaches himself from entanglements in the mundane world, and becomes a monk. In Jin Yong's text, Xu Zhu (whose name suggests "humility" according to a Chinese expression, but also "nihilism") begins as a Buddhist monk. Although Duan Yu does not become a monk, his story invokes Baoyu's journey to Buddhist enlightenment in *Dream of the Red Chamber* and thus stands as the polar opposite of Xu Zhu, the monk who turns into a desiring subject. Xu Zhu's adventures in the novel, while embellished with and inflected through the martial arts idiom, symbolize the Buddhist concept of one's "entry into the world" (*rushi*), while Duan Yu's name 段譽, homophonic with 斷慾 (the termination of desire), stands for the concept of *chushi*, surrendering one's attachment to the earthly world of "red dust."

Duan Yu's story, like Baoyu's, serves as a commentary on desire. Duan Yu meets and falls in love with several women in the novel. Without exception, every one of them turns out to be his half-sister, a product of his father's numerous extramarital relationships, and hence unavailable to desire. The prohibition against incest, however, is resolved with a dramatic twist when the novel finally reveals that Duan Yu himself is the product of his mother's infidelity with another man, and hence he is biologically unrelated to the women the Duke of Dali fathered. The "half-sisters" suddenly become legitimate objects of desire again, and with this surprising resolution of his drama, the Duan Yu story has a happy ending.

Xu Zhu's character is the polar opposite of Duan Yu's. Xu Zhu is a devout Buddhist monk devoid of worldly desires who shows interest neither in martial arts nor in the political intrigues around him. While Duan Yu is perpetually entangled with various female characters, Xu Zhu embodies the refusal of desire. Like Duan Yu, however, Xu Zhu is a product of forces beyond his control. He ends up breaking all the

Buddhist vows he has taken. He is first tricked by another character into eating meat. Soon after, he is forced to learn non-Shaolin martial arts, which breaks the oath or code of loyalty. Then he is forced by circumstances to kill, breaking another Buddhist vow. Finally, he falls victim to the plot of a powerful martial arts master and commits the carnal sin of the flesh with a woman. In the end he is punished by the elders of the Shaolin temple for his deeds and is excommunicated. As Xu Zhu removes his Buddhist attires in the ritual, Ye Siniang, one of the villains in the story, sees the tattoo on his body and rushes to cover him in tears, revealing that Xu Zhu is in fact the secret love child of herself and the head of the Shaolin Temple. Like the Duan Yu story, the narrative of excessive carnal desire is displaced back onto the parental generation, whose identity and history replace the story of the children as the true object of investigation and emotional cathexis.

The Cold War in Asia

On October 16, 1964, China successfully detonated its first nuclear bomb and became a nuclear state. In 1963, Chen Yi, China's Foreign Minister Marshall, had stated that China's development of nuclear weapons would put an end to white supremacy and prove wrong both the United States and the Soviet Union—neither of which believed at the time that an economically and technologically backward third-world country like China would ever acquire nuclear capabilities. Chen Yi said, famously, that "we are determined to go ahead and build our own atomic bombs (*yuanzi*) even if we have to lose our pants (*kuzi*). Otherwise we will end up as a second- or third-class nation."[16] "Pants" stands for the principle of sustained livelihood, which in Chen Yi's mind is less important than military development. Newspapers in Hong Kong reported China's acquisition of nuclear weapons as the pride and glory of all third-world countries in their common struggles against the domination of the Soviet Union and the United States.

Ming Pao, the newspaper founded by Jin Yong, was the lone dissenting voice in Hong Kong's intellectual circles. Jin Yong himself published a series of political commentaries on the subject in his newspaper. The editorial on October 20 states that "we refuse to take pride in the invention of the atomic bomb in China. … We do not support the Chinese Communist Party's development of the nuclear bomb. We do not think the bomb is the pride of all Chinese people." Jin Yong's essay on October 23 calls the bomb a "crime against humanity" (*youhai renlei de zui-e*) and proposes a conceptual distinction between a weapon and its use. His essay criticizes the Chinese Communist Party's claim that the purpose of the atomic bomb is to save lives and also criticizes the Chinese adoption of the doctrine of Mutually Assured Destruction (MAD) and nuclear deterrence (*yi zhan zhi zhan, yi he zhi he*). Jin Yong argues that nuclear weapons themselves are inanimate objects and not the source of evil; he writes, "A sword is a sword, but in court, the same sword can be the instrument of justice, or the exhibited evidence that convicts the criminal." It is, rather, the purpose for which weapons are used that establishes a crime, and if objects are created for military aims, even if this is for retaliation, self-defense, or deterrence, their purpose is already wrong. Jin Yong invokes the classical Chinese proverb, "The water that carries a boat is the same substance that capsizes it" (*shui neng zai zhou, yi neng fu zhou*) to convey his stand that acquiring atomic bombs will only lock China into the global arms race. His critique is not leveled at the absolute value of the weapons themselves; rather, his point is directed at the futile social cycle of violence and exploitation that a militant response to the threat of imperialism perpetuates. Instead of securing "sovereignty" and "national independence from American and Soviet imperialism," the arms race will only allow external relations to determine the distribution of China's resources. The creation of increasingly potent weapons of destruction as a response to the history or continued realities of Western colonial violence only begets more violence, and in developing nuclear weapons as an answer to Soviet and American threats, we forget our responsibilities to our citizens and the rest of humanity. In his criticism of Chen Yi's "pants versus atomic bombs" speech, Jin Yong states that Mao's brand of socialism has shifted its aim from the creation of sustainable livelihood for the exploited classes to the creation of advanced means of destruction against the Soviet Union and the United States. By choosing atomic bombs (*hezi*) over pants (*kuzi*), socialism has been officially derailed.

Jin Yong's commentaries enraged the nationalists in Hong Kong. Liang Weilin, the head of the Hong Kong branch of the Chinese newspaper *Xinhua News*, branded *Ming Pao* as an "anti-Communist, anti-Chinese, unpatriotic propaganda machine that worships England and America."[17] The strongest criticisms of Jin Yong were published in Hong Kong's newspaper *Dagong bao*. In the October 25 issue, an article written under the pseudonym of Ranxi ("burning and sharp tongue") characterizes *Ming Pao* as an American puppet created to distort, defame, and destroy the Red Flag. Ranxi charges Jin Yong with "Soviet revisionism," stating that Jin Yong's critique of Chen Yi's "pants versus atomic bomb" speech is a rephrasing of Khrushchev's racist remark: "These Chinese—you know—five of them share one pair of trousers." Ranxi writes:

> Since China detonated its first atomic bomb, every citizen of the globe, except the Americans, Chiang Kai-shek and a few self-hating Chinese, has been celebrating this achievement. The consensus of the Continents of Asia, Africa, and Latin America is that China is finally going to put a stop to the American monopoly of nuclear weapons. … Any Chinese person, after witnessing their brothers finally achieve the means of independence and their fatherland advance into the age of high technology by securing this achievement for national security and the ability to defend world peace … should be dancing in the streets.

The issue of *Dagong bao* further points out that Jin Yong, like the characters in his "pernicious, unpatriotic wuxia fiction," is an agitator who uses "concealed weapons" (*anqi*) and "pressure-point hitting techniques" (*dianxue*) to hypnotize Hong Kong's public sphere. Another writer, Cha Chawei, repeats the idea that a nuclear China is the only means to "national independence" and "self-reliance" (*zili gengsheng*), a "glorious achievement" (*weida chengjiu*) in the service of world peace.[18] The most sustained criticisms of Jin Yong were published by one of *Dagong bao*'s associates, the columnist Chen Fan, under the pen name of "Zhang Hennu" 張恨奴 ("I hate being a slave"), which I mentioned in the previous discussion of the debate between Elder Song and Elder Xu over Xiao Feng's membership in the Clan.[19] Zhang argues that China's development of nuclear weapons was a reaction to America's strategy of containment, which, after the Sino-Soviet split, had effectively isolated China from the international community and threatened its survival.

Jin Yong's invocation of the precariousness of human life against the advancement of military technology began with his coverage of Hong Kong's 1962 refugee crisis. In the months of April and May, after the Three Years of Natural Disasters and the Great Leap Forward took an unprecedented human toll, tens of thousands of people began to cross the border into the British colony, which already had a population of over three million. Unknown, and untold numbers of refugees simply drowned, and those known (the Hong Kong government "captured" 300 to 600 illegal immigrants daily during the two month period) were deported back to mainland China. The Chinese government, however, accepted only deportees who could be proven to have escaped on land, with the result that those who swam to Hong Kong (or traveled to Hong Kong via Macau) were simply denied entry and citizenship by both governments. The refugees became, in other words, literally stateless people. Various newspapers called on the Hong Kong government to extend humanitarian aid to "our mainland brothers and sisters." The crisis escalated when, answering the *Singtao Daily*'s criticisms of the "inhuman manner" in which immigrants were handled, the Hong Kong government issued a statement defending the deportation programs as an effort to protect "the living standards of 3,200,000 Hong Kong residents."[20] Responding to this crisis, Jin Yong published a series of essays in *Ming Pao* between 1962 and 1963 that characterize the Great Leap Forward as an erroneous prioritization of industrialization over the livelihood of human beings.[21] The value of a human life always exceeds the military or industrial competitiveness of a nation-state.

In an essay entitled "*Juda de dingshi zhadan*" (The big time bomb), Jin Yong uses the metaphor of weaponry—a bomb, again—to analyze the Hong Kong and the Chinese governments' responses to the crisis, comparing the illegal immigrants to a "bomb" the governments have ignored, which could explode anytime. This tropical turn is founded on the idea that the undocumented immigrants are invisible to the eye (since they exist outside the census). Jin Yong reasons that there is no way to fully calculate the real damage the invisible bodies are causing and suffering. The essay prefigures the dichotomy between the visible and the invisible that he later uses to characterize the difference between open armed conflict and the danger of stockpiling nuclear weapons. A nuclear China is not actively, visibly engaged in war, but its very principle of existence has been compromised by its self-perception as a state of permanent emergency.

Just as Mao discovered the secret published long ago by pre-Marxist economists—that the true source of all value is nothing but human labor—he also discovered in the figure of the peasant the "Asiatic mode of production question." Instead of characterizing a hydraulic society in need of a despotically managed irrigation system, the unique nature of China's agriculture in Mao's vision delineates the fundamental differences between Chinese and non-Chinese, rather than Asiatic and non-Asiatic, modes of production. The "Asiatic mode of production" was then replaced by the "Chinese mode of production" in the work of Guo Moruo's [Kuo Mojo's] three-stage theory, which was the CCP's official statement on the problem since the 1930s. The theory held that, unlike the West and the rest of Asia, China went through three stages—the slave societies of the Xia, Shang, and Zhou dynasties; the feudal centuries between the Warring States period and the Ming dynasty; and the beginning of an indigenous Chinese capitalism after the Ming dynasty. With the official sanction of the three-stage theory, the "Asiatic Mode of Production" (AMP) was then given its decent burial in Chinese intellectual circles, and those still wondering about its existence (such as He Ziquan and Fan Wenlan) were quickly condemned as "Trotskyite." The AMP debate did not command much critical attention again until the 1980s, when a new

wave of interest eventually culminated in the belated appearance
of a Chinese translation of Wittfogel's *Oriental Despotism* in 1989.[22]
Even though Marx's speculation on the existence of the AMP was
discredited in Chinese Marxism, Chinese critics have nonetheless
assumed that a historically unique relationship between *agriculture*
and the state was only to be found in China. Against the backdrop
of the 1930s debate, Mao argues in a 1938 speech on "China's
Characteristics and Revolutionary War" that China is distinct
from the capitalist West, the Soviet Union, and other parts of the
world on two counts: China's peasant economy, and the necessity of
armed struggles for a uniquely "semicolonial, semifeudal" country.[23]

In the face of international hostility, the urgency of industrialization in China became conceptually linked with the urgency
to incorporate the peasantry—the self-sufficient sector of the
population historically situated outside of the immediate
development of capitalism—into a rational national economy.
How did Mao's anti-imperialist struggles make industrialization a
priority and the peasantry the agent for realizing that social goal,
while claiming at the same time that industrialization could be
diametrically opposed to "capitalism"? In his analysis of romantic
anticapitalism (his own example being National Socialism), Moishe
Postone connects the apparently contradictory glorification of
industrial capital and demonization of finance and interest capital
to the split between use value and value within the commodity
form itself.[24] If we comprehend Maoism as a form of romantic
anticapitalism, it begins to make sense how and why the Great Leap
Forward and the Cultural Revolution affirmed the peasant as the
"honest" producer of use-values, against which the "feudal class"
were made out to be the parasites responsible for China's "failure."
The description of society as divided into classes of productive and
unproductive citizens (small peasantry, the landed class, artists and
intellectuals, etc.)[25] became a vital component of Maoist discourse
only because there was a prior historical event, namely the rise
of capitalism itself, that made such an antinomy a useful and
comforting explanatory principle for many. Historical capitalism
made labor in modern times a form of *wealth* by turning labor-

power into a commodity, and gave the commodity its "double-character" as the objectification of socially productive activity and the representation of relations of exchange. The unproductive segment of society, to be reeducated by the peasantry, served as the personification of "exchange value" or "capitalism." The value-producing segment of society, by contrast, appeared to be *noncapitalist*, and its origin in capitalist relations, in the antinomy between use value and exchange value, was denied. Thus Postone argues:

> Forms of anticapitalist thought that remain bound within the immediacy of this antinomy tend to perceive capitalism, and that which is specific to that social formation, only in terms of the manifestations of the abstract dimension of the antinomy; so, for instance, money is considered the "root of all evil." The existent concrete dimension is then positively opposed to it as the "natural" or ontologically human, which presumably stands outside the specificity of capitalist society. Thus, as with Proudhon, for example, concrete labor is understood as the noncapitalist moment opposed to the abstractness of money. That concrete labor itself incorporates and is materially formed by capitalist social relations is not understood." (309)

Furthermore, the Maoist demonization of finance capital took the form of "self-reliance" against the "free market" of international trade. Maoism then represented itself as an asceticism, and capitalism a consumerism. Concrete labor was therefore not seen as constituting the antinomy specific to capitalism, but exterior to it.

Although from time to time China sought to obtain technology and modern weaponry from abroad (in particular Western Europe) the consistent focus of its state policy in the postwar era was on making China's own military-industry complex self-sufficient.[26] Self-sufficiency, however, is a paradoxical concept, for it refers to the belief that the nation must have a sufficiently strong industrial and economic base to fully utilize its "natural" comparative advantage in *international* trade (rather than on the domestic market) and develop the sufficient military strength comparative to other states that makes future imperialist encroachment at least a costly endeavor if not an impossible ambition. The misnomer of self-sufficiency thus cannot be taken at face value as the drive to optimize the conditions of self-reproduction within Chinese borders; in reality it is the interiorization of a set of exterior relations.[27] A great portion of aggregate social labor is thus extracted from productive workers to meet a demand that is outside of China itself, while these "needs" are constantly changing in accord with developments in the world system that cannot possibly be harnessed to national control through "planning." The international arms race is a structuring condition of the whole social order that affects differently situated states differently. The impossibility of self-sufficiency as such in the face of perpetual international competition suggests that the permanent arms economy produced a global "compulsion," a global condition in which nation-states are forced to constantly revolutionize their means of production and "modernize" their military in order to survive.

Jin Yong's writings help revaluate the meaning of independence and freedom in a context when the idea of economic self-sufficiency was rhetorically justified and sustained by the imperatives of war. The doctrine of "self-reliance" was born in response to a perception of powerful external threats: a virtual military encirclement by antagonistic nations—the United States and its Asian allies, the Soviet Union, and India. A long and entangled history of territorial disputes with virtually all neighboring states from the Ussuri River to the Philippines only confirmed this perception. Even before a U.S.-led embargo excluded China from normal diplomatic and commercial relations with other states, and before the split with the Soviet Union ended the illusion of socialist solidarity without borders, political policies in China were already guided by the humiliation brought by the division of the country at the hands of nineteenth-century Western powers, decades of civil war, and Japanese occupation in the twentieth century. The perception of an isolated, imperiled China resulted in the expropriation of the Chinese peasantry, and the melting of many woks. Once these state efforts transformed the agricultural hinterland into a source of internal surplus for the capital needed to upgrade the nation's industrial development, it became more difficult to characterize capitalism in China as simply the presence or absence of an immediate network of commodity consumption, for the source of the labor-power expended in the creation of a commodity can "ultimately" be found in a place where that commodity is neither consumed nor available. As the confrontation between socialism and capitalism becomes an increasingly less meaningful description of the society of either bloc, the idea of "permanent arms economy," depicted by Jin Yong's fiction, provides a much more realistic account than state-based political theories.

NOTES

1. See Ed Gunn, *Rewriting Chinese,* and Lydia Liu, *Translingual Practice*, for the standard accounts of this process.

2. On "necropolitics," see Achille Mbembe, "The Banality of Power and the Aesthetics of Vulgarity in the Postcolony."

3. Wang Shuo, "Wo kan Jin Yong," in Liao, ed., *Jin Yong xiaoshuo lunzheng ji*, 3–7; for a complete account of this debate and its cultural implications, see Hamm, 250–260.

4. Commenting on the incident, Kong Qingdong argues that the canonization of Jin Yong represents elite culture's successful modification of popular culture, not the other way around. See Kong's *Jin Yong Pingzhuan.*

5. English translation of the interview is available at http://www.cscse. com.cn/publish/portal20/tab863/info7077.htm

6. Wolfgang Kubin, "Ban the Poet Lu Xun!" 17.

7. Jin Yong, *Collected Letters*, 39.

8. See Sharon Lai, "Translating Jin Yong: A Review of Four English Translations" for some of the difficulties with translating Jin Yong. Critics point out, among other things, Jin Yong's use of a particularly "local" "structure of address" that interpellates his reader.

9. Currently, only a few titles of Jin Yong's works have been available in English. An abridged and simplified version of *The Book and the Sword*, translated by Graham Earnshaw and edited by John Minford, was published by Oxford University Press in 2005. The same Press has also published Minford's own translation of *The Deer and the Cauldron* and announced his work-in-progress, *The Legend of the Condor Heroes*. An earlier and less fluent translation of *Fox Volant of the Snowy Mountain* by Olivia Mok in 1993 has attracted relatively little attention in the United States.

10. John Minford, "Louis Cha through the Translator's Eyes," 314.

11. Unless otherwise noted, citations in this book refer to the second edition (the Revised Edition) of Jin Yong's works rather than the first (the Old Edition) or the third (the Millennium Edition), since the second edition was the most widely read (between 1970 and 2000), and most works that created the "Jin Yong phenomenon" (dissertations, scholarly books, academic conferences, movies, TV series) were based on the events and characters in the second edition, some of which do not exist in the other editions.

12. See, for example, Chen Mo, *Wuren buyuan youqing jienie—xishuo Tianlong babu*.

13. Rojas argues that these "processes of subject formation and ideological interpellation" are accomplished through a structure of specularity between the "screen" of the pictorial manual in the novel and the culturally conditioned "gaze" of the reader-as-viewer. "Jin Yong and Picturing Nationalism," 138, 151.

14. In *Taiwan wuxia xiaoshuo fazhan shi*, Lin Baochun and Ye Hongsheng define the treasure hunt, martial arts training, revenge, and tournaments as the four standard motifs in martial arts literature.

15. Xiao Feng leaves out a word from the original poem, which would mean "The sage only uses it when he has no other choice." The original Li Po version states, "Sheng ren bu de yi er yong zhi," while Xiao Feng says, "Sheng ren bu de er yong zhi."

16. An English translation of Chen Yi's speech appears in "Red China: Who Needs Pants?" *Time* magazine, November 8, 1963.

17. Zhang Guiyang, *Jin Yong and Ming Pao Daily Legend*, 143.

18. *Dagong bao*, October 28, 1964.

19. Zhang Hennu's real identity as Chen Fan is discussed in Zhang Guiyang, 144–146.

20. Kwai-Yeung Cheung, *Jin Yong yu bao ye* (Jin Yong and the press), 100–110; Hamm, 126

21. Yang Lige argues that these political essays played a pivotal role in Jin Yong's own intellectual development in *Jin Yong chuanshuo*, 99–113.

22. In 1980, the *Shijie shanggu shigang* (world ancient history studies)

collective published an article, "The Asiatic Mode of Production—A Problem That Is Not a Problem," in *Lishi yanjiu* (historical research), which initiated a new discussion on the subject in Chinese intellectual circles. In response to the publication of *Oriental Despotism* in Chinese (*Dongfang zhuanzhi zhuyi*, trans. Xu Shigu et al., Beijing: Zhongguo shehuikexue chubanshe) , a collected volume of essays by Li Zude, Chen Qineng, and other prominent social scientists appeared in 1997. *Ping Weitefu de dongfang zhuanzhi zhuyi* (Essays on Wittfogel's *Oriental Despotism*) (Beijing: Zhongguo shehuikexue chubanshe, 1997). These writers rejected Wittfogel's thesis as "Eurocentric," "racist," and "a product of the Cold War."

23. "When the time comes to launch such an insurrection and war, the first step will be to seize the cities, and then advance into the countryside, and not the other way about. All this has been done by Communist Parties in capitalist countries, and it has been proven correct by the October Revolution in Russia. China is different … Basically, the task of the Communist Party here is not to go through a long period of legal struggle before launching insurrection and war, and not to seize the big cities first and then occupy the countryside, but the reverse. When imperialism is not making armed attacks on our country, the Chinese Communist Party either wages civil war jointly with the bourgeoisie against the warlords … or unites with the peasants and the urban petty bourgeoisie to wage civil war against the landlord class and the comprador bourgeoisie … All this shows the difference between China and the capitalist countries. In China war is the main form of struggle and the army is the main form of organization." *Selected Works of Mao Tse-Tung*, Vol. II, 220–221.

24. Moishe Postone, "Anti-Semitism and National Socialism," in *Germans and Jews Since the Holocaust: The Changing Situation in West Germany*, 302–315.

25. Jean-Francois Billeter argues that the Maoist class status system is a *moral* inversion of the class of each individual (rather than individuals of a certain class) in the pre-revolutionary economic structure (itself a conceptual aporia) that leaves class division intact. See Billeter, "The System of 'Class-Status.'"

26. See Maurice Meisner, *Mao's China and After*.

27. In this sense Gordon White and Robert Wade are entirely right to observe that, contrary to popular opinion, Chinese reformist policies "defined agriculture as an obstacle rather than an impetus to industrialization and imposed an organizational form (the collective), the purpose of which was to enforce state claims on agricultural surplus rather than raising productivity and rural incomes." White and Wade, "Developmental States and Markets n East Asia," 16.

Chapter 4

JIN YONG'S ISLAM IN THE CHINESE CULTURAL REVOLUTION

"Not all mutants survive. Or, consider him sociopolitically: most migrants learn, and can become disguises. Our own false descriptions to counter the falsehoods invented about us, concealing for reasons of security our secret lives."
—Salman Rushdie, *The Satanic Verses*

Jin Yong's interest in Islam began with his first novel, *Book and Sword* (1955). The novel depicts the adventures of an underground society of Han Chinese "resistance fighters" called the Red Flower Society seeking to rid China of the foreign rule of the Manchu and restore the nation's sovereignty to the Han ethnic majority (*fanqing fuming*). In mainstream Chinese historiography, the period of the Qing dynasty that Jin Yong chooses as his novel's setting—the reign of Qianlong—is typically remembered as a phase of economic expansion, cultural efflorescence, and bureaucratic consolidation. Jin Yong rewrites the political history of the reign of Qianlong as a story about individual racial identities, conflicts, and fantasies. In the novel, the Manchu Qing emperor Qianlong is said to be Han Chinese himself and the biological brother of Helmsman Chen, the leader of the anti-Manchu Red Flower Society. As a result of a "baby swap," Qianlong becomes emperor of the powerful Manchu state, an empire built on the backs of his own embittered and shackled brethren, the Han Chinese. The emotional crux of the text is placed on the final revelation of Qianlong's birth to the emperor himself, at which point he must choose between his loyalty and obligations to the Qing state, his sympathy for the Chinese cause, his entangled relations with his biological brother (who is also the leader of the resistance movement), and his desire for a mysterious Islamic woman, Hasli. Qianlong's final choice is not politically but sexually driven. He betrays his friends and foes alike and breaks his pact with the Red Flower Society in order to satisfy his desire with Hasli. By juxtaposing Hasli and racial politics as the moral choices Qianlong must make, Jin Yong outlines a complex but subtle relation between gender and nation.

I propose that neither Islam nor women can be viewed as incidental details designed merely to embellish the text. Instead, gender and Islam are integral to the structural design and emotional import of the tale about the rise and fall of empire, and the loss and recognition of selves. During their travels, Helmsman Chen and other heroes of the Red Flower Society encounter Uyghur tribespeople who are pursuing a convoy that has stolen the Qur'an from them. Chen helps the Uyghurs recover the holy text and subsequently becomes romantically involved with the Uyghur chief's two daughters, Hasli and Huo Qingtong. Toward the end of the novel, Qianlong invades the province of Xinjiang in an effort to pacify the Uyghurs. Chen and the heroes come to the aid of the Uyghurs, but prove unable to save the tribe from annihilation. The victorious Qing army captures Hasli and brings her back to Beijing. Emperor Qianlong is stunned by Hasli's beauty and tries to make her his concubine. In an effort to secure a truce between her people and the Qing Empire, Hasli agrees to Qianlong's proposition, but when she realizes that the Qing Emperor will betray her Han Chinese allies, she commits suicide as a warning to the incoming heroes of the Red Flower Society.

The traditional interpretation of *Book and Sword* is that it is yet another familiar Manichean political fable that exalts the virtues of the Han Chinese at the expense of the Manchu. The Manchu's historical rule of the territory of China from 1644–1911 is considered by ethnocentric Chinese historians as an illegitimate episode of "foreign" rule in Chinese history. According to this Manichean logic, the Manchu in China are oppressive foreigners rather than proper citizens; the Han Chinese are the martial heroes who bravely defy their rule. This interpretation of the novel, however, fails to account for the symbolic and political significance of Islam in the organization of the text. This "Islam" differs from the historical religion of Islam and serves as a metonym for social differentiation in general. It complicates the emotional texture of this tale, disrupts its dichotomous racial logic, and prevents it from turning into a naïve nationalist text. It is crucial that in *Book and Sword*, the epic struggles between the Manchu and the Chinese unfold through the mediation of the Muslims rather than from a straightforward or authentic "Chinese" perspective, but exactly why the Muslims are so important to a text whose aim appears to be a conservative and ethnocentric celebration of Han culture remains a political paradox. Although most critics see *Book and Sword* as an ideological text that seeks to naturalize the equation between the political identity of "China" and the ethnic identity of the Han Chinese by marginalizing non-Han Chinese peoples who in fact make up much of what is known as Chinese culture, this common interpretation fails to explain the centrality of Islam in Jin Yong's literary imagination.

Conversely, the interpretation of Han Chinese nationalism as an assimilationist ideology—a melting pot discourse that derives its legitimacy from the recognition of minorities in China—does not explain the text's derogatory attitude toward the Manchu. The foreignness of the Manchu and the necessity of the Muslims for what appears to be a Han Chinese–centered nationalist project constitute a logical problem for the interpretive categories of race and nationalism. Consequently, critics who characterize *Book and Sword* as the product of an essentialist and romanticized nationalism are either forced to ignore the novel's invocation of Islamic cultures altogether, or to dismiss it as an Orientalist strategy that mixes in the "exotic flavors of central Asia" with the "sensational rumor" concerning the birth of the Qing Emperor.[1] Critics who explain the novel's reliance on Islam as nothing but a commercially driven Chinese Orientalism naturally make similar claims about its representation of women as another "exotic" or "sensational" element in the text.

Contrary to these views, I would argue that the political matrix of *Book and Sword* refuses an axis of good and evil, and unfolds instead as a dialectical process of absence and presence, whereby not two but three terms or perspectives alternate and succeed one another.

Han Chinese identity is not the dominant term in this triangulated relationship or the sole occupant of a victim discourse; rather, Chineseness is both a figure of inclusion and one of exclusion, whose binary relationship to the Manchu is disrupted by their common dependency on the representation of Islam. This figurative Islam differs from the historical religion or culture of the name and provides deconstructive leverage to the novel that prevents the closure of the category of the nation. This Islam is, furthermore, consistently and intimately intertwined with the problem of gender in ways that are too complex to be dismissed as mere eroticism or exoticism. Compounded with the problem of gender, Islam plays a central and formative role, often under names that are not immediately recognizable to the readers, in Jin Yong's political imagination throughout his literary career. Instead of seeing such tropes through critiques of Orientalism and male fantasy, I suggest that we view Islam and gender as two related forms of minority agency that Jin Yong invokes to develop an interventionist tactic in the politics of the Cultural Revolution. I insist that the Cultural Revolution is the indispensable historical context for the representation of Islam in Jin Yong's mature novels, and the immense appeal of Jin Yong in Chinese-speaking communities must be attributed to his unique capacity to employ political history in a way that is emotionally and intellectually compelling to his local readers.

Gender and Islam converge into a mode of minority agency that synthesizes transgressive energies against the Manichaean political logic of the Cultural Revolution. Rather than essentializing either term, Jin Yong dramatizes the failures of nationalist claims to represent their constituencies, and the complex ways in which nationalist thinking comes undone by its own claims. Gender, as one of the axes of power along which one becomes socially marked and intelligible, yields fertile grounds for Jin Yong to foreground the constitutive failures of nationalist claims. The complexity of gender, in other words, provides Jin Yong with the requisite material to develop a theory of the social conditions of subject formation that defies categorization of race and nation. Islam refers simultaneously to the experience of racialization and gender disidentification; minority agency is then derived from a common experience of oppression—sharable but not exchangeable between groups. Muslims, antistatist Han Chinese, and sexual dissidents in the text are represented not as identity categories, but as intimately related positions in a universal structure of power. The novel suggests that racial and gendered struggles against political persecution and assimilation cannot take place as the assertion of an individual's political interests; rather, they have to be articulated to other experiences of oppression and marginalization, other memories, institutions, and means of livelihood that are overshadowed and eradicated by the expanding state.

The scholarly tendency to dismiss both tropes of gender and Islam as commercial opportunism has its roots in the erroneous perception of martial arts fiction as a form of mass entertainment derived from film, which in turn leads critics to attribute the influence of the genre to the popularity of fantastic actions and spectacles in Chinese society. On the cover of the English translation of *Book and Sword*, for example, Oxford University advertises it as "*The Lord of the Rings* meets *The Magnificent Seven* in an Oriental setting! … This is *Crouching Tiger, Hidden Dragon* or *Hero* brought thrillingly to the page." As I have argued in previous chapters, however, *Crouching Tiger, Hidden Dragon* and other internationally successful martial arts films are actually cinematic adaptations of Chinese novels, and the written imagination of *wuxia* preceded its visual culture. The publisher's promotional statement not only reverses the historical relationship between film and literature for the American reader (films "brought thrillingly to the page"), but also infantilizes the martial arts novel as a Chinese equivalent of young adult fantasy fiction. In the original Chinese context, Jin Yong did not become the cornerstone of postwar Chinese literature by winning the hearts of moviegoers with action and thrills in a consumer-oriented society. Rather, he did so because of his insight into the political realities of contemporary China, a history that his English-language publishers' analogies with Kurosawa and Tolkien evacuate and discount. Jin Yong's novels capture, in a language more powerful than journalism, the ethical and political dilemmas of revolutionary China. His works provide an intellectual platform for political debates over human nature, progress, national leadership, unity, and the role of the media. Deeply entrenched in the local, contemporaneous politics of their times, his novels can be neither abstracted into nor explained away as a timeless or transcultural set of fantasized images on the screen. Instead, Jin Yong's success and appeal drew on a very historical reference: the Cultural Revolution. As the critic Hong Qingtian noted, Jin Yong first rose to fame as a dissident public intellectual and critic of the Cultural Revolution.[2] The so-called Jin Yong phenomenon must be explained in terms of its proper context of the politics of the Cultural Revolution, a period when radical intellectuals began to question the dogmatic aspects of Chinese Marxism-Leninism.

In both Chinese domestic and international opinions today, a bipolar lens has dominated the historiography of the Cultural Revolution. This interpretive framework takes on a moralizing language and either celebrates the Cultural Revolution as the greatest revolt against bureaucratic privilege in global twentieth-century history and an inspiration to humankind as a whole that promises a "universal liberation, a global unbinding of energies" (in the words of Fredric Jameson), or condemns it as the emblematic example of pure barbarism, comparable to the Holocaust.[3] Recent historians of the Cultural Revolution seek to overcome this moralizing tendency (whether nostalgic or dismissive), characterizing the Cultural Revolution as a legitimate, if misguided, intellectual movement of rational content and historicity.[4] While the historiography of the Cultural Revolution has been effectively rehistoricized in this way, the history of counter–Cultural Revolution thought has not received similar revisionist treatment. If the Cultural Revolution has been too easily dismissed as an embodiment of political irrationality and madness, the history of counter–Cultural Revolution discourse has been overlooked as empty Cold War propaganda from Hong Kong and Taiwan. Seen in this context, Jin Yong's works represent a nonconservative effort from the 1960s to deconstruct the historiography of the Cultural Revolution.

State of Divinity

Jin Yong's most important work during the Cultural Revolution was *Xiao-ao jianghu* (hereafter cited as *State of Divinity*, 1967).[5] The novel has been adapted many times for film and television, but the most famous reproduction of the story on the silver screen is Tsui Hark's trilogy: *Xiao-ao jianghu* (*Swordsman*, 1990), *Xiao-ao jianghu zhi Dongfang bubai* (*Swordsman II: Asia the Invincible*, 1991), and *Xiao-ao jianghu: Fengyun zaiqi* (*The Swordsman III: East Is Red*, 1993). Based on the general plot of Jin Yong's novel, *Swordsman* is a landmark and a major breakthrough in Hong Kong cinema that uses computer-generated imagery (CGI) instead of wireworks and trampolines to create the visual effects of spectacular, fantasy-like martial arts. The move proved to be a resounding success and a sequel was made immediately, this time focusing on a single character from the novel, Asia the Invincible. Although the title character presumably dies at the end of the movie, *Swordsman II: Asia the Invincible* was once again such a critical and commercial success that the producers (Ching Siu Tung and Raymond Lee Wai Man) decided to bring Asia the Invincible back to life in a third installment, *East Is Red*, but this time with a script that is completely independent of the original novel authored by Jin Yong.

Even before the film adaptations, Asia the Invincible stands as one of Jin Yong's most memorable characters of all time. Most readers, however, are unaware of the fact that Asia the Invincible was invented as an allegory of Mao during the Cultural Revolution and hence must be understood within the unique framework of Chinese politics. The third film in the series, *East Is Red*, further highlights the connection between the Maoist allegory in *Asia the Invincible*. More specifically, the figure developed, through the lens of transgressive sexuality, a sustained analysis of "human nature" grounded in a rejection of the competition between the Communist and Nationalist Parties.

Tsui Hark's *Swordsman II: Asia the Invincible* is one of the most iconic films in early 1990s Hong Kong cinema. Tsui casts a cheerful and somewhat boyish-looking Jet Li as the story's protagonist, Linghu Chong, and the luminously beautiful, phenomenally popular actress Brigitte Ching-Hsia Lin as the antagonist, Asia the Invincible. Both commercially successful and critically acclaimed, *Swordsman II* is one of the most important milestones in Hong Kong cinema and cultural history. Hong Kong's veteran film scholar, Stephen Ching-kiu Chan, identifies the film as a forceful articulation of the cultural logic of the era precipitated by the imminent 1997 handover of Hong Kong, which produced a feeling of crisis as well as an ambivalent sense of hope from the "ruined culture for utopian longings" and "an unknown and unknowable future" for Hong Kong.[6] While the film's cultural authority and representative-ness is commonly acknowledged, critics do not always mention that the film is an adaption of one of Jin Yong's most important novels, whose original historical touchstone is not a Hong Kong threatened by a collapsing real estate market, but Mao's China. In 1966, as part of his power struggle with other leaders of the Communist Party such as Deng Xiaoping and Liu Shaoqi, Mao launched the Cultural Revolution and placed the party organs in the control of the Gang of Four, led by Mao's last wife Jiang Qing. During the Cultural Revolution period, the structure of power was particularly volatile. A powerful leader of the Party today could wake up one morning and find himself charged with treacherous crimes the next day; a doting mother might get turned over to the authorities by her own children and persecuted as a "capitalist roader"; a champion of the socialist cause might wind up imprisoned as a counterrevolutionary. In a world turned upside down, the teachings of Confucius were not the only thing called into question: friends were not to be trusted, enemies were invisible and ubiquitous, and nothing was what it seemed.

The theme of *Swordsman II* is the cyclical nature of violence. Violence begets violence, and as one of the principal characters puts it, "As long as there are human beings in the world, there are conflicts." Martial arts, the ability to enforce justice where law and state power fail, appear to be cursed blessings. The characters are tormented by their martial powers and caught in a cycle of violence, revenge, and debt from which they cannot escape. The film begins with the protagonist's (Linghu Chong) plan to "retire from the world of martial arts" with his comrades by "going into seclusion" in a distant place called the Ox Mountain that never appears in the film. On their way, the swordsmen find themselves constantly entangled in a series of intrigues, power struggles, and gratuitous violence against the weak and the powerless. Linghu keeps promising his comrades that "this is our last mission" in each act of intervention; in the end, the entire band of Linghu's sword brothers dies at the hand of Asia the Invincible, ruler of the Demon Cult, and Linghu joins forces again with Asia's enemies to claim revenge. Invading the capital of the Demon Cult, Linghu comes face to face with the dreaded Asia for the first time, only to discover that Asia is a beautiful woman rather than a man and, in fact, the same person as a mute, helpless, and mysterious lady he has spent a night with and come to regard as his soul mate. Unbeknownst to Linghu is the fact that Asia has been practicing the arts of the *Secret Scriptures of Sunflowers*, a martial arts manual that requires the practitioner to pay the unthinkable price for the acquisition of superhuman powers: he must castrate himself. As a result of his castration, Asia transforms from a man into a woman and falls in love with Linghu during their chance encounters. In the final battle, Asia singlehandedly defeats Linghu and his army of allies, but at a critical juncture decides to spare Linghu's life, at which point the invading army seizes her moment of weakness and indecision to administer a fatal attack. Asia uses all of her remaining energy to try to kill her competition, the two other women Linghu is involved with, and falls off the cliff. Linghu jumps off with her and demands the truth of her identity: "Tell me you are Cici [the woman I slept with]"; Asia answers with an enigmatic smile, "I won't tell you; I want you to regret this for the rest of your life," then throws Linghu back to safety with her martial powers while falling to her own death.

The overarching theme of *State of Divinity* is the critique of the indoctrination, guised as political education, into dogmatic beliefs in Manichean binaries, which take form as distinctions good and evil, orthodox and heterodox, and the gentleman and the rogue. In the novel, Jin Yong cleverly uses the convention of the Secret Scripture in martial arts fiction to deliver a trenchant critique of

Mao's *Little Red Book,* the only text that people were allowed to read during the Cultural Revolution. In the novel, several characters meet their doom due to their dogmatic belief in a single book, *The Sunflower Scripture*, whose complex role in troubling these binaries I examine later in this chapter.

State of Divinity is a lengthy, extremely elaborate and complex novel about political intrigues, betrayals, and secret deals between various martial factions. The events, characters, and plots in the novel are reminiscent of many well-known acts of power struggle within the Communist Party during the Cultural Revolution, including the rise and fall of the Gang of Four and other famous personalities. Schematically, the novel centers on the perpetual struggle between two forces. Set during an unknown dynasty, the novel is famous for the portrayal of two martial arts masters who are also master politicians. Yue Buqun and Zuo Lengchan are heads of powerful martial clans, the school of Mount Hua and the school of Mount Song. Mount Hua and Mount Song are two of the five sacred mountains in China, and the martial arts of the schools are derived from and inspired by the landscape of their respective dwellings. For years, the five Sacred Mountain schools have joined forces with Shaolin and Wudang to defend themselves against a dreaded common enemy, the Sun-Moon Sect, which has been attempting to unify China under its rule. The Sun-Moon sect is referred to as the "Demon Cult" (*mojiao*) by the heroes of the "orthodox" martial clans, including the Shaolin and Wudang, in addition to the clans of Zuo and Yue. Describing themselves as the "orthodox" martial schools (*zhengpai*), the schools in the alliance prohibit their disciples from fraternizing with members of the Demon Cult, of whom the disciples of the orthodox sects learn the admonition to "kill-on-sight."

While part of a political alliance, each of the Sacred Mountains schools has its own style of martial arts, history, and culture. The school of Mount Heng, for example, is a secluded monastery that admits only female disciples. Zuo Lengchan, however, is not satisfied with being the leader of the five-mountain alliance. Mobilizing his people under the cause of defending the Alliance against the Demon Cult, Zuo seizes the opportunity afforded by the political crisis to attempt to merge the other orthodox factions into a unitary school under his sole control. For the dissidents who cannot be persuaded, he sends out minions to assassinate them, or else resorts to blackmailing, deal-cutting, and bribery to quell his opposition. While Zuo is a coldblooded, ruthless man of boundless ambitions, Yue is nicknamed "Gentleman's Sword" and known throughout the martial world as a man of great intellect, modesty, and integrity. Yet, though Yue pretends to disagree with the proposal of unification, he cunningly piggybacks on Zuo's brutal tactics to advance his own political interests. The overt use of brute force (Zuo) and the covert operations of psychological warfare and mind games (Yue) turn out to be two sides of the same coin. The novel deconstructs the opposition it sets up, suggesting that such moralizing discourse is a ploy that politicians resort to in order to achieve their own political objectives.

Within the Sun-Moon Sect/Demon Cult, power is equally corrupt and unstable. A coup occurs, and the old leader is arrested and locked away by a newcomer called Asia the Invincible. Linghu becomes entangled with the politics of the Sun-Moon Sect after meeting and befriending several "royalists" (which includes the old leader's daughter Ying Ying) who are trying to defeat Asia the Invincible through a countercoup. Linghu is Yue's student and foster son, and he has been taught since birth that mingling with members of the Demon Cult is a sin. The tension between his responsibilities to his new friends and his ties and promises to his own "orthodox" clan constitute the central drama of the text.

Although Linghu regards Yue as his role model, he is nothing like his master. Even before he becomes involved with the Demon Cult, Linghu is frequently punished for violating the strict and numerous codes of the Huashan school. Unlike the majority of Jin Yong's major characters, who typically embody certain degrees of the Confucian ideal of chivalry, Linghu is a free-spirited person who does not believe in dogmas. In ways that do not befit a martial arts "hero," Linghu is widely known for his vices rather than his virtues. A Don Juan–like philanderer, he is given to wine, gambling, frequenting prostitutes, and street-fighting with petty gangsters, standing in stark contrast to the type of gentlemanly mentality upheld by Yue.

That Yue and Zuo, the Gentleman's Sword and the evil villain, turn out to be two sides of the same coin (different forms of political hypocrisy) is mirrored by Linghu's experience with his friends and foes in the Demon Cult. After he and Ying Ying defeat Asia the Invincible and restore Ying Ying's father to power, the new leader turns out to be just as ruthless and ambitious, and declares another war on the Alliance. Linghu tries to lead the Alliance in a defensive war against the Sun-Moon Sect, but he also realizes that Yue, his martial arts teacher and surrogate father, is the mastermind behind the schemes. Good and evil keep switching sides in this dramatic text, which is fraught with tension, twists, and surprises. Most of the principal characters turn out to be other than who they initially appear as—including the protagonist in the first five chapters, himself the sole survivor of a tragedy. A sense of disenchantment with political promises and hypocrisy, and an outcry against moralizations and sloganeering, pervade this text.

The opening event in the novel is the massacre of the Lin family who are rumored to be in possession of a Secret Scripture. Jin Yong begins the story with the perspective of the young son Lin Pingzhi, the sole survivor of the tragedy, and misleads the reader into believing that Lin is the protagonist of the novel. Until the middle of chapter five, the third-person omniscient narration is filtered through Lin's consciousness and limited by his knowledge. Lin will eventually turn out to be one of the villains, consumed with rage and corrupted by the powers of the Secret Scripture that Linghu fights to contain. Jin Yong's choice to begin the novel with Lin's consciousness, however, serves multiple purposes. It gives the villain character a childhood and a psychology and humanizes that figure—a project that is consistently important to Jin Yong. More important, by initially placing the reader in a consciousness external to the principal character and representing Linghu as an alien character rather than the immediate locus of moral identification, the novel forces the reader to experience virtually what Linghu later discovers: the disintegration of the entire spectrum of values and beliefs with which one grows up.

The primary function of Lin's character in the beginning chapters is to introduce and define the morally unambiguous villains. Several important characters, such as Master Yu and Hunchback Gao, are developed at this point through their greedy and murderous activities in the downfall of the Lin estate. Constructed as blatantly despicable rogues, Master Yu and Hunchback Gao provide a ready foil against which Yue's noble, gentleman-like nature receives definition and substance. Yue arrives in time to rescue Lin Pingzhi from the persecution of Master Yu and Hunchback Gao, and takes him in as a protégée and a disciple of Huashan. The novel at this point shifts to the perspective of Yue's other disciple, Linghu, who will learn, through a series of rude awakenings, that both the young survivor of a massacre and his own foster father are capable of evil-doing.

Yue Buqun is the real mastermind behind all the schemes, and his gentlemanly demeanor is merely a façade designed to further his own political goal—the elimination of competing schools, the seizure of unquestioned political power under a "one-party" rule, and the unification of "China" (*tianxia*, "all under heaven"). In short, Yue and Zuo's political visions are identical, where they differ is their approach. Linghu, however, has difficulty moving beyond the teachings he has internalized since birth and coming to terms with the loss of his father figure as he recognizes Yue's hypocrisy. As soon as the novel's perspective shifts to Linghu, he begins encountering and befriending a number of characters from the Demon Cult who employ heterodox, sinister, and underhanded martial skills. Among these characters are Blue Phoenix, head of the Five Venom Sect and universally feared for her mysterious poisons; licentious monks and nuns who pay no heed to the vows of chastity; Master Ren, Head of the Demon Cult who uses bloodworms to control the minds of his minions; and, finally, Ying Ying, the daughter of Master Ren and an unrepentant, coldblooded assassin herself, whom Linghu eventually marries. Linghu is constantly torn between the code of conduct he was brought up with and the apparently evil intentions and deeds of the friends he meets by chance. The novel depicts Linghu as a victim of moral education, who seeks to "retire" to a world beyond good and evil, but is ultimately unable to do so.

These events depicted in the novel are inspired by happenings and policies during the Cultural Revolution, especially the familiar stories about how moral "reeducation" and "rectification" campaigns for the virtues of socialism turned family members against each other. The world in which Linghu finds himself is one turned upside down, and one whose violence he despises, but an exit does not seem anywhere close. One of the earliest major episodes in the novel is the "hand-washing ceremony." A senior member of Mount Heng, Liu Zhengfeng, announces that he has decided to retire from the Martial Order. According to the protocols, Liu will wash his hands in a golden basin in a public ceremony. By doing so, he clears his debts and responsibilities to all members of the Martial Order, and will not be allowed to use martial arts for the remainder of his life. The real reason behind Liu's retirement is that he has become friends with an elder in the Demon Cult, who, like Liu himself, is a talented and passionate musician. The two bond over a shared interest in music, and the innocent songs composed and compiled by the accursed friends give birth to a music manual that is the title of the novel, *State of Divinity*, which is subsequently mistaken by greedy martial arts characters as a Secret Scripture and hence becomes the cause of many unnecessary conflicts.

Zuo, however, declares Liu's act as one of treason and secession, and sends an army of minions to interrupt the ceremony by force. When Liu defies Zuo's order, Zuo's convoys take his family hostage. To force Liu's surrender, Zuo's men execute his wife and children in front of him, and force his youngest son to denounce his father in public.

> Seeing his dead mother, brother, and sister lying in the blood pool and Shi Dengda's sword point at his face, Liu Qin was scared out of his wits.
>
> "Please, please, I beg of you to spare my life, and spare … spare my dad's life," he said to Lu Bai.
>
> "Your dad collaborated with the villains in the Demon Cult. Do you think it's right or wrong?" Lu Bai pressed.
>
> "It's … wrong!" Liu Qin murmured.

"Should this kind of person be executed?" Lu Bai
asked.
"Yes … yes, they should!" Liu Qin muttered
immediately. (Vol.1, 257)

The political resonance of this scene is unmistakable. During the
Cultural Revolution era, both governments across the strait exercised
terror to control the thoughts of the people. The execution of "KMT
collaborators" "and "capitalist roaders" by the Communist authorities
in China, like the execution of "Communist sympathizers" and
"bandits" by the KMT government in Taiwan, were familiar, everyday
media stories. The most distinguished legacy of the Cultural Revolution,
however, was the practice of "self-criticism" and reeducating one's
politically incorrect parents by denouncing and humiliating them in
public. The conversation between Lu Bai and Liu Qin, in which the
young son of the Liu family is terrorized into denouncing his own
father as a traitor and a separatist, is an easily recognizable fragment
of the trauma of the Cultural Revolution.
    In Tsui Hark's 1991 film rendition, the directors take much artistic
license and change the story into a romantic encounter between Linghu
Chong (Jet Li) and the head of the Demon Cult, Asia the Invincible
(Brigitte Lin). Linghu and Asia are political enemies, but like Liu
and his friend from the Demon Cult in the hand-washing ceremony
story, they bond over music and wine. Again like Liu, Linghu has
decided to "retire" from the Martial Order and is already on his way
to Ox Mountain, where he and his sword-brothers will live as ordinary
peasants. Linghu invites Asia to go with them, not knowing that the
beautiful woman with whom he shares a jug of wine and sublime
music is the dreaded master of the Demon Cult. Asia falls in love with
Linghu and feels tempted by his offer, but he is torn because he is in
the midst of launching a full-scale military campaign to suppress the
dissidents and, for the first time in a long history, finally unify China.
Asia and Linghu end up sleeping together, but in the dark before they
undress, Asia asks his own concubine to "stand in" for him. In the final
battle of Blackwood Cliff, Linghu realizes that Asia used to be a man
and experiences a crisis in masculinity. Although Asia's martial skills

are vastly superior, he spares Linghu's life, loses the battle, and falls off the cliff. At this point, Linghu jumps off after Asia and demands to know if it was really "her" with whom he spent a night, and how that could have been possible. Smiling, Asia refuses to answer, uses what strength remains in her to throw Linghu back to safety on the ground, and falls to her death.

The oppositional values that structure the two scenes, one from the film adaptation and the other from the original novel, are similarly derived from a classical liberal-humanist framework: music is characteristically considered private, personal, and apolitical, linked to the sphere of life that is putatively most private and hidden from public scrutiny—sexuality or what transpires in the bedroom. Music is directly opposed to martial arts, which are collapsed with politics in both scenes. Politics, in turn, is defined as that which limits and prevents individual pursuit of freedom (music and sexuality) at the expense of a social collectivity, although one's membership in that social collectivity is inherently violent. Conversely, the violent nature of the social field maims and deforms human nature, transforming it beyond recognizable terms. The thematic emphasis on the impossibility of extricating oneself from the chain of violence is not new; many other films and literary works in the genre (*Kung Fu Hustle* and *Tianlong babu*, for example) depict skilled martial arts masters who prefer the peace and quiet of an ordinary lifestyle to the constant bloodshed and the responsibilities that come with the privileges of martial arts, but who falter in their attempts to find an exit to the world to which they have already been initiated. What is new about *State of Divinity* is that the idea of the inherent violence in the Martial Order is directly configured as *realpolitik*. Liu and his family are not simply prohibited from retiring from the Martial Order; their decision is branded as political secession in a novel written in the context of the Chinese civil war, in which both the CCP on mainland and the KMT governments in Taiwan are busy educating their citizens about the urgency of reclaiming the other part of China from the hands of the puppets of American imperialism or the bandits of Chinese communism.

The Religion of Light

Asia's gender is crucially connected to a figural use of the concept of Islam in the novel. In *State of Divinity*, Asia is a tyrannical, ambitious ruler of critical intelligence and formidable martial powers. After disposing of his predecessor and seizing political power through a scheme, Asia acquires the coveted and powerful treasure of the clan, *The Secret Scripture of Sunflowers*. He begins practicing the martial arts of the Scripture. However, the Scripture explains that in order to access such mysterious and superhuman powers, the aspiring martial arts master must pay a price—castration. Asia complies, and becomes an invincible hero in the Martial Order as the Scripture promised. The Scripture's superhuman powers, however, also have unexpected results. After the castration, Asia no longer finds women attractive, and orders all of his concubines beheaded. Instead, he finds himself enamored with a masculine but low-ranking subordinate in his clan. Although now Asia possesses the power to rule the world, he is no longer interested in politics and instead builds a boudoir, where he takes up sewing and other domestic duties. In the final battle, the Alliance forces, commanded by the novel's protagonist, Linghu Chong, invade the headquarters of the Sun-Moon Sect and meet the enigmatic Asia face-to-face. The dramatic scene in Asia's boudoir begins with a detailed description of Asia's fantastic martial moves. Three supreme martial arts masters gang up on him but are unable to defeat him. In an attempt to distract Asia, the resourceful daughter of Master Ren starts attacking, mutilating, and torturing Asia's lover, who is watching the ensuing battle in the room. Asia falls for her ploy and sacrifices his own life in an effort to protect the life of his lover. Tsui Hark's film version changes this detail and makes protagonist Linghu Chong the object of Asia's affection; but in the final battle in the movie, Asia similarly loses a winning war in a moment of weakness when he hesitates to take Linghu's life.

Jin Yong represents political power as inherently corrupting. After Linghu Chong and his allies help defeat Asia the Invincible and restore Master Ren to power, Ren simply becomes another Asia the Invincible, and history ends where it began. Ren creates a blacklist of clan members he intends to purge, revealing his own ambition to launch an attack on the other political factions—the five martial arts schools of the sacred mountains, the school of Shaolin Temple, and the school of Wudang—in order to "unify all of China." Whereas the ending of the movie sends Linghu and Ren's daughter into peaceful exile, the novel resolves the cycle of violence by bringing Master Ren to an untimely death as a result of excessive and incorrect practice of martial arts.

State of Divinity is a political allegory. The fear of the Demon Cult depicted in the novel refers to the "red scare," anti-Communist hysteria; however, the novel's sympathy with the misunderstood or, more accurately, demonized Sun-Moon Sect does not present the Communist Party in a romantic light either, since the Sun-Moon Sect itself is corrupt and politically unstable. Asia the Invincible, "Dongfang Bubai," is Jin Yong's code name for Mao Zedong; the name "Dongfang Bubai" is a deliberate allusion to Mao's first name ("Zedong," the one who brings prosperity to Asia) despite the fact that in several interviews Jin Yong denies that the similarities between the ruthless, power-hungry character Asia the Invincible and Mao Zedong was intended. What he wanted to create in 1966–1967, the year of the onset of the Cultural Revolution, was a "timeless" story about "human nature" as such. In the 1980 postscript to *State of Divinity*, Jin Yong explains:

> In writing martial arts fiction stories, what I really want to write about is human nature, just as writers of most other genres. The years when I was writing *State of Divinity* saw the height of the power struggle during the Chinese Communists' Cultural Revolution. In order to gain power and profit, both the dominant political faction and the oppositional faction [referring to the Gang of Four] resorted to the foulest means but showed no moral compunction whatsoever. During these years I was given a sobering picture of the inherent ugliness of human nature. At that time, I was writing a daily political column for *Ming Pao*, and my disgust with the dirty dealings in

politics was naturally reflected in my novel, which I also worked on daily. This novel is not an intentional *roman à clef* or political innuendo aiming at the Cultural Revolution. I simply wanted to depict certain general phenomena found in three thousand years of Chinese politics through my fictional creation of certain characters. (Vol. IV, 1682)

However, in a scene where Jin Yong depicts one of these "certain characters"—Asia the Invincible—the actions and events surrounding Asia bear an unmistakable resemblance to the Cultural Revolution. The text uses Asia as a focal point to construct a story of the destruction of the Chinese family during the Cultural Revolution, where members are forced to denounce each other in public to reeducate their own political consciousness. Like Mao, whose "personality cult" is commonly used as an explanation for the irrational dimensions of the Cultural Revolution, Asia is deified as a "Holy Master" in this allegorical novel. In this scene, an old comrade of Asia's, Tong, witnesses his own family tortured by Asia's boyfriend.

> The boyfriend said, "Of the entire family, which one of you remembers Article 3 of the Holy Master's teachings?" And a boy about ten years old said, "Article 3, The Teachings of the Erudite, Righteous, Merciful, Enlightened Holy Master: 'Show no mercy to your enemies. Spare no one in their family— men, women, or children—and leave no roots.'" The boyfriend said, "Excellent, excellent, little boy! Can you recite all ten Articles by our Holy Master?" The boy answered, "Yes, all ten of them. If I don't study the teachings of the Holy Master for one day, I can neither sleep nor eat. When I do study His teachings, I make great progress in martial arts and I have strength in battles against our enemy." Asia's boyfriend said with a smile, "Who taught you to say these?" The boy said, "Daddy." Asia's boyfriend

pointed at Hundred-Bears and asked, "Who is he then?" The boy said, "Grandpa." Asia's boyfriend said, "Your grandpa doesn't read the teachings of the Holy Master, and doesn't obey the Holy Master, what do you say we should do?" The boy said, "Grandpa should be denounced. Everybody should read the teachings of the Holy Master and obey his instructions." (Vol. IV, 1682)

The injunction contained in the Holy's Master's teachings, "Show no mercy to your enemies. Spare no one in their family—men, women, or children—and leave no roots" are almost a verbatim quotation of a famous line from Mao's essays "Our Friend, Our Enemy," written after the Sino-Soviet split as an attack on Soviet "revisionism" and itself an example of Manichean discourse. The Teachings of the Erudite, Righteous, Merciful, Enlightened Holy Master is undoubtedly an allusion to Mao's *Little Red Book*. The practice of self-criticism, as well as the denunciation and public humiliation of one's own family members, were hallmarks of the Cultural Revolution.

The novel, however, is not a simplistic critique of the Cultural Revolution. Like the fictional Demon Cult, the Chinese Communist Party has been demonized by historians and critics for events in the Cultural Revolution. In positing an analogy between the Communist Party's radical politics and the social position of the Muslims within China, the novel presents an experience of the powerless, the persecuted, and the oppressed that is significantly distinct from the moral judgment of traditional pro- or anti-Communist historiography. Muslims constitute one of the most important non–Han Chinese communities in China; their cultural and economic specificities remain inassimilable to and underrepresented by a party based on the interests and perspectives of Beijing. The Chinese state is not at all isomorphic or coterminous with the people it claims to represent; instead, the identity of the state is constituted by precisely what it excludes from social signification, what it suppresses under the banners of national sovereignty, political stability, and territorial integrity, and what it silences through the invocation of colonial dismemberment.

Islam in Jin Yong names a different kind of border that is traversed under the idiom of martial arts, and a different kind of cultural affinity to the history of Chinese civilization that is erased from view in the official struggle and mass mobilization against the imperial West and the Soviet Union. Islam is the forgotten "West" to China, a site of cross-fertilization that Jin Yong seeks to recuperate in his alternative imagination of Asia. In Jin Yong's novels, the West as defined by the official language of Maoist national struggles— America, Europe, and the former Soviet Union—does not make an appearance. As in *The Journey to the West*, Jin Yong's West (*xiyu*) refers to India, Persia, Turkey, and Tibet—the high civilizations that have served for centuries as China's interlocutors. The "enlightened monk from the West" (usually Tibetan or Indian) is a recurring character type in Jin Yong's fiction. Jin Yong's novels delineate a transcultural process of contact and exchange within Asia that does not take the European West as its normative point of reference. In the novels, the identity of China is constantly thrown into crisis and then renewed by its contact with one of its neighbors in Central or South Asia. *State of Divinity* builds on a cross-identification between two kinds of minorities in China. The underground Red Flower Society is defined against the government by their antistatist activities.

State of Divinity is unique among Jin Yong's works in many ways. Although all of Jin Yong's martial arts novels are historical novels, *State of Divinity* is the only major Jin Yong work whose time frame is deliberately left unspecified because of its sensitive political subject.[7] It is, moreover, a rewrite of an earlier theme, one that begins with *Book and Sword*. In many ways the story strikes the reader as the "already read," now inflected by the vocabulary of the Cultural Revolution. In the rest of this chapter, I would like to consider the continuities between *State of Divinity*, *Book and Sword*, and another major Jin Yong novel—*Heavenly Sword, Dragon-slaying Saber*— all of which take a surprising interest in Islam, in ways that are not immediately transparent to their readers.

Heavenly Sword, Dragon-slaying Saber was written in 1961 as a 112-chapter work, before being reorganised into forty longer chapters in the 1970s. Part of the story concerns a Persian spy who operates under the martial name of "The Dragon King of the Purple Gown" (*Zishan longwang*). This character disguises herself as a middle-aged Chinese woman in an attempt to steal a Secret Scripture, *Qiankun da nuoyi*. The Scripture is the prized possession of a Chinese secret society called "Manichaeism" (*mingjiao*). The novel, set in the fourteenth century, erroneously identifies Manichaeism as a "Persian" religion. By contrast, *State of Divinity* is set in an unidentified, mythical time period, although some scholars speculate that its historical setting is most likely the seventeenth century.[8] The anachronism of the former and the ahistoricism of the latter in the descriptions of Manichaeism and Persia embody a sedimented interest in present-day Islam rather than in the pre-Islamic Middle East or historical Persia. While Islam is never explicitly named in the stories, the assumptions the author makes about "Persia" derive from Chinese understandings of Islam as a fossilized object of knowledge, rather than of the historical Persian Empire.

Although Jin Yong scholars today do not typically see the representation of Manichaeism in *Heavenly Sword* as an effort to depict Islam, Manichaeism is, in fact, another name Jin Yong has invented for the Demon Cult in *State of Divinity*, whose official title is "The Sun-Moon Sect." The Chinese name for "The Sun-Moon Sect," *Ri yue shen jiao*, is a coded way of saying "The Religion of Light." The two pictograms, "sun" (*ri*) and "moon" (*yue*), together form the ideogram "light" (ming). The Chinese characters for sun and moon written next to each other in expressions such as "The Sun-Moon Sect," in other words, are tantamount to the Chinese character for light. In the two novels, the characteristics and attitudes of the adherents of the two sects are strikingly similar.

As with Islam, Jin Yong deliberately misrepresents Manichaeism as a confused tangle of knowledge about Persia, Arabs, Nestorianism, Zoroastrianism, and other fragmentary ideas associated with the Middle East. For example, the Manichees in the novel are said to be fire-worshippers like Zoroastrians, while historically adherents of Manichaeism worshipped symbols of the Sun and the Moon but not fire;[9] in fact, the teachings of Mani were abhorrent to the Zoroastrians. Here the author's efforts form a distinct Chinese "Orientalism" whose provenance lies in European scholarship rather than China's direct interactions with the Middle East. The European roots of Jin Yong's imagination of "Persia" in that Oriental discourse on "Islam" are visible, for example, in Jin Yong's emphasis on Persia as an "oil-supplier" (Vol. IV, 1531). These associations are more commonly made in reference to "the Middle East" than China's own Muslim minorities, who are understood as a "problem" insofar as they pose the threat of secession, but not of the scarcity of oil. Similarly, the adherents of Manichaeism in the novel are characterized by a natural penchant for martyrdom, an envy of Chinese modernity, and religious fanaticism (Vol. II, 421, 709; Vol. III, 1017; Vol. IV, 1602). These stereotypes are not found in indigenous Chinese writings in premodern times, which did not treat Islam as necessarily more foreign or threatening than Christianity. By contrast, Christian-based insurrections such as the Taiping Rebellion—in which the leader Hong Xiuquan proclaimed himself God's Chinese son—have given birth to numerous negative representations of Christianity in modern Chinese culture.

The representation of the Manichees is distinctly marked by the conflation of race and religion. Whereas certain characters in the novel may be said to be "Taoist" or "Buddhist," these differences are understood as different styles of martial arts rather than religious beliefs or cultural differences. Taoism and Buddhism are diacritical differences on a plane that remains uncomplicated and untroubled by religion as such, and the race of a character that practices Taoist or Buddhist martial arts is neither marked nor framed by such differences. Rather, Taoism and Buddhism denote a common Chineseness that is consti-tuted precisely through the exclusion of such ethnic and religious differences as "Manicheaism" or "Islam." The actions, views, and values of the Manichees in the novel, by contrast, are determined and homogenized by Manichaeism as a religion, leading to a conflation of religion with a psychopathological essence that only applies to Manichaeism, while Buddhism and Taoism are not represented as religions.

In *Heavenly Sword, Dragon-slaying Saber* Jin Yong has a character present the following view of Manichaeism as the bearer of stigma in China:

The Religion of Light originated in Persia, where it was formerly known as Manichaeism, and was introduced into the Middle Kingdom during the reign of Empress Wu in the Tang dynasty. At the time many Persian travelers to China brought with them the sacred text of Manichaeism, *The Scripture of the Three Principles*, which became the Manichean canon commonly studied by the Chinese. On the 29th of the sixth lunar month of the third year of the reign of Dali, the Temple of the Light was founded in Luoyang. Afterward the Temples of the Light were built in major cities such as Taiyuan, Jingzhou, Chezhou, Hongzhou, Yuezhou, and others. In the third year of the reign of Huichang, the imperial court issued an edict to purge the Religion of Light, after which its influence greatly declined. Ever since then, the Religion of Light remained a secret society that was persecuted from dynasty to dynasty. In order to survive under a hostile climate, the Manichees adopted a perverse way of life. As a result, the character "Mani" in its name was changed into "mo" (demon) to describe their strange ways, and Manichaeism became known as the Demon Cult [*mo jiao*] in China instead. (HSDS, Vol. III, 1017)

Throughout this martial arts novel, Jin Yong describes several instances of the "strange ways" of the Manichees in China and Persia, which include nude burial for deceased members (Vol. II, 421), a lineage of virgins as the successive rulers of the Persian Orthodoxy, vegetarianism, the elevation of fire to a sacred symbol, and demon-worship. The last two are identified as the twin pillars of this religion (Vol. II, 417). While the more exaggerated rituals are clearly the author's own invention, certain descriptions of Manichaeism in the novel can be traced to a twentieth-century Chinese discourse on the Middle East that was already in circulation by the time of the novel's composition. In an influential study published in the

1940s, "The Religion of Light (*mingjiao*) and the Ming Dynasty" (*mingjiao yu da ming diguo*), Chinese historian Wu Han speculated that the Ming dynasty (1368–1644) was named "ming" by its first emperor Zhu Yuanzhang because the majority of the members of the rebel group called the Red Turbans that helped him overthrow the Yuan (Mongolian) dynasty also belonged to an underground religious society, The Religion of Light which, as Jin Yong's character correctly claims in this passage, is what Manichaeism was called in medieval China.[10] According to Wu Han's theory, "ming," the Chinese word for "light," was chosen to be the name of the new dynasty after China's liberation from the Mongols as the new Emperor's way of thanking the Manichees for assisting him in the revolution.

The structural parallels between *Heavenly Sword, Dragon-slaying Saber* and *State of Divinity* are found in the common concern with the Manichaen axis of good and evil, which both novels set out to deconstruct in different ways. In *State of Divinity*, the protagonist Linghu Chong wrestles with realities of a corrupt Martial Order and the dogmatism of the Good. He has been conditioned by the injunction to eradicate evil, which he has learned since his childhood to equate with the Demon Cult, or Religion of Light. The grand mastermind behind all evil schemes turns out to be his own teacher, one of the leaders of the Alliance. Good and evil switch places, and Linghu marries the daughter of the Demon Cult leader, but he refuses to join their faction when he is offered the position of vice leader. He stands by his childhood oath and allegiance to the Good, which is represented as a dogma in the book that determines the thoughts and actions of the protagonist. By contrast, Zhang Wuji in *Heavenly Sword, Dragon-slaying Saber* makes the opposite decision. Zhang's story bears many structural similarities to that of Linghu Chong. Like Linghu, Zhang is born a member of the so-called Good forces and encounters members of the opposing faction that he is conditioned to hate and kill on sight. He, too, becomes entangled with members of the Demon Cult and learns that there are human beings behind these faces and names. Eventually, like Linghu, Zhang is offered a chance to join the Demon Cult but, unlike the protagonist of the later novel, Zhang accepts the offer and becomes its new leader. He saves the Manichees from extinction and persecution from the sanctimonious, bloodthirsty wrath of the crusading Good, and eventually joins forces with Zhu Yuanzhang in his rebellion against the Mongols.[11] The connection between what may be a mere linguistic coincidence (the word *ming* in the title of the Ming dynasty, and the historical name for Manichaeism, *mingjiao*) is elaborated in a dramatic fashion in *Heavenly Sword* that adds much flavor to the theory Wu Han first propounded. Jin Yong's adaptation of Wu Han's theory as his source material for a novel bears critically on the question of nationalism. As captured by the recurring slogan of "fanqing fuming" (overthrow the Qing dynasty and restore the Ming), spoken by many characters in Jin Yong's novels, the Ming dynasty is exalted as a true "native" dynasty in Chinese nationalist historiography, sandwiched between two foreign dynasties—the previous Mongol-ruled Yuan dynasty and the later Manchu-ruled Qing dynasty. The word "ming" is also the name Jin Yong chose for the newspaper he founded in 1959, *Ming Pao*.[12]

The protagonists of the two novels, *Heavenly Sword, Dragon-slaying Saber* and *State of Divinity*, have similar experiences when it comes to their encounter with the demon(-ized) Sun-Moon Sect or Manichaeism. In *State of Divinity*, after Linghu helps Ying Ying and Master Ren defeat Asia the Invincible, Master Ren offers Ying Ying's hand in marriage to Linghu, and offers to make Linghu the vice leader of the sect as well. Adhering to his childhood promise to his foster parents never to mingle with the members of the Demon Cult, Linghu refuses, incurring Master Ren's wrath. Master Ren later dies abruptly from a medical condition associated with the "essence-draining" martial technique he practices, giving the novel a happy ending. Ying Ying and Linghu are thus able to marry each other without the father's disapproval, and the contradiction between Linghu's obligations to his own foster parents and Ying Ying's filial piety, both embodying the same value in traditional Confucian order of things, finds a facile resolution and grants the novel a sense of closure.

The Interpretation of Gender

Despite their different decisions and outcomes, however, Linghu and Zhang are protagonists of two different major Jin Yong novels that signify the same form of minority agency Jin Yong is constructing. It is, in fact, possible to read Linghu and Zhang as being the same character. Although he does not become the leader of the Demon Cult, Linghu does leave the School of Mount Hua and becomes the leader of Mount Heng, the nunnery martial arts school that has never accepted a male disciple. By violating this social taboo, Linghu enacts a gender-based transgression, which is structurally analogous to Zhang's ascension to leader of the Demon Cult in the other novel.

Asia's sexuality is another kind of productive transgression, a socially marginalized form of existence that disrupts the interior and exterior boundaries of the self. Originally a character in *State of Divinity*, Asia the Invincible has taken on a life of its own, and its meaning in Chinese culture today has been molded and remolded by a wide range of cultural practices. Since his creation, Asia's enduring presence in the Chinese cultural imaginary has destabilized the relation between body parts of social norms. The reception and re-creation of Asia the Invincible amplifies a contradiction inherent in the very concept of gender.

After the castration, Asia undergoes a series of unanticipated transformations as he begins to master the mysterious arts of the Scripture, eventually finding himself in love with a muscular male subordinate in his clan. These changes do not trouble Asia; he embraces his new feelings wholeheartedly and he willingly "plays the role of a submissive housewife" (Vol. IV, 1274). The story can be read as a narrative of how one discovers the pleasures of bottom-hood, or how queerness might be understood as the unexpected, the new, the culturally unsanctioned, rather than a fixed and stable identity. In fact, the multiplicity of interpretations this narrative produced in the subsequent years suggests that it is marked by an irreducible queerness whose shape cannot be decided in advance. In television adaptations of the story, Asia is conventionally played by an unattractive male actor, and his transformation after castration represents a "fall" into "homosexuality." In Tsui Hark's 1991 *Swordsman II: Asia the Invincible*, Tsui offers a significantly different view of Asia's transition, which is certainly a testament to the malleability of the Jin Yong story and to the way in which Asia signifies an internal incoherence of gender that may be reread and redeployed in unanticipated ways. In *Swordsman II*, Asia's change is reinterpreted as a change in *gender* rather than sexual orientation. The character Asia begins as a man (unconvincingly played by Brigitte Lin) and ends as a woman whose love interest is changed to the protagonist Linghu Chong (played by Jet Li) instead of the minion in his own clan as depicted by the original novel. The film adds a female character that did not exist in Jin Yong's text, Shi Shi, as Asia's concubine before he becomes a woman. The addition of Shi Shi allows the film to explain Asia's transgendered experience as the transformation from one heterosexuality to another. His sex change neatly coincides with the transition between his attraction to two objects of desire—Shi Shi and Linghu Chong. Asia's gender is retroactively established by his object of choice. Whereas the original novel states that Asia beheads all of his "concubines" (Vol. IV, 1283) after he starts acquiring the power of the Scripture, these "concubines" are not mentioned anywhere else in the novel and thus do not have the status of full characters. In lieu of these invisible and multiple concubines, in the film Shi Shi serves to embody the heterosexuality of the preoperative Asia as a concrete and individuated instantiation of a heterosexual desire that can be counterposed to Asia's postsurgical heterosexual desire for Linghu Chong.

Chou Wah-shan's reading of the story places Asia the Invincible in a long lineage of homophobic constructions in Chinese culture. Focusing his attention on the film, Chou understands Tsui Hark's choice of a "biological woman," Brigitte Lin, for the role of Asia to be a critical strategy that saves a homophobic film from the embarrassment of placing two male actors in a sex scene, even if one of them is playing a woman.[13] Chou's interpretation suggests that the film's casting was constrained by a problem that was internal to the Asian film industry: the star system.[14] The constellation of mental, physical, physiological, and social changes that Asia experiences, however, cannot be reduced to the abject figure of "the homosexual," and Chou's criticism itself shows a limited understanding of queer or antihomophobic struggles.

The novel states that Asia cuts off his testicles but not his penis, and he becomes feminine and submissive but not female-identified. In his postcastrated state, Asia is a man who desires men. The novel asks its reader to consider a relationship between a psychic scene of desire and a physical, visible scene of anatomical change. Asia's psychic change is clearly the result of a "sex" change, but what is that gender change? Is the castrated Asia the Invincible a heterosexual woman with a penis, a male homosexual who prefers to be penetrated, or a transvestite? The wording of the original novel implies that Asia's most significant postsurgical transformation is not from a heterosexual man to a homosexual but from a polygamist to a monogamist, who is now singularly obsessed with just one man instead of many men. The novel repudiates the static cultural lens that would read sexuality as gender. Asia changes, sexually, in a number of ways, from polygamy to monogamy, from top (the penetrating partner) to bottom (the penetrated partner), from testicleful to testicleless, and these changes form a complex set of materials that are used to mark his gender. His gender, however, is radically dissociated from bodily life and shown to be constituted through social norms that are opaque to the subject formed in their matrix. The difficulty of interpreting Asia's sex offers a platform for investigating the discursive production of differences that are never fully captured by the sign of sex. This explains why the choice of gender transgression as a theme for a novel about "Islam" and martial arts rests upon a historically determinate compatibility between queerness and the author's conception of the spiritual world, and why sexuality is able to signify other differences, other "secrets" that the novel seeks to bring to light.

Three different characters in *State of Divinity* castrate themselves to acquire the forbidden but powerful arts of *The Secret Scripture of Sunflowers*: Lin Pingzhi, the protagonist's rival in a love triangle; Yue Buqun, the protagonist's master and surrogate father; and Asia the Invincible, the leader of the Demon Cult. Of all three characters, though, Asia is the only one who experiences a change in sexual *orientation* (beginning to desire men instead of women) as a consequence of his castration; the other two men who castrate themselves become effeminate men with high-pitched voices but remain heterosexual in the orientation of their desire. In singling out Asia as the sole character whose gender is transformed by the powers of the sacred text, Jin Yong implies a connection between Asia's political experience and his sexual aberration. Before the start of the final battle between Asia and the royalists that takes place in Asia's boudoir, Asia explains to the invaders that before he acquired the *Sunflowers* Scripture, his ambition was to "unify the world of martial arts" (*yi tong jiang hu*). However, once he had castrated himself and started practicing the martial arts of the Scripture, he realized that "true joy in life does not lie in political power; rather, it is in being loved by a man" (1278). Asia then says to the daughter of the former Head of the Clan, "So long as a person was born female, she is already infinitely luckier than a dirty man. But when a person is not only born female, but young and pretty like you … If I could switch places with you, I wouldn't even be interested in being the Emperor of China, let alone the Holy Master of this clan" (1278).

The juxtaposition of politics and sexuality in the narrative seeks to characterize Asia/Mao as a tyrant who tortures his own political subjects. However, the characterization significantly departs from the conventional portrayal of Mao as an inane ruler who launched the Great Leap Forward and the Cultural Revolution out of foolishness and irrationality. Instead, the novel characterizes Mao's allegorical figure, through the vocabulary of aberrant sexuality, as a cunning and competent ruler whose efforts are derailed by sexual desires. Asia's failed political programs are out of character, and the strangeness of his policies is conjoined to the strangeness of his sexuality. The political critique relies on a cultural imagination of the stigma of sodomy, the social meanings produced by the image of a dictator being, and taking pleasure in being, sodomized. The signifying power of the fiction depends on and reinstates a prior cultural discourse on sex that institutes a historically determinate form of social power. *The Secret Scripture of the Sunflowers* constitutes part of this cultural discourse on sex: The "sunflowers" are a metaphor for the anus, "flowers" that open up for "the sun" or male energy. In Chinese slang, *kui hua* (sunflower) and *ju hua* (chrysanthemum) are both euphemism for the anus.

Within the parameters of the novel as well as the cultural idiom underlying its construction, male homosexuality appears to be founded by anal intercourse, which is not only presumed to be a necessary part of the definition of "true" homosexuality, but also endowed with the power to define the "genders" (understood as "roles") of the partners. One character comments that Asia "likes to wear women's clothes and does needlework in a boudoir and is infatuated with a muscular, unrefined man like Yang Lianting ... and turned himself into a half-man, half-woman monstrosity" (1460). Asia's preference for needlework and housekeeping *despite* his martial powers is discursively produced as a contradiction in need of explanation, just as his "sex" becomes culturally unintelligible ("half-man, half-woman") but nevertheless accounted for (*"because* he castrated himself") in the novel. Asia has assumed a *sexed* position in language, but that position proves to be an unviable one that language does not adequately describe.

The power of language to produce sexed positions must be examined in conjunction with the cultural logic that makes having a gender that is not quite one's own—Asia's own acceptance of his status as a "half-man, half-woman monstrosity"—a position consistently preferred to having no gender at all. The reason living without a gender, even a false one, is not an option to many is simply the requirement of survival: without a gender, one cannot relate to others in the political community that one does not choose for oneself but depends on for one's livelihood. Symptomatically, the contradiction between Asia's power and his chosen lifestyle derives from a cultural division of achievements between the male/public domain (Asia's martial power) and female/domestic labor (needlework).

Jin Yong's most complex account of gender is found in *The Giant Eagle and Its Companion*, whose female protagonist, Xiaolongnü, is one of Jin Yong's most memorable characters.[15] Jin Yong uses Xiaolongnü's character as an illustration of the necessary interdependence of gender and culture: gender is a social construction that has no meaning and no basis outside of culture. Xiaolongnü is a character who grows up in a tomb with almost no human contact. As a result of living in complete social isolation, Xiaolongnü evinces many traits that are incompatible with the social definition of femininity. The novel connects Xiaolongnü's martial arts and her imperfectly formed gender to each other. The tomb functions as a symbolic site where Jin Yong articulates two points simultaneously: his view regarding the relation between sex and gender and his distinction between nature and culture. Living in a tomb and shielded from exposure to sunlight, Xiaolongnü is naturally white-skinned and unobservant of all rules of the "adult world." The choice of a tomb as a narrative locale conveniently explains her ignorance of the male sex as well as social rules, serving at once as insulation from the domain of culture and the domain of sex.

Jin Yong highlights the connection between her childlike ways and the incomplete nature of her "gender" through a misunderstanding of her age.

> At this time, Xiaolongnü was actually already over twenty years old, but since she spent all her life in an ancient tomb and never saw any sunlight, her skin was unusually soft. In addition, her internal martial arts power [*nei gong*] was highly developed, so she looked like she was only sixteen or seventeen. Before she and Yang Guo met each other, she did not know any human emotions. Desires and passions were most damaging to the body and the face, so for someone like her who could be free of desire, two years passed only as one. If she could really obey the instructions of her master and rid herself of all her worldly thoughts, not only could she expect to live no less than one hundred years, even when she did turn one hundred, her face and strength would be no different from a fifty-year-old. Huang Rong naturally assumed that she was actually younger

than Yang Guo. Besides, Xiaolongnü was more clumsy
and innocent like a child in her mannerisms than
Guo Fu. No wonder Huang Rong thought Xiaolongnü was a little girl. (Vol. II, 498)

Here, her martial power apparently works better than the best
age-defying facial cream. Understood as a magical, spiritual healing
art, martial arts in the world of *wuxia* fiction is the cultivation of
one's spiritual essence, and this equation, maintained by other
martial arts stories, allows Jin Yong to make a number of strategic
choices. He represents Xiaolongnü's sexuality as detachable from the
worldliness of the world, as the presocial, pregendered interiority
of her personhood, as her "virginity." Paradoxically, however, this
virginity acquires its visibility and intelligibility in the text only when
it is posited as a sexual matter, as a relation between men and women
and as a movement or trajectory of desire. What is said to be presocial
turns out to be permeated with the social, and it is only in the social
that her virginity acquires its meaning and significance. Her virginity
is therefore from the beginning figured as a play of desire rather than
an absence of desire.

Jin Yong makes a continuous effort to paint Xiaolongnü as a
desirable object whose desirability comes precisely from the fact that
she grows up in a tomb. Xiaolongnü's coming-of-age becomes an
act of border-crossing—from the underground world hidden away
from view to the social, visible world—and border-crossing becomes
inextricably linked with gender-crossing, as her movement from a
pre-gendered being to a gendered one. Xiaolongnü is viewed as a
desirable person not only because she is physically a virgin, but also
because she is mentally and socially a child. Jin Yong emphasizes
this by depicting Xiaolongnü's loss of virginity as her entry into
"culture." While she is still living in the tomb, all her human
passions are inhibited by her special martial arts. Before her first
sexual experience, Xiaolongnü is cold, unresponsive, devoid—and in
fact incapable—of "human emotions." She never sheds a tear when
her nanny, who is more of a parental figure to her than her master,
is murdered in front of her. Xiaolongnü's first sexual experience

ignites feelings she did not know she was capable of and sets into motion a chain of events. By Jin Yong's design, her sexual awakening is also her initiation into "society," the inauguration of her role as a social agent.

> Xiaolongnü had been living in an underground tomb for a long time without any sunlight, so her face was usually extremely pale, with a white glow. But right now she was extremely pleased, and started to blush like a blossoming flower. She said with a bright smile: "Yes, I am indeed his teacher, but now his martial arts is just as great as mine. He really likes me, and I really like him too. Before ..." At this point, she lowered her voice. Even though she was innocent and did not understand any social rules, a woman was born with a natural shyness. She said slowly, "Before ... I thought he did not like me, did not want me to be his wife. I ... I was really hurt, and I thought I'd be better off dead. Only today did I find out that his love is true, I ... I ..." In the hall, hundreds of people listened in silence to her pouring her heart out. Even if a girl was madly in love, how could she share that information in public like this? How could she tell that to a stranger like Guo Jing? But Xiaolongnü did not know anything about the etiquette and ethics governing human society, so once she felt as if she had things to say, she simply followed her impulse. (Vol. II, 545)

The emphasis on the social motivates the text to construct a narrative apparatus that weaves together feminine objects and feminine sex into coherent scenes. Xiaolongnü's "gender" is expressed through a number of codes signifying the female sex; these codes, in turn, derive their signifying power from a set of conventions and rules outside the parameters of the novel itself and in this sense the novel is merely the reworking of the "already written." The novel describes her femininity in a combat scene with a Taoist, Hao:

Xiaolongnü said, "You've killed someone. You must pay for your mistake with your life. Kill yourself now and I'll spare the lives of the rest of the Taoists at your Temple."

Hao smiled grimly, "I killed Grandma Sun by accident. I will forgive your rudeness, young lady. I'll grant you and the kid safe passage. You may leave the Temple now."

She slowly took from her pocket a mysterious piece of material as if made of ice, and put on a pair of white gloves. It turned out that the material was a silk belt. She quietly said, "Old Taoist, you are a coward. Since you're afraid of taking your own life, I'll take it for you. Defend yourself." She raised her hand slightly, and the strip of silk suddenly flew from her hand, heading straight for Hao's face. Under the candlelight, he saw only a gold-colored sphere tied to the silk belt flying at him, without a sound and out of nowhere. Hao realized that she administered her attack deftly, and the weapon she used was mystic. Unsure of how to react, he tried to dodge her attack by jumping to the left. But he didn't know that Xiaolongnü's belt could turn direction in midair. As Hao leapt to the left, the belt followed him. Three "dings" were heard as the golden sphere shook three times, each time aiming at the "Receiving Aroma," "Holding Tears," and "Central" pressure points on his face. The speed and precision of this young woman's pressure-point hitting technique rivaled the most renowned masters of martial arts. (Vol. I, 188)

In this passage, Xiaolongnü's femininity is defined by the kind of weapon she uses, a silk belt. The novel also takes pains to emphasize that before she can enter combat, she needs to put on a pair of gloves to protect her chastity. Later on, we also learn that Xiaolongnü's powers come from her virginity, and her powers become severely curtailed the moment she loses her virginity. Earlier in the story we are also told that her teacher was also a virgin who had learned her own martial arts from a secret scroll called "The Heart Sutra for the Pure [Jade-like] Women" [*Yunü xinjing*], where "jade-like women" is a euphemism for virgins. The novel hence effects a displacement of several material objects at once. Jade is somehow made to denote the qualities of being a virgin, and a book is somehow able to infuse superhuman martial arts powers in the person who reads it. This displacement of material objects is the precondition for the constitution of Xiaolongnü's gender, which in the passage is constructed through a discourse of material objects. Xiaolongnü uses as her preferred weapon in combat a pair of white gloves and a silk rope that are not only perpetually pristine white but also apparently dirtproof, as her preferred weapon in combat. The eternal whiteness of Xiaolongnü aims to create a sense of correspondence between the color white, female chastity, and female martial power. She practices martial arts on a bed made of ice (suggesting that she is sexually frigid) and is the sole heir of the ancient martial arts secret scroll for virgins. Her martial power is then symbolically (in a hyperbolic manner) derived from her virginity. Xiaolongnü, hence, is most emphatically a cultural notion of virginity—the virginity complex itself—masquerading as a full character with psychological depth.

The text therefore constructs an interpretive framework that causally links Xiaolongnü's sexuality to her gender through a surplus of specificity, a surplus of objects, and narrative detail. She uses a silk belt rather than a sword because her martial power is feminine; she is feminine because she grew up around and was trained by feminine objects. This circular logic suggests that this 1959 story understands gender to be produced by sexuality rather than anatomy. Crucially, however, in the passage there is no mention of the biological strength of the woman character. Her martial arts is theorized as independent of her biology and of the physiological differences between men and women, and her gender is made intelligible in purely social terms, that is, as dependent on the social meanings and conventions already ascribed to the objects that are used to depit it. Cultural norms produce a stable relation between anatomy, desire, sensations, pleasures, and acts by instituting an evidentiary procedure between these elements, whereby one element is inter- preted as explanation or evidence for another. The fact that we see in this text a tautology where an inanimate object is understood to be gendered first, and the gender of a person is then under- stood to be derived from the gender of that inanimate object, is a historical accomplishment of a long cultural process of reifying gender, a process in which Jin Yong's novels participate.

The Incest Taboo

The Giant Eagle and Its Companion is often considered to be the most romantic of Jin Yong's novels.[16] Jin Yong, however, includes in the romance between Yang Guo and Xiaolongnü a highly contro- versial scene: Xiaolongnü, while blindfolded, is raped by a Taoist priest, and, thinking in her innocence it is Yang Guo (at the time still her student and a young boy) "playing a game with her" becomes sexually excited. Even after the event, Jin Yong does not allow Xiaolongnü to understand that the man who deflowered her was not Yang Guo, and this disjuncture between the reader's knowledge and the character's knowledge is precisely what makes the pornographic effect of the text a legitimate, culturally acceptable, construction. In fact, Xiaolongnü comprehends her sexual excitation with innocence, and this innocence allows her to "discover" her feelings for her student Yang Guo, and unbeknownst to her, break the taboo of cross- generational love. Before Xiaolongnü is raped, the love between her and her student is purely platonic, respectful, and in accordance with the Confucian martial arts ethics in which one ought to respect one's martial master as one would a biological parent. Since Xiaolongnü mistakes the rapist for the protagonist, she *legitimately* enjoys the intercourse and thanks to this misunderstanding also legitimately enjoys her love for a student, a love repressed by the cultural prohibition against "cross-generational" (defined by status, not age) desire between master and disciple. In return, the protagonist's love for his martial master, Xiaolongnü, is legitimated by the fact that he, after all, is not the one who raped his own teacher. On the contrary, he remains "quite a gentleman" throughout the years of their companionship and never feels, let alone expresses, any immoral desire for his teacher until Xiaolongnü confesses her love to him. The romance between master and disciple is thus enabled by a double-legitimating discourse: the man's abstinence from sex and the woman's ignorance about sexual matters. Their "incest" is exculpated by their "innocence," but their innocence is defined in asymmetrical terms.

Modern TV reproductions of the story invariably, and simply, excise the rape scene from the story, for the producers are either uncomfortable with the explicit sexual content or fail to see the point of a narrative digression from the proper development of a love story. However, Jin Yong's point has to be understood strictly in conjunction with another function he assigns the couple: that they are utterly disrespectful of social conventions—one out of pure innocence and improper socialization (obliviousness of "culture"), the other out of a boyish arrogance and a willful defiance of established authorities that is, when embodied by the male sex, considered to be attractive. It is therefore not a coincidence that Jin Yong also arranges the plot in such a way that the rape scene narratively resolves and absolves the prohibition of incest; once displaced, the horror of rape becomes obscured by the horror of incest and the remainder of the story deals only with the oppression Xiaolongnü and her student suffer in the face of more conservative characters appalled by their "beastly union"—the copulation between Master and Disciple.

But why does the novel have to represent the loss of Xiaolongnü's sexual innocence as her initiation into womanhood, and why does that event have to be emplotted as an "accident" rather than the culmination (and consummation) of romance? I have noted above the double-legitimating move this plot-arrangement allows in relation to the incest taboo. In the larger context of Jin Yong's narrative idiom, however, this incident must be reconstructed as a component of a sex/gender system against which Asia's aberration can be discursively produced. The fantasy of deflowering a virgin who is not only sexually inexperienced but also powerless contributes to the top's sense of being a top. The "homosexual" plot of Asia's story and the "heterosexual" plot of Xiaolongnü's story turn out to be different versions of the same fantasy—a culturally maintained and reproduced relation between power and manhood.

Deciphering the Secrets

The preservation of martial arts fiction (the reason these texts continue to be read) hinges crucially on its function as an antidote to a frustrated desire—a materially and historically produced lack. At the same time, this unacknowledged capacity of the narrative text for serving as wish-fulfillment also operates in concert with its openly acknowledged function as an object of pleasure, as popular literature. In this sense *Heavenly Sword, Dragon-slaying Saber* must be situated squarely within the vernacular tradition of popular fiction whose hallmark is the mechanism of suspense: the series of surprises and plot twists that engineer and propel its narrative movement. Cast in this light, this familiar narrative device of *transgendering*, already developed by Wang Dulu and further exploited by Jin Yong, acquires an additional symbolic value. In *transgendering*, the novel misleads its reader into believing that a particular character is supposed to be a man and later reveals that character, much to the reader's consternation and thrill, to be a woman. The pleasure this reading experience yields depends on a chasm between such surprises and a cultural expectation of the continuum between exterior attributes and a binaristic notion of sex that can be said to be either male or female, an expectation these "surprises" frustrate and exploit for the pleasurable effects they produce.

In *Heavenly Sword, Dragon-slaying Saber*, the tension between transgender and the rigidity of established cultural norms finds expression in several female martial artists who cross-dress to avoid male harassment while they "roam the world of martial arts," such as the character Zhaomin. These actors understand cross-dressing to be the prerogative of women who practice martial arts—a requirement of their vocation, as it were—but their crossing over also provides important (albeit unexpected) occasions for eroticization. Although Zhaomin pleads convenience as her excuse to wear men's clothes in public, her inconsequential decision has the additional, instrumental value of turning the (otherwise banal) love story between her and the male protagonist into the restoration of a female "top" to her proper place as a female bottom when a "true" man arrives on the erotic scene. The novel therefore has to represent the beginning of Zhaomin's feelings for the protagonist as coinciding with the termination of her preference for men's clothes. The issue of "transgender" in the case of Zhaomin and others also serves as the engine of narrative movement, for the transgendered or transgendering (in a permanent process) person in these stories, despite the nuances in their individual experiences, is inevitably returned to the same relation of sexuality. Because the restoration of her "true" *gender* is facilitated, in fact achieved, by the deferred use of her *sexuality*, the deferred establishment of her true gender is necessarily structured in accordance with the movement of the romance plot, which often involves the overcoming of external obstacles (usually a father, or a factional vendetta, or ethnic differences) between lovers.

The reader's expectation that the butch woman, even in the most masculine attire, will *eventually* succumb to a man, is obviously a culturally produced expectation of the novel's responsibility (and ability) to resolve any dissonance between gender and anatomy, but it is also an expectation and comprehension of the finitude of the novel as a material object—that is to say, the story has to end "somewhere." Because the denouement of the story is made emphatic by position, the sequentiality of its events usefully reflect the precedence of anatomy over gender, and the desire reflected in the woman's final, properly heterosexual union with the man appears to be "truer" than the pleasures she enjoys in cross-dressing prior to that moment, despite the length of the novel devoted to each style of embodiment. Hence, the drive to finish the story is animated in part by the desire to see the "woman" in question returning to a culturally legitimate mode of eroticization. We might conclude that the element of suspense that is most characteristic of this genre (together with detective fiction, and a number of other forms of "popular" literature) was historically developed in tandem with a culturally policed experience of gender and sexuality.

The implied reader is a constitutive component of a narrative, not exterior to it. The implied reader also names a culturally contingent structure of desires and expectations that a novel mobilizes. In *Heavenly Sword, Dragon-slaying Saber*, Jin Yong incorporates the reader's desire into the structure of the text through the deployment of four characters' appearances in the novel, the four Kings of the Dharma (*fa wang*) in the Manichaean Sect. After introducing the Eagle King of the White Eyebrow, the Vampire King of the Blue Wing, and the Lion King of the Golden Mane, all of whom readily joined the protagonist's cause, the whereabouts and true identity of the fourth King—the Dragon King of the Purple Gown—is withheld until the end of the novel, where she is revealed to be neither male nor Chinese, but a female Persian spy, in fact a former Holy Virgin sent on a mission by the Persian orthodoxy (Vol. III, 1161). The revelation of Dragon King's gender in *Heavenly Sword* is structurally parallel to the surprise that organizes the narrative of *Tianlong babu*, when Qiao Feng undresses the spy and realizes she is a woman, as well as the narrative in *State of Divinity*, where the reader discovers, along with the protagonist of the novel, the secret of Asia the Invincible's martial power—his self-castration. But just as the true surprise in *Heavenly Sword* is the Dragon King's connection to Islam and not her gender, the latter novel is less interested in dramatizing Asia's loss of penis as it is in emphasizing that he is now a *bottom*. The reader makes that crucial discovery through the perspective of the protagonist, Linghu, when he meets Asia's boyfriend for the first time.

> A man appeared from behind the screen. Linghu stole a glance at him, who seemed to be under thirty years old, wearing an elegant dark red fur coat that could barely hide his muscular body. His whole face was rugged with a bushy beard, which made him

extraordinarily manly and stately. Linghu wondered
in silence: "Ying Ying told me that Asia the Invincible
is extremely fond of this guy, and said that the two have
a dirty relationship that she doesn't care to comment
on. I then assumed that Asia is keeping a girlie boy
with a pretty face. Who would have thought that it's
such a manly guy? This is not at all what I expected.
Perhaps I got the wrong guy?" (1255)

Linghu then learns that Asia's lover, in addition to an impressive
amount of facial hair and a manly stature, also has a "husky voice"
(1256) and a "hard" attitude (*ying qi*, "fortitude," 1281), even though he
is utterly unskilled in martial arts. Linghu's plan is to use Asia's lover to
lead him and the royalists into Asia's secret hiding place, which again
turns out to be a surprise.

The minute they entered the house they detected
a thick, flowery fragrance. In the main hall there
hung a painting depicting three beautiful women
and each chair was padded with an embroidered
cushion. Linghu then thought, "He took us to a
woman's boudoir. Why is Asia living here? Oh, I see,
this must be the bedroom of his favorite concubine.
He's indulging himself in the tenderness of a certain
woman and that's why he became uninterested in
politics and left all things to that guy. (1273)

Linghu's surprise is that Asia is not keeping a catamite, an
effeminate boy-toy, but rather himself "playing the submissive role of
a wife" (1274). In the process Linghu discovers Asia to be a bottom,
not by sleeping with Asia (as he does in Tsui Hark's film version of
the story), but dialectically by meeting his lover who turns out to be
a top. The refreshing quality of the "turn" is quite similar to drag or
camp in general in the sense that, insofar as the performance of the
fictional text and the performance of the living person both subvert
the dominant paradigm and remain tethered to the paradigm, they

crucially derive their liberating and pleasurable effects from the paradoxical distance from and dependency on the form of power they displace. In this scene, what is introduced is the coexistence and incompatibility of two incommensurable perspectives, Linghu's and Asia's. Both characters implicitly emphasize the radical dependency of one's sense of one's own gender on the presence of an Other whose "gender" is relational to the subject, infinitely displaced, and only capable of emerging on the horizon of cognizance when it figures as an object of desire. The very readability of the text in turn is predicated on the assumed coherence of gender and the stigmatization of being "topped." Asia's bottomhood therefore reinstates a cultural interpretive framework according to which sexual roles appear to derive from positions of power.

According to the novel, the aspiring martial artist must castrate himself as a prerequisite for learning the secret Sunflowers martial arts because the one who learns this forbidden dark art will be immediately consumed and driven to dementia by an uncontrollable rise in libido. In the story, however, Asia does not become desexualized; rather, he becomes oversexualized and ultimately ruined by his affection for his male lover, whose life he saved by sacrificing his own. The question the novel never asks is, of course, what would happen if a woman were to attempt the martial arts of the *Sunflowers* scripture? That this question is not even posed is not so much evidence of Jin Yong's bad logic but rather the attachment of his logic to a fixed notion of "gender," with the result that, in the idiom of martial arts fiction, women are by definition excluded from consideration by things that appear to be gender-neutral, and that the possibilities of development are themselves gendered. Jin Yong retains a hopelessly stubborn and naturalistic conception of gender that requires his female characters to learn martial arts from a text called "The Sutra of Nine Forms of Feminine Energy" (*Jiu yin zhenjing*) since, as Jin Yong's novels explain again and again, women's bodies produce only female energy or *yin qi*, which makes it impossible for them to learn masculine martial arts moves and stances. But insofar as these martial arts manuals merely stand for prescriptions on how to develop individually (within fictional terms) or nationally (allegorically), and while these prescriptions presuppose and reproduce gendered categories (prescriptions for men versus prescriptions for women) in a manner that makes the text vulnerable to criticisms of misogyny, it is important to interrogate the more complex process in the story and in the culture of the story's production whereby an individual is compelled to have a sexed position in language. The analysis of the ways a person is compelled to have a socially legible gender in order to "be" is fundamentally different from the analysis of masculine dominance. The injunction of achieving a socially recognized gender is compelled by the motive of survival and interpersonal dependency, while the effects of masculine and heteronormative hegemonies appear to be powerful and inescapable only on the assumption that the process of achieving a gender is complete and invariant. The social actors in these martial arts novels realize that one cannot survive by oneself, and the necessity of entering a set of social relations—a linguistic community that has a structure and a set of rules made without their participation or endorsement—is represented in hyperbolic terms as the "ethics" of martial arts.

The World

Xiaolongnü in *The Giant Eagle and Its Companion* prefigures the character Dragon King that appears in *Heavenly Sword, Dragon-slaying Saber*. In the latter novel, which begins with a poem praising Xiaolongnü's chastity, whiteness, and hermitage, Xiaolongnü is represented as an immaculate existence untainted by worldliness.

The world that Jin Yong's characters live in is free of real commodities and the need to labor to sustain one's livelihood but the erasure of these worldly matters from view serves—much like the "closet" in Sedgwick's analysis of gender—as a performative silence. This performative silence, or erasure, produces a certain truth by *not* verbalizing its negating forces; it functions as a truth-*effect* that counts as truth by being constantly and successfully reiterated. While a novel such as Jin Yong's *Heavenly Sword, Dragon-*

slaying Saber seeks to police its terms of representation and its themes within these limits, it cannot help but betray its anchorage in the concrete system of domination that at once makes "citizenship" the very engine of narrative and precludes the possibility of its representation.

Jin Yong's martial arts novels construct a warped space in which characters travel at science-fictional speed. The apparently "historical" cities in the stories were selected rather arbitrarily. For example, between the various editions published between 1972 and 2003, Jin Yong changed the locations of important events in *The Eagle Shooting* novel from one city to another city miles apart, without feeling the need to alter the nature or sequence of events. Against the backdrop of the 1962 refugee crisis, during which Jin Yong defended the Hong Kong government's decision to close its borders to refugees from mainland China, the apparent ease and mobility with which characters move in and out of "the Middle Kingdom" in the fourteenth century acquires a symbolic significance that exceeds the parameters of the stories' manifest content. While many factors of social life and political power treated in Jin Yong's political writings—the Cultural Revolution, citizenship, territory, political cadre, the state—are conspicuously absent in his fictional stories, these concerns press upon the novel contextually, enjoin a response in fictional terms, and form the novel's latent thoughts and interests. At the same time, it is important to explain Jin Yong's conscious refusal to engage contemporary realities despite its vested interest in late nineteenth-century and early twentieth-century anti-imperialist struggles, as more than merely the honoring of a convention that "Old School" martial arts fiction writers established and solidified. With respect to the 1962 refugee crisis, it becomes clear that only with the modern rise of the system of states—namely the division of political authority into mutually exclusive jurisdictional domains— did it become ideologically fulfilling or therapeutic to fictionally represent a lost wholeness marked by a magical porosity between Persia, the Middle Kingdom, and other quasi-states. To many of Jin Yong's readers in Hong Kong, the severance of the port city from mainland China was sometimes a historical trauma and sometimes quite a blessing. In the case of Asian political formations, what is perceived as the recent "colonial desire for the sovereign" might in fact be the result of a cultural amnesia.[17] In these incommensurable discourses, however, some object is posited as an "originary" human condition of wholeness, a state of affairs where the constraints anchoring subjects in particular locales appeared to be technological and economic but not political. The imagination of a political space extending from "the Middle Kingdom" to "Persia" acquired a wish-fulfilling function only on the condition that such an originary wholeness can be thought and represented in language.

The "femininity" of all these "women" (Xiaolongnü, Dragon King, Asia the Invincible, or Ah Zhu, the spy in *Tianlong babu*) is imagined on the basis of, and receives much of its definition from, these women's shared distance from the worldliness of the world (the tomb, "Persia," the boudoir). But what is this world? The novel imagines an exit from that world and returns the reader to a world and a space of inequalities when its terms betray their entanglement in the structure of political domination. To the residents in the British colony, there was nothing subtle about the fact that Hong Kong citizens needed a visa to visit the United Kingdom. The inescapabilities and particularities of places were brought into relief when the most basic right according to liberal ideology—the right to live—was not even guaranteed by the very system that organized birth-accidents into nations and positions of power. While clearly no one has ever lived or lives in a tomb, in an imaginary Persia, or in a boudoir without outside human contact, these stories from Hong Kong record a poignant condition of modern life, designated by the dual symbolism of gender and Islam, that gestures toward a world much larger than the geopolitical confines of Hong Kong itself.

NOTES

1. Cover of Louis Cha, *The Book and the Sword*, translated by Graham Earnshaw.

2. Hong Qingtian, "Jin Yong zuopin yu zhonggang shehui," 191.

3. Fredric Jameson, *The Ideologies of Theory: Essays 1971–1986*, vol. 2, 188.

4. See Yiching Wu, *The Other Cultural Revolution: Politics and Practice of Class in the Chinese Cultural Revolution, 1966–1969*; and Alessandro Russo, "The Probable Defeat: Preliminary Notes on the Chinese Cultural Revolution."

5. The novel is more commonly referred to by its literal translation as *Smiling, Proudly Wanderer* in English.

6. Stephen Chan Ching-kiu is attentive to the ambiguous nature of the film and reads it as a "figure of hope and despair" produced in response to crisis of the 1997 Hong Kong handover. "Figures of Hope and the Filmic Imaginary of Jianghu in Contemporary Hong Kong Cinema," 486–514. Stephen Ching-kiu Chan, "Figures of Hope and the Filmic Imaginary of Jianghu in Contemporary Hong Kong Cinema."

7. The time frame of *State of Divinity* is unspecified; Jin Yong states that it is intentionally left ambiguous because the novel is allegorical in nature. In *Swordsman II*, the story is set during the reign of the Wanli Emperor in the late Ming dynasty.

8. Lin Fushi, for example, defends this position in "Healers in the World of Martial Arts," *Proceedings of the International Conference on Jin Yong's Novels*, 104.

9. Samuel Lieu, "Fact or Fiction: Ming-chiao (Manichaeism) in Jin Yong's I-t'ien t'u-lung chi," *Proceedings of the International Conference on Jin Yong's Novels*, 62–63. See also Lin Wushu, "Jin Yong's Manichaeism vs. Historical Reality," *Historical Monthly*, 1996(3): 66–67. Samuel Lieu's detailed study on the subject traces both the actual history of the diffusion of Manichaeism into China as well as the discrepancies between the historical sources and Jin Yong's novels.

10. Samuel Lieu, "Fact or Fiction," 60–62.

11. Jin Yong discusses the role the Manichees played in the founding of the Ming dynasty toward the end of the novel. See *The Heavenly Sword and the Dragon-slaying Saber*, Vol. IV, 1629.

12. On Jin Yong and his collaborators' choice of the newspaper's name, see Sun Yixue, *Jin Yong zhuan*, 115.

13. Chou, Wah-shan, *Tongzhi Lun* (Theory of the Chinese queer), 289–302.

14. Tabloids and paparazzi have a particularly strong presence in the culture industry of Hong Kong, and actors and actresses are seen as performing both the fictional characters and their star personae on the screen.

15. Her name is literally "little dragon woman"; Jin Yong changed her name to Dalongnü, "big dragon woman," in the millennium edition.

16. For a representative statement, see Chen Mo, *Qing ai Jin Yong* (Love in Jin Yong), 273–276. Chen identifies the representation of martial moves in this novel as a function of its romantic plot, the "true story" Jin Yong wishes to tell.

17. Lydia Liu suggests in her work on the history of international law that the very concept of sovereignty was developed in a complex process that historically has always involved non-Western states and peoples and their agency. The existing network of interstate relations in the East that the European powers came upon during colonial expansion was incorporated into rather than obliterated by the law of nations. Asian maritime custom, for example, was invoked as a legal precedent in the Dutch-Portuguese dispute over the East Indies. The popular view that Asian countries were denied legal status and only later admitted into the family of sovereign nations turns out to be itself an (ahistorical) imagination of nineteenth-century positivist jurists who were unaware of this fact. See Liu, *The Clash of Empires*.

Chapter 5

A TALE OF TWO CHINAS

Gu Long and Anomalous Colonies

"If mainland Chinese military forces ever land on Taiwan, the Taiwanese will fight them to the last American."

—American joke

Today, two nations in the world, the People's Republic of China (PRC) and the Republic of China on Taiwan (ROC), both refer to themselves as China. The creation of two Chinas was a consequence of Taiwan's historical role as America's island fortress for the crusade against Communism in the Pacific. However, since Taiwan's "democratization"—its first multifactional presidential election in 2000—ethnic identity has replaced anti-Communism as the dominant political issue in Taiwan.[1] Currently, the Taiwanese polity is divided into two color-coded camps: the Pan-Green Coalition led by the Democratic Progressive Party (DPP) and devoted to the promotion of Taiwan's *de jure* independence, and the "One China" Pan-Blue Coalition centered on the nationalist Kuomintang Party (KMT) platform of unitary Chinese national identity and close economic cooperation with the People's Republic of China. The Green Camp made the creation of a distinctive Taiwanese identity and "de-Sinicization" (*qu Zhongguo hua*) major campaign issues, emphasizing the KMT's long record of oppression and martial law, its massacre of Taiwanese protestors in the 228 Incident, and its regime of White Terror that imprisoned and executed 45,000–90,000 intellectuals in the 1950s. At the same time, support for the Blue Camp reflects the realities of the growing geopolitical importance of the PRC and cross-strait economic linkages. Since its electoral victory in 2000, the DPP's dire record of corruption scandals, including those that led to the conviction and imprisonment of former President Chen Shui-bian, has somewhat reoriented Taiwan's political culture in Blue Camp's favor.

While democratization is typically celebrated as an achievement, the competition between the Blue and Green Camps has radically impoverished the meaning of *politics* in Taiwan, preventing other issues from entering public debate and having an impact on the electability of candidates. Same-sex marriage, environmentalism, labor unionism, reproductive freedom, and health care are obscured by the project of Taiwanese independence in this political climate. Partisan passions for or against Taiwan's quest for statehood decide in advance what constitutes a political dialogue. In this context, Taiwan's tradition of stateless martial arts novels acquires a newfound significance. In this chapter, I seek to recast Gu Long, Taiwan's most celebrated martial arts novelist, as a creator of stateless subjects instead of the indigenous national genius of Taiwan. Gu Long's works represent the possibility of forming political solidarity *without* a national community. In Gu Long, a human life is sustained, symbolically and materially, by a field of discursive practices, social norms, and cultural ideals independent of that person's knowledge. The recognition of this field necessarily implicates a person in a web of responsibilities. While these responsibilities might constrain one's life and actions, they also open up a different order of political action, critical inquiry, and social solidarity. I argue that these lessons of Gu Long's fiction have been obscured by common interpretations of him as an *ethnic* writer. My reading of Gu Long's thematic and stylistic features seeks to reveal a different imagination of China(s) that can help us, I hope, reclaim the political status of *wuxia*.

Gu Long and Taiwan

Together with Hong Kong's Jin Yong and Liang Yusheng, Gu Long is commonly recognized as one of the three greatest postwar martial arts novelists. From 1960 to 1985, Gu Long's productivity, talent, and influence were unrivaled in the martial arts literary market in Taiwan—a country that, during his lifetime, was more commonly referred to by its official name, the Republic of China. Partially as a result of the movement to create a distinctive Taiwanese identity, Gu Long's writings are now being politicized and reinterpreted as the product of an ethnic writer who can contend with Hong Kong's and China's literary celebrities. After Gu Long's untimely death in 1985, the only luminary to emerge was the controversial Wen Rui-an (b. 1954), who is noted for his experimentations with hybrid narrative forms rather than his attempts to preserve the idiom of *wuxia*. The genre is therefore essentially a historical artifact, and Gu Long remains the last major Taiwan-based martial arts novelist in literary history.

The figuration of Gu Long as a minority author from Taiwan issues from a multilayered historical amnesia. It denies, first of all, Gu Long's birth and education in Hong Kong. Indeed, important cultural continuities underlie Gu Long's writings and earlier Republican martial arts novels.[2] Furthermore, this figuration contradicts the historical lessons of Gu Long's fiction, which provide an alternative conception of cultural affinity we can retool to unlearn the political map we have inherited from the Cold War's division of East Asia into mutually hostile and temporally desynchronized camps—the two Chinas.

The theme of orphanhood figures centrally in Gu Long's fiction. The protagonist of *The Eleventh Son* (1973), Xiao Shiyi Lang, is the only surviving member after various tragedies claimed the lives of all ten of his elder siblings. But Gu Long's interest in the trope is not limited to his best-known works, one of his earliest novels was originally entitled *Tale of the Orphans* (*Guxing zhuan*, 1960) before the 1974 reprint changed it to *The Storm-seeker* (*Fengyun nan'er*). *Legendary Siblings* (1966) deals with twin brothers, orphaned at birth, who grow up under different masters who instruct them to kill each other when they come of age. These fictions invite allegorical interpretations, where the "legendary siblings" may very well stand for the two brothers at war, the ROC and the PRC. However, such allegorical readings must be qualified by a closer examination of the historical context in which these fables of kinship are fabricated, and the transnational (as opposed to domestic) political culture to which these novels may be responding. Reducing Gu Long's works to state-based political allegories often plays into efforts to determine the author's nationality—whether his fiction is expressive of Chineseness or Taiwaneseness—and misses the point of his works altogether. A critical reading of Gu Long as a stateless author might help us deconstruct the political allegories, foundational fictions, and fantasized boundaries that circumscribe our lives and limit our imagination to existing juridical states. More significant, such a reading practice might recover Gu Long's contributions to theories of power in postcolonial societies so that we may resituate his place in the canon of modern Chinese-language literature, not as the genius of Taiwan, but as a theorist of universal human affinity. Kinship, in Gu Long's martial arts novels is conceived in nonbiological terms, as historically formed and formative. Questions of biological origins, cultural continuity, and ethnic purity are suspended in favor of the question of the self's historical—as opposed to filial— relation to the world.

Gu Long in the Sinophone Pacific

Comprehended as a phenomenon instead of a person, Gu Long is properly pan-Asian rather than Chinese or Taiwanese. Even if we limit our analysis to biographical facts, Gu Long is a transnational and not a Taiwanese author. Né Xiong Yaohua, Gu Long was actually born and raised in Hong Kong, only immigrating to Taiwan with his family at the age of thirteen. His father, Xiong Pengsheng, was an obscure martial arts novelist. Both Gu Long's birth year and the exact number of his works have been subjects of scholarly controversy. While some sources claim that he was born as early as 1936, and most scholars accept 1937 or 1938, more recent scholarship establishes 1941 as a more reliable year based on the records of Zhenshanmei Publishing House (the official copyright holder of his works) and on inductions from reconstructed fragments of his autobiographical writings.[3] We do not know the exact number of works Gu Long has penned, either. Various biographies of Gu Long and general histories of martial arts literature published in Taiwan, mainland China, and Hong Kong attribute anywhere from sixty-eight to seventy-eight works to his name.[4] The undecidability of his birth year and the subsequent speculations have only added to his mystique and fame.

Gu Long's birth and education in Hong Kong have not troubled critics who seek to secure a proper place for him in the pantheon of Taiwan martial arts literature, just as Jin Yong's birth and education in mainland China have not prevented critics from declaring that his novels express the psychic pain of colonial Hong Kong. Unlike Jin Yong, whose identification with and cultural ties to classical China are unambiguous, Gu Long evinces and embodies, in his work and in his life, a transnational subjectivity that is more properly termed Sinophone than Taiwanese. Jin Yong studied international relations in China in his youth and after retiring chose to pursue a doctoral degree in Chinese history at St. John's College in Cambridge. Gu Long's undergraduate major was English literature, and his sources of influence were characteristically eclectic. His novels draw on Japanese detective fiction, American popular culture, and various non–martial arts literary trends in Chinese. In *Duoqing jianke wuqing jian* (*The Heartless Sword of a Sentimental Swordsman*, 1968–1969), for example, he combines motifs from Wang Dulu's *Crane-Iron Pentalogy* with those from Jack London's *The Call of the Wild*. In an even wilder transcultural allusion, Louisa May Alcott's *Little Women* make appearances in his *Huanle yingxiong* (*Joyous Heroes*, 1971–1972). His *Liuxing, hudie, jian* (*Falling Star, Butterfly, Sword*, 1971), while still a recognizably *wuxia* novel, is punctuated by the language of the *Godfather* film series. The result is an unexpected, idiosyncratic, and delightful vocabulary of new martial arts fiction that is characteristically his own.

Currently available Chinese-language scholarship on martial arts literature tends to focus on the theme of history as the main distinction between Gu Long and Jin Yong. It is well known that Jin Yong's martial arts novels are also historical fiction. With the exceptions of *The State of Divinity* and *Ode to Gallantry*, whose time frames are ambiguous (but most likely the Ming dynasty), Jin Yong's novels are consistently set in specific imperial reigns and tied to well-known historical events.[5] Real historical figures, including Chinese emperors and court officials, serve as martial arts characters in Jin Yong's fiction. By contrast, Gu Long's works are patently unconcerned with Chinese history.[6] In addition, the idea of martial schools or clans, a staple of the genre since Huanzhu Louzhu, is conspicuously absent in Gu Long's works. Although certain characters in his novels are said to be members of the standard schools such as Emei, Wudang, and Shaolin, for the most part Gu Long's characters are unbound outlaws, or members of small independent groups (such as the "Twelve Zodiacs" in *Legendary Siblings*). His characters employ individual martial techniques instead of those derived from "Wudang" or "Shaolin."[7] If factional feuds between the schools constitute the major theme in Pingjiang Buxiaosheng's works, by the time of Gu Long, generational conflicts and large-scale battles are replaced by individually defined skirmishes. The emphasis on individually created styles of martial arts further detaches Gu Long from the notion of collective history Jin Yong's works represent.

Gu Long's protagonists are invariably freestanding heroes unconnected to any sects or schools. Indeed, his most famous protagonists, Chu Liuxiang, Lu Xiaofeng, Xiao Shiyi Lang, and Fish, are free-spirited bandits, thieves, and tricksters who are also social outcasts. Traditional martial arts novels, whether written by Gu Long's predecessors in the Republican period or by his contemporaries, such as Jin Yong, typically focus on the development of a glorified hero and fall into the genres of *Bildungsroman* or quest narratives.[8] By contrast, Gu Long's novels are marked by a conspicuous absence of the familiar tropes of martial and psychological maturation such as training, treasure hunting, Secret Scripture, tournaments, and bonds between master and disciple. Instead, his characters arrive in the novel as already developed martial masters, without a discernible or relevant past. No account of the origins of their martial power is given, nor is the story structured around the quest for a legendary weapon or Secret Scripture. In light of the well-established generic conventions of the martial arts novel, Gu Long's deviation from these norms and formal experimentation constitutes a performative statement about the relation between his works and the Chinese masters from whom he has inherited his vocabulary. In *Legendary Siblings*, the protagonist Fish stumbles into a forlorn cave and finds a Secret Scripture, an event we have seen repeated in many of Jin Yong's novels (Zhang Wuji, Yang Guo, and Linghu Chong). After reading the martial arts manual, however, Gu Long's protagonist casually tosses it into a river, as if mocking the tradition itself. The techniques he learns from the Scripture also prove to be entirely inconsequential in terms of the novel's plot development. Whereas the knowledge acquired from Secret Scriptures always play a decisive role in Jin Yong's novels, in *Legendary Siblings*, Fish consistently relies on his wits rather than his martial skills to defeat his enemies. The tradition of Secret Scriptures is both consciously represented and trivialized by Gu Long.

These characteristics seem to suggest that Gu Long's style is a conscious rebellion against the tradition established by pre-1949 authors on the mainland in the service of a new form of martial arts fiction that is entirely Taiwan's own. To a certain extent, this current scholarly attempt to redefine Gu Long's status in literary history and "demystify" Jin Yong against Sinocentrism, Hong Kong–centrism, and the "minoritization of Taiwan" (to use Shih Shu-mei's phrase) is not entirely unjustified. Historically, though, Gu Long's reputation and influence as a martial arts novelist predated those of Jin Yong, and Gu Long's works cannot be seen as a conscious refusal of Jin Yong's China-centered historical martial arts novels. Only after Gu Long's death did his fame begin to be eclipsed by Jin Yong. Subsequently, martial arts literature was conflated with Hong Kong, which was in turn conflated with the singular achievements of Jin Yong. Taiwan's contributions to the development of the genre were largely unaccounted for. An outstanding example of Taiwan's unique martial arts culture is the phenomenon of *budaixi*, a local form of "puppet opera" that combines "martial arts" and period drama typically performed in the Taiwanese (Minnan) dialect instead of Mandarin. Some critics call *budaixi* "digital knight-errant puppet" shows.[9] In 1965, *budaixi* was transformed into a television show that combines *wuxia* themes and characters with the traditional aesthetic of puppet opera by a family of talented producers, script-writers, and voice actors. In 1985, the Huang family created the enormously successful *Pili* TV series, which further popularized the genre in the Taiwanese dialect.

As a corrective to the perception that Hong Kong has monop-olized the production of martial arts fiction, numerous cultural projects have been developed to revive, promote, and domesticate the martial arts literary tradition in Taiwan. Foundations, news-papers, and cultural bureaucracies regularly offer literary prizes and contests for *wuxia xiaoshuo* to encourage young writers to pursue this narrative form. In 1995, under the auspices of the Ministry of Education, Lin Baochun founded the Center for the Study of Martial Arts Fiction at Tamkang University, Gu Long's alma mater.[10] The Center is devoted to the research on martial arts novelists in Taiwan, with the explicit mission of canonizing Gu Long. Following the model of previous international conferences on Jin Yong held in the United States, China, and Taiwan, Lin's center has organized similar events on Gu Long; in 2006, conference proceedings produced a major book on Gu Long, *Aoshi guicai—Gu Long* (*The Prodigy of Martial Arts Literature—Gu Long*).

The most influential landmark study of Taiwan's martial arts literature, however, was the 2005 *Taiwan wuxia xiaoshuo fazhan shi* (*The Development of Martial Arts Literature in Taiwan*), coauthored by Lin Baochun and Ye Hongsheng. This book is the culmination of a decade of research undertaken by the two scholars and Lin's graduate students at the Center for the Study of Martial Arts Fiction. It converts a colossal archive of reconstructed newspaper microfilms and rare copies of out-of-print books into five hundred pages of narrative history, complete with tables, figures, graphs, images, and appendices. The book's primary argument refutes the myth that Gu Long's work is derivative of Jin Yong, offering instead a revisionist history that casts Gu Long's oeuvre as the product of a vibrant dialogue with other important but forgotten martial arts novelists in Taiwan such as Sima Ling (Wu Siming, 1933–1989), Wolongsheng (Niu Heting, 1930–1997), and Zhuge Qingyun (Zhang Jianxin, 1929–1996).

Lin and Ye divide the development of martial arts fiction in Taiwan into four distinct eras, separated by watershed events that are unique to Taiwan's local culture: the embryonic stage (1951–1960), the golden age (1961–1970), the autumn (1971–1980), and the eventual decline (1981–2000). The year 1951 saw the publication of the first martial arts story in Taiwan: Lang Honghuan's (b. 1897) *Guse aixian* (*Sorrows of an ancient zither*). It was also the year when the KMT government instituted its notorious censorship system under martial law (*Jieyan shiqi chubanwu guanzhi banfa*), which by 1959 had led authorities to ban the majority of martial arts novels. The 1960s then marked the beginning of Taiwan's "economic miracle" and an efflorescence of literary production. Lin and Ye estimate that during this second stage of martial arts fiction's development in Taiwan, there were over three hundred different authors writing *wuxia* stories and ten publishing houses dedicated to the genre. By the end of the 1960s, however, martial arts fiction met new challenges and went into a period of steady decline.

Lin and Ye attribute the changing fortunes of martial arts fiction to several factors, the most important being the advent of martial arts film and TV programs in the early 1970s. Instantly accessible and easily more exciting than the written originals, visual renditions of martial arts adventures took over the mass market after the first martial arts TV drama series was aired in 1971 in Taiwan. Within three years, the three television networks (the only three in Taiwan at the time) tried to meet the demand of an insatiable audience by creating thirty different martial arts TV series. Martial arts television was certainly riding on the success of martial arts movies, which had already begun to flourish in the 1960s through the works of legendary directors King Hu (Hu Jinquan, 1932–1997) and Chang Cheh (Zhang Yiyang, 1923–2002). Many of the movies were adaptations of Old School martial arts stories, but all the major works of Wolongsheng, Gu Long, Sima Ling, and Zhuge Qingyun have graced the silver screen. The explosive success of Bruce Lee's *Fist of Fury* in 1972 brought about a sea change in martial arts cinema, turning it further toward action-based "kung fu" and away from the narrative traditions of *wuxia* and *shenguai*. Interestingly, however, the power vacuum created by the quantitative decline of martial arts fiction helped solidify Gu Long's reputation as the master stylist of martial arts fiction. The immense popularity of film turned out to be a blessing for his career. The director Chor Yuen (Zhang Baojian) alone made fifteen movies based on his novels.

Ye Hongsheng is a seasoned critic of martial arts novels who has written many commentaries on the genre since the 1970s. He is also the editor of the authoritative, annotated Lianjing series of martial arts novels.[11] Lin Baochun is the founder of the Center for the Study of Martial Arts Fiction. Lin has organized a number of national and international conferences on Gu Long, based on the model of similar academic events in Colorado, Taipei, and Beijing that have greatly facilitated the fin-de-siècle canonization of Jin Yong.[12] In his own *Deconstructing Jin Yong* (*Jiegou Jin Yong*, 2000), Lin endeavors to show that Gu Long's literary reputation, which has in fact preceded that of Jin Yong, has been unjustly eclipsed by the rise of the latter to stardom and Gu Long's own untimely death. As Lin shows, Jin Yong's status as the godfather of martial arts fiction was retroactively constructed by Jin Yong criticism in the 1980s, before which Gu Long was considered to be the true heir of the martial arts tradition from the Republican Old School. According to Lin, the invention of the inventor, the myth that Jin Yong somehow "created" martial arts fiction out of thin air, was itself the result of a convergence of business and political interests that could be explained only with attention to cross-strait politics.

In film history, Gu Long's significance by far exceeds Jin Yong's. Gu Long was a prolific novelist, but his career first took off when he started working as a producer and script-writer in Hong Kong. According to the official records of Taiwan's broadcasting bureau, during the brief years between 1976 and 1982 alone, Gu Long directed twenty-five movies himself, and over sixty additional movie adaptations of his novels were produced by other directors.[13] Many major stars in Hong Kong and Taiwan, such as Ti Lung (Di Long) and Adam Cheng (Zheng Shaoqiu), rose to stardom by playing martial arts characters in film adaptations of Gu Long's works, and in the 1960s all the Shaw Brothers movies were based on his work, mostly starring Chu Yuan. Gu Long's longstanding partnership with Chu Yuan is well known. The cultural critic Qin Tiannan once described Gu Long and Chu Yuan as two "spiritual twins," the real-life legendary siblings.[14] During his life, Gu Long also participated in the production and screen adaptations of many of his own martial arts novels in Hong Kong and Taiwan. Famous film adaptations of Gu Long's works include *Killer Clans* (1976), *The Magic Blade* (1976), *Death Duel* (1977), *The Sentimental Swordsman* (1977), *Legend of the Bat* (1978), *The Proud Twins* (1979), and *Bloody Parrot* (1981).

Today, endless adaptations and remakes testify to the continuous popularity of Gu Long's works. As an example of his enduring appeal, Gu Long's first novel, *The Spirit of the Sword* (1964), was produced as a TV series starring Leslie Cheung in 1979; nearly three decades later, in 2007, another Taiwan production of *The Spirit of the Sword* appeared, featuring Nicholas Tse. Across these many adaptations of Gu Long's works, the figure of Chu Liuxiang, who recurs in a dozen Gu Long novels, has been an important and iconic character. In 1980 alone, five movie companies in Taiwan made six different Chu Liuxiang films. This was only three years after the release of the very first Chu Liuxiang film, *Chu Liu Xiang* (*Clans of Intrigue*), produced by the Shaw Brothers in Hong Kong in 1977, and one year after the first Chu Liuxiang television series, *Chor Lau Heung* (*Chu Liuxiang*), originally created by Hong Kong's TVB in 1979. This 65-episode *wuxia* drama *Chor Lau Heung* (*Chu Liu Xiang*) began airing in Taiwan in 1982 and forever changed television history. To date, this series remains a legendary phenomenon, holding many unmatched records. The first two episodes of *Chor Lau Heung* aired in Cantonese and immediately attracted national attention. China Television Company (CTV, one of the only three television networks in Taiwan at the time) purchased the series and redubbed it in Mandarin. The series achieved 70 percent television viewership (TVR) in 1982. Taiwan newspapers reported that the "taxi-drivers stopped working, and night markets closed down businesses" during the times *Chu Liu Xiang* aired because the streets were simply empty. The enormous influence of this TV series forced the Taiwan government to change its broadcasting regulation laws and reclassify Hong Kong–produced TV series as "foreign programs" in order to limit the number of episodes and hours (up to two hours of airtime per week) they could be broadcast.

The argument that Gu Long's fiction represents a native Taiwanese writer's heroic efforts to resist Chinese assimilation logically rests on the assumption that there must be an empirically observable and nationally homogeneous set of values, beliefs, and practices that defines Taiwan's culture. The most simplistic formulation of this difference issues from the Taiwanese and Chinese governments themselves. Despite their apparent simplicity, these generalizations are deeply entrenched across various registers of discourses, and thus prove difficult to challenge. Observers often view China as the sole proprietor of authentic Chinese culture, whose revolutionary outlook and traumatic emergence in the twentieth century has produced serious, politically oriented literature devoted to the collective reflections on the fate, future, and sufferings of the nation. By contrast, Taiwan is viewed as a capitalist society and usually celebrated either as a success story of East Asian democratization, or condemned as a Westernized, consumer-oriented bourgeois society, corrupted by American influences and a sensationalist media, and dominated by materialism and an ethos of individualistic profit pursuit.

Such characterizations necessarily invoke the language of temporal markers (pre- and post- this or that mode of production) in the discursive production of the differences between China and Taiwan, and this reliance on morally differentiated temporalities within the same region institutes a political teleology that produces the impression of a "time lag" between actually contemporaneous cultures. As Johannes Fabian argues, the "allochronism of racial time" constitutes an imperialist tactic through "the denial of coevalness" that explains the economic inequality *between* nation-states as the presence or absence of modernity *within* each nation-state.[15]

Viewed from a standpoint that sees Taiwan as an economically more advanced but morally corrupt nation compared to China, Gu Long's writings embody precisely all the characteristics associated with decadent, bourgeois postmodern culture: sexual and chemical escapism, instant gratification, and an underlying sense of malaise. Chen Kangfen, for example, attributes the development of Gu Long's entire corpus to the rise of consumerism and postindustrial mode of production in Taiwan.

> Because Gu Long lacked Jin Yong's traditional intellectual background, and Gu Long was limited by the circumstances of contemporary society, he sought innovation for the sake of innovation. What was exemplified by his fiction was a "worldview" of contemporary Taiwan, which was radically different from Jin Yong's "culturalist view." Jin Yong's works reflected the life philosophy of classical China, while Gu Long explored the problems of human nature and human desire in contemporary Taiwan. Unlike Jin Yong, who relied on the intellectuals' projection of a shared identity with a mythical, traditional China, Gu Long mainly appealed to what was familiar to the masses in urban parts of Taiwan.[16]

Elsewhere Chen Kangfen characterizes Gu Long as the product of "a conspiracy between industrialized society and mass culture"; she explains his popularity as the result of his ability to fulfill a "spiritual gap" (*xinling yu duanlie*) and "identity crisis" (*ziwo zhuixun de kunjing*) created by Taiwan's rapid transformation from an agricultural economy to an urban, industrial economy in the 1970s.[17]

As I have been arguing, the actual reason critics have paid more attention to these themes in Gu Long has more to do with cross-strait politics than Gu Long's aesthetics or personal agenda. Analyses of Taiwan literature today are dominated by the statist politics of the unification versus independence debate. Consequently, the scholarship on Gu Long has focused on his distinctions from Jin Yong, who in many ways remains a self-consciously "Chinese" writer. The stylistic differences between these two authors are well known. Jin Yong's works are all historical novels that are keyed to specific dynasties in imperial China. Gu Long's fictions are characteristically unconcerned with (Chinese) history and devoid of distinct time frames. Jin Yong's novels thematize grand scale, epic-like struggles between Han Chinese and other races that have historically invaded and occupied China, such as Manchus and Mongols, as well as tensions between Han Chinese and the minorities in China who have been marginalized or oppressed by Sinocentric hegemony, such as Tibetans, Miao, Khitan, and Uyghurs. Not only are race and ethnicity absent from Gu Long's thematic arsenal, his works reject the tradition of *menpai*, martial schools or martial clans, that has been a staple of this genre since the Republican period. Instead, Gu Long's characters are individuals. Gu Long himself suffered from alcoholism, grew up with a traumatic childhood with divorced parents, and had a series of failed relationships with women he neglected and abandoned. All of these factors contributed to the impression that Gu Long's works represent the stereotypes about Taiwan: a libidinal, hedonistic, Westernized and individualistic bourgeois culture in contrast to the somber political realism in Jin Yong.

In an illuminating article, the prominent Taiwan novelist, cultural critic, editor, and historian Yang Zhao characterizes Gu Long's project as the destruction and reconstruction of a "genealogy."[18] For Yang, "genealogy" is both a theme that Gu Long consistently represents in his fiction, and a relation to a prior body of Chinese literature that Gu Long destroys and reconstructs through his writing. Yang identifies Pingjiang Buxiaosheng as the "father" of martial arts fiction and Gu Long as his "heir." However, Gu Long consciously deconstructs this "intertextuality" with the Chinese canon by fundamentally changing the ways in which his characters relate to and associate with each other. If the *wuxia* formula of martial arts "clans" (*menpai*) seems to resurrect a "feudal" form of social organization and subliminally interject it into modern life, the sociality of Gu Long's heroes represents instead an "anti-*jianghu*," a chaotic dissociation or dissolution of that precapitalist mode of human connectedness. The performative gesture whereby Gu Long destroys his own relation to the tradition of Chinese martial arts fiction renders his reader's accumulated knowledge, in Yang's words, "useless." Proposing a more Hegelian reading of Gu Long's work as the simultaneous invention and destruction of a tradition, Yang Zhao's article reminds us that Gu Long's genealogical relation to Chinese culture and his textual representations of genealogy are two sides of the same coin, and both are too complex to be reduced to a reflection of Taiwan alone.

The Eleventh Son

One of the most frequently cited examples of Gu Long's writings as bourgeois decadence is *The Eleventh Son*, to this date the only Gu Long novel to be translated into English. Riveting, absorbing, and compulsively readable, *The Eleventh Son* is a page-turner structured around twist after twist, revelation after revelation. Readers of this text are frequently surprised by how little martial arts "action" it offers compared to character and plot development. Like most of Gu Long's other novels, *The Eleventh Son* reads more like a mystery novel than a traditional martial arts novel. Its complex and numerous plot twists are ingenious and too intricate to summarize. Instead the focus here is on the unusual narrative structure of the text and the problem of novelistic closure, which intimately relate to the conception of kinship and Chineseness at the heart of Gu Long's literary practice. Understanding this relationship provides an alternative to the domestication of Gu Long as allegory for Taiwanese independence.

Structurally, *The Eleventh Son* consists of three parts, each defined by a theme or set of characters that initially appears to be independent. The organization of the text certainly suggests a kaleidoscope of schizophrenic fragmentations, while its characters are hedonists who believe in instant gratification, *carpe diem* worldviews, and individualism. While these features may seem to be traits of the postmodern, postindustrial society that is Taiwan, the novel's textual logic reveals a different order of affinity that serves as the novel's latent thought against its manifest content or rhetorical style. This comes to the fore only if comprehended through a restructured, deimperialized narrative of Taiwan's political history outlined above.

The novel begins with the character of Feng Siniang, a beautiful, strong-willed, and manipulative thirty-three-year-old woman experiencing what, in contemporary language, may be called a midlife crisis. Feng is an accomplished martial arts master, feared by all in the Martial Order. A typical Gu Long hedonist, Feng knows "what to wear for each occasion, what to say to any sort of people, what to eat with a particular liquor, and … which kind of kung fu would kill which kind of people. She [knows] about life and how to enjoy it" (2). Contemplating her age, however, she realizes how lonely she has been, and wishes for the company of the men she has rejected (or murdered) and for a child. In particular, she longs for the sight of one friend, Xiao Shiyi Lang, a notorious bandit to whom she feels a special connection. Like her, Xiao Shiyi Lang is a social outcast. In the novel's terms, Xiao is a socially unintelligible being whose existence exceeds or contradicts the grid of culture: "Xiao was an enigma. Some cursed him, some hated him, some loved him … but few understood him. He didn't expect to be understood" (32).

In the first part of the novel, however, instead of meeting Xiao, Feng encounters a succession of minor characters, all of whom are famed martial arts masters, each more powerful than the one before. These minor characters (Flying Doctor, Hua Ping, the strange-looking lad) reveal to Feng that they have been maimed and mutilated by Xiao Shiyi Lang. A swordsman had his left arm cut off in a battle with him. A kung fu master renowned for his speed and agility lost his legs to him. Xiao himself does not appear until the third chapter. This structural oddity of narrative deferral and indirection serves as a symbolic feature of his character.

When the protagonist finally appears in the text, his and Feng's first conversation in the book concerns two legendary weapons, forged by China's renowned ancient smiths, which Feng has acquired from a mysterious man, Count Carefree. One of these ancient weapons has been broken by a newer weapon, a sword called the Deer Carver.

> "Deer Carver? The name is fancy. Why haven't I heard of it before?"
> "Because this saber was made less than six months ago."
> Xiao raised his eyebrows. "A newly forged saber can cut fine weapons made long ago? Is it possible that the man who made this saber is as good as the distinguished swordsmiths of the late Zhou dynasty [such as] … Ganjiang, Moxie, and Ou Zhizhi?" (33–34)

This dialogue between Feng and Xiao hinges on a deliberate contrast between the accumulated wisdom of ancient China and the power of a "newly forged" upstart, the Deer Carver, which miraculously trumps the authority of the ancient, the traditional, the Chinese. The relation between Taiwan and China is symbolically and metafictionally staged here as an encounter between innovation and tradition. The Deer Carver's symbolic status as an allegory for Taiwan is clear, and this political allegory is further sustained by Gu Long's choice of the weapon's name. In Chinese, the deer is a common metaphor for politics, as in the expression *zhulu zhongyuan* ("hunt the deer in the central plains," the Chinese equivalent of "throw one's hat into the ring"). Jin Yong's last novel about the Manchu emperor, *The Deer and the Cauldron*, derives its title from the same expression. *The Eleventh Son*'s omniscient narrator, in fact, defines the meaning of the Deer Carver as follows: "In ancient China, the deer was used to symbolize the coveted throne" (34), making a political reading of the item unavoidable.

In terms of both their narrative structures and language, Gu Long's novels seem to be a radical, postmodern departure from the traditional form of martial arts fiction. His novels are full of plot twists and composed in short, choppy sentences that are mostly dialogues. Some of his works read like novelized movie scripts, an impression that is fortified by Gu Long's dual role as novelist and movie producer. In turn, Gu Long's crossings between literary and visual cultures further reinforce the perception of his works as products of postindustrial or mass culture.[19] Indeed, *The Eleventh Son* was first conceived and composed as a film script.[20] However, while both the Deer Carver and the schizophrenic organization of the text, taken independently, might be facilely translated into a straightforward political allegory of postmodern consumer culture, the combination of the two poses an interpretive problem. The Deer Carver, mentioned at the beginning as a mysterious, legendary weapon, promises to make the novel into a quest narrative and serves as the primary plot driver for the first third of the text. However, since *The Eleventh Son* is a typical Gu Long and a schizophrenic text as well, the mention of Deer Carver only creates expectations that the novel later thwarts. This setup allows Gu Long to mislead his reader into believing that the novel bears a resemblance to the plot of Jin Yong's *Heavenly Sword, Dragon-slaying Saber*, which hinges on various martial heroes' pursuit of the titular items and the ultimate secret each contains. After the first third of *The Eleventh Son*, however, the narrative thread about Feng Siniang and the fate of the Deer Carver abruptly disappears, and the novel shifts its focus to the tangled and tortured romance between Xiao Shiyi Lang and Lady Shen. The rest of the novel deals with the couple's struggles with their feelings and with two new villains introduced in the second half of the novel: Little Mister and Count Carefree. Feng Siniang becomes a minor character, and for the rest of the novel the Deer Carver is never mentioned again. In other words, the political allegory is constructed and given status as the narrative motor only to be deconstructed, and supplanted by the novel's true theme, historical affinity.

Gu Long's literary style thus exemplifies the art of narrative misdirection. The first six chapters of the text are narrated from Feng Siniang's perspective, with a focus on the discovery. The Deer Carver, like Xiao Shiyi Lang, is introduced to the reader first through a foil, an inferior object. In her first conversation with Xiao in the text,

Feng reveals that she has already acquired two legendary weapons from Count Carefree. Of the two weapons she has equipped, Blue Jade is still intact, but Crimson Glow has already been broken by the Deer Carver. Feng displays the broken instrument in an attempt to intrigue Xiao and enlist his help in securing the Deer Carver, but Xiao refuses. Feng concocts a plan and proceeds without Xiao. She disguises herself as a prostitute and engages the master, who is guarding the Deer Carver, in a protracted psychological battle. She outwits the master and incapacitates him, but just as the reader is about to congratulate Feng on her scheme, the master launches a surprising counterattack, stating that he was only pretending to have fallen for her tricks so that Feng would let her guard down. He overpowers Feng and is about to rape and kill her, at which point Xiao unexpectedly arrives to steal the Deer Carver and free Feng. When the couple escapes to a location of safety, however, they soon discover that the Deer Carver they have managed to steal is a fake.

The story of the Deer Carver exemplifies Gu Long's narrative style of *zhengyan ruofan* (stating truth by negating the negation), a common term often employed by Gu Long critics.[21] Constantly switching back and forth between narrative points of view, Gu Long's text violates many rules of traditional literary aesthetics at once in order to achieve an immersive, cinematic effect of twist after twist, revelation after revelation. In chapter seven, Xiao and Feng meet Lady Shen, and the novel takes another surprising turn, this time on the organizational level. Feng, who has served as the novel's primary site of narrative focalization and eroticization up to this point, suddenly recedes into the background and becomes a minor character, while Xiao and Lady Shen usurp the narrative motor and become the protagonists in her stead. The substitution of one focalizer and love interest for another stands as another example of the narrative technique of "negating the negation." Shen is an extraordinary beauty who is already married to one of the most respected gentlemen in the Martial Order, Lian. Like her husband, Shen is well mannered, polite, refined, soft-spoken, cultured, and conservative. The personalities and social values of Lian and Shen stand in stark contrast to those of Xiao and especially Feng, who is described in the novel as an exhibitionist and a narcissist. On several occasions, Feng bares her breasts in public, either as a diversionary tactic in combat, or simply to cause embarrassment to her male comrades. The opening scene of *The Eleventh Son* has Feng taking a bath with seven skilled assassins around her, whom she murders by lifting hands that are "as delicate and graceful as orchids" while sitting naked in the bathtub (5). By contrast, Lady Shen is always fully clothed. In a later scene her feet are swelling from poison, and when Xiao tries to remove her shoes and socks to examine her wounds, she blushes and screams, wishing "she could just chop off her leg" instead because "even her husband has never seen her feet" (131).

As aptly suggested by the title of the chapter in which they first meet—"The Lady and the Bandit"—the relationship between Shen and Xiao stages the conflict between two characters who differ not only in their social class but in their relation to human collectivities, rules of culture, and the disciplinary force they exert. Lady Shen is a character who simultaneously thrives on and bemoans her enslavement to what society thinks of her—her reputation, or what the novel calls her "honor" (*mingyu*). By contrast, Xiao is a loner without family or friends (other than the equally notorious Feng). Shen considers Xiao "vulgar" (129), but finds herself strangely attracted to him despite the fact that she is already married to a perfect husband.

Xiao is known throughout the Martial Order as the Great Bandit who has violated every social rule and incurred the wrath of every powerful martial leader. However, at the age of twenty-seven, Xiao is also the most feared and powerful martial arts master in the known world. An uncouth, callous man burdened with the ill reputation that preceded him, Xiao often compares himself to a wolf. Much of his superior martial skill, indeed, issues from animal instincts. He is described as a savage and honest misfit who has never mastered the rules of culture, trying to survive in the emphatically social world of martial arts.

Most of the rest of the novel centers on the tortured and tangled romance between Xiao and Shen. As the target of a deadly plot hatched by Count Carefree and his disciple, Shen repeatedly comes close to death. Although the two characters try to keep their distance, Shen's precarious situation continually forces Xiao to return to her side. Shen struggles with her own feelings and her vows to Lian, whom she also loves and whose child she is already carrying. Shen is, in short, caught between the "civilized world of hypocrites" and the brutal scene where human beings are nakedly exposed in all their flaws and imperfections (217).

In the last third of the novel, Xiao and Shen find themselves trapped in Count Carefree's "dollhouse." The couple is first led to Count Carefree's mansion, which is tastefully decorated with paintings, trinkets, and an elegantly crafted dollhouse that is "more elaborate than any child could ever conceive" (276), with remarkably life-like animals, trees, men, mountains, gardens, and pavilions. It also contains two figurines that appear to be in the midst of a chess game. Xiao and Shen become unconscious after drinking tea offered by their host, and when they wake, they realize they have magically "shrunk" to the size of dolls and trapped inside the dollhouse. The miniature dogs and other creatures they have seen the previous night come alive, and the chess-playing men inform them that they too have fallen victim to Count Carefree's spells and will be living inside the house for eternity. Upon hearing this news, Shen feels as though "she might go insane," and Xiao is "on the verge of losing his mind" (286). The dollhouse, however, is merely an illusionist's trick. As Xiao eventually figures out, there is no such thing as magic. The chess players who work for Count Carefree are lying, and Xiao and Shen are simply trapped in a mansion in the real world, adjacent to the house where they originally saw a replica of their current prison.

On the surface, the dollhouse section of the book seems to be another break with expectations invoked by the previous two-thirds of the book, since this subplot has nothing to do with martial arts. The entire section includes no exciting martial battles nor any mention of the familiar ingredients of a *wuxia* tale that the novel had previously suggested, such as the Deer Carver sword or any Secret Scripture. Moreover, neither Count Carefree's scheme nor Xiao's insight stems from the character's superior martial abilities. Xiao defeats Count Carefree not because our protagonist is a better martial artist, but because he is an ordinary human being who understands human greed, need, and despair. Gu Long's text, however, is only superficially incoherent. The continuity between the dollhouse plot and the rest of the novel lies instead in the fact that martial arts in Gu Long never simply refer to kung fu to begin with; rather, martial arts stand for the forces of history. In Gu Long, martial arts are more accurately interpreted as the burden of the past that decenters the human subject and resituates it in a social field of Others. The three sections discussed here—the traditional martial arts story of the Deer Carver, the tangled love story between the married lady and the bandit, and the fantastic mystery story of the dollhouse and its "alternate universe"—are Gu Long's ways of showing the power of history in the production of the self. The Deer Carver, which never materializes, is only a linguistic construct and as such the embodiment of the forces of language in a way that is similar to the "reputation" question that constructs Shen's character. Evaluated in this context, the derailed or lost narrative of the Deer Carver becomes part of a coherent narrative design whose thematic nexus is the recognition of the historicity of the self.

After Xiao breaks out of the dollhouse trap, Count Carefree smugly explains his intention:

> Many of them either went insane or slit their own throats. It's definitely entertaining. If you had seen the expressions of those who were shocked to find themselves shrunk, and how they kept drinking or using other ways to numb themselves until they finally went insane, you'd agree that nothing in the world is more entertaining. In order to survive, those people discarded everything they'd once believed in, including morality, integrity, reputation, or social status. Sometimes, they'd even trade their wives for a mere jar of wine. (323)

In this scene, Xiao and Shen's dilemma is reconfigured as the question of the relationship between human nature and the power of culture and history. Since Shen's "honor" prevents her from beginning a relationship with Xiao, their perpetual entrapment in a parallel universe, if they believe the illusion, provides a perfect opportunity for them to distill and separate their identities that belong to the sphere of the (Lacanian) Law, from whatever might remain when one is removed from all the teachings and rules of society and "magically" restored to a primordial state of nature. In this sense, Count Carefree's design is essentially a social experiment. Gu Long's invention of this subplot foregrounds the conflict between the forces of culture, which he calls martial arts, reputation, chivalry, or honor, and the notion of a "presocial" self, which, as Xiao and Shen discover, can never be fully restored or recovered even in the doll-house.

This aspect of the text allows us to reconsider the apparent autonomy of Xiao himself. In Gu Long criticism, Xiao is conventionally interpreted as a *langzi*, a free-spirited and hedonistic, but socially marginalized, person with no attachment to or respect for society.[22] The polar opposite of a *langzi* is a *junzi*, the ideal gentleman, exemplified by Shen's husband, Lian. Throughout *The Eleventh Son*, Xiao plays on this difference by singing a song about wolves and sheep:

> It's March. It's early spring.
> Sheep rejoice at the tall grass.
> It's cold. The earth is frozen.
> Who is going to feed the wolf?
> Men's hearts take pity on the sheep.
> Wolves' hearts are lonely and sad.
> The heart of heaven is hard to fathom.
> The hearts of the world are cold as frost. (221)

Xiao's character and ideals should not be conflated with the overarching message of the text. On the contrary, the figuration of Xiao as the lone wolf independent of society, like the Deer Carver, is a narrative ploy that delivers the opposite message through its negation.

Gu Long often repeats the aphorism "renzai jianghu, shenbu youji": "A human being in the Martial Order is a human being whose self does not belong to himself." *Wuxia*, martial arts, are not physical skills in Gu Long's literary imagination; they indicate the extent to which one becomes a socially viable subject by virtue of being subject to the will of Others. It is impossible for any human being to truly "belong" to himself or herself. Ultimately, rather than being a celebratory vision of pluralistic, individual agency, the story reveals the impossibility of dissociating oneself from the constraints of history, seen most clearly in the fact that Xiao and Shen fail to transcend or rise above the burdens of social opinions and the rules of culture.

The burdens of history also present opportunities for a renewed understanding of the relation between self and society—between the "I" and the faceless Others whom we do not know but remain bound up with. History is cumbersome, but also productive in Gu Long: it designates our kinship to and dependence on those we recognize as family. By recasting history as nonbiological kinship in works such as *The Eleventh Son*, Gu Long reconfigures the traditional *langzi* figure that he seems to celebrate. To understand the precise meaning of history as productive constraint, however, we need to turn to another text about orphans and orphanhood: *Legendary Siblings*.

Legendary Siblings

Legendary Siblings is Gu Long's longest and best-known novel. The standard edition comprised ten volumes, totaling around two thousand pages. The setup of this convoluted saga, however, is simple. Two exceedingly beautiful, powerful, yet lonely sisters who rule a mysterious martial clan called The Palace of Shifting Flowers (*Yinhua gong*) rescue a handsome swordsman at the point of death. The two female rulers have elegant names: Yaoyue (She who invites the Moon) and Lianxing (She who takes pity on the Stars). They nurse the handsome swordsman to full health with tenderness and both fall in love with him. His heart, however, is captured by an ordinary-looking maid in the Palace. Once the swordsman recovers his strength, he elopes with the maid. He plans to seek protection from his friend, Yan Nantian, the Supreme Swordsman in the Martial Order. Sadly for the newlyweds they run into several deadly thugs before they can reach Yan Nantian, and die after a brutal battle. The wife manages to give birth to twin boys before she dies. Yaoyue and Lianxing arrive just in time to dispose of the thugs and collect the corpses of the traitorous couple, but they decide not to kill their orphaned sons right away. Instead, the jilted sisters concoct a much more fulfilling and elaborate revenge plot: they will raise the brothers to be mortal enemies. Each will be instructed to duel the other at the age of eighteen, and after one of them dies, the sisters will reveal their true identities to the victor, and laugh at his remorse and agony. The surviving brother, they believe, will also be cursed with the unspeakable karmic sin of fratricide. They adopt one boy and name him Hua Wuque (the Flawless One) and send the other boy to Yan Nantian. An epic battle between good and evil is thus scheduled between the heir of the Palace of Shifting Flowers and the disciple of the Supreme Swordsman.

The sisters' grand design, however, is derailed by a series of accidents. Before the other infant gets to safety, Yan Nantian is attacked by five master criminals from the Valley of Evil and falls into a coma. Seeing the infant as a blank slate, the five criminals decide to conduct a social experiment of their own by raising him to be the "greatest evil in history." Instead of learning martial arts from the Supreme Swordsman, Little Fish, as his new foster parents now call him, grows up to be a cunning criminal. The anticipated meeting between the two siblings who are destined to kill each other nonetheless continues to propel the narrative as the central conflict that animates the text and awaits resolution. At this point, however, Fish begins to monopolize the novel's narrative focal point, and Hua Wuque becomes a secondary character that the reader will meet in a much later chapter when both men become adults.

While *Legendary Siblings* appears to be a straightforward Bildungsroman about two brothers, it is also a tale of orphans and parents. It is a text about nonbiological kinship, unconventional parenting, and social engineering that intervenes in the nature-versus-culture debate. The novel is clearly concerned with kinship—

the obligations, bonds, and exchanges between human beings who share a common genealogical origin. It is, however, also an affirmative and provocative reflection on the viability of nonconventional parents and parenting. Both protagonists are raised by parents we would describe in contemporary U.S. political parlance as nonheterosexual life partners—two unmarried sisters, or five friends, who decide to raise a child together. The children, who become the center of narrative attention, obscure and eclipse the parents, whose queer parenting continues to inform and build up the characters that we have come to recognize as the proper object and vehicle for the novel. Both fictional examples are condensations of social energies that rebel against the regulatory ideal of the nuclear family as Freud defined it. Indeed, much narrative space is devoted to the development and descriptions of the parental characters' deviations from traditional gender roles.

The title of the work, *Legendary Siblings*, suggests that both brothers will play an equal role in the story, and that over the course of the novel they will emerge "legendary" by becoming subjects of exciting martial adventures. The "legendary siblings" may equally refer to the two unmarried sisters who decide to raise a child together and create a family of their own, rather than the twins. The relationship between the two sisters that contemporary U.S. idiom would describe as a "domestic partnership" is mirrored by the parallel example of the five parental figures to Fish. The title of the novel might equally refer to the hidden origins of the two brothers in the two sisters. Yaoyue and Lianxing are described as ill-tempered spinsters and cold-blooded murderers, but Wuque is not presented as a traumatic victim whose character-formation is hopelessly damaged by the lack of a male model. Rather, his story is an affirmative one that challenges the presumed naturalness and indispensability of a father figure. The unconventional parenting Wuque receives is mirrored by Fish's fate. While Wuque grows up without a male model, Fish grows up without a female one. In Fish's mind, he has not two but six parents—the five felonious martial teachers, and a "corpse" he talks to every day in private that is the comatose Yan Nantian. Among his five parent-teachers in the

Valley of Evil, only one, Tu Jiaojiao, is biologically a woman but Gu Long resists the presumption of heterosexual parenthood by making her character a fulltime transvestite, skilled in identity-theft and metamorphosis. As reported by the characters, nobody can ever tell if she is really a man or a woman.

Just as Yaoyue and Lianxing's decision to raise the child of their enemy is a social experiment, the five master criminals' adoption of Fish after defeating Yan Nantian also reflects a conviction that nurture outweighs nature, and life can be fashioned, molded, and designed by will.

> Tu Jiaojiao said, "Wait … You cannot kill this baby."
>
> Haha'er laughed, "Don't listen to Tu's crazy talk. Why should we leave the seed of revenge alive? If the roots are not removed during weeding, the weeds will grow again."
>
> Tu Jiaojiao did not respond immediately. She asked around: "We are all evil people, but who is the most evil one in the world? … Each and every one of us here has done roughly the same amount of ruthless, vicious, and immoral deeds. Nobody out-evils anybody else. Before today, true evil has not been born yet! … Until we met that crying baby over there."
>
> Everybody was startled. Li Dazui said, laughing, "You mean he is the greatest evil in the world?"
>
> Tu Jiaojiao ignored him and continued, "This kid does not know anything. His life is a blank slate. If we tell him that crows are white, he will believe us. If he grows up as our baby, everything he hears and sees will be our evil. Not only will he grow to be an evil man, he will out-evil anybody we know! Think about it: if a single person can master all of the dirty tricks in the Valley of Evil known to the five of us, how evil, wicked, and ruthless will he be?

Haha'er laughs, "Even demons would run away from him!"

"Right. If even demons fear him, imagine what is going to happen when he leaves the Valley and enters the Martial Order?" (125–129)

The true parallel between the siblings, Wuque and Fish, concerns the state-of-nature hypothesis: What happens when human beings are raised by nonbiological parents? Even more dramatic than Jin Yong's orphan figures and unconventional parent-child relations— for example, Guo Jing, who grows up among foreigners, and Yang Guo, who is raised by a young woman of the similar age in a tomb— Gu Long's characters represent the experience of social autonomy and the limits of social autonomy. Before the story is about martial arts, it is first a story about the social effects of, fantasies about, and desire for an unconventional family.

Hua Wuque, raised by the sisters, is the only man after his father ever allowed entry into The Palace of Shifting Flowers. He becomes a man who is slightly effeminate, but refined, elegant, emotionless, and, above all, unparalleled in martial arts in his generation. Fish, on the other hand, is an antihero who relies more on wit and trickery than on martial arts for survival. He is street-smart but not intellectual. He is an accomplished martial artist as well but prefers to fight dirty, with guile rather than brute force, using such tricks as poisons, concealed weapons, feigned-death, lock-picking, traps, stealth, and deceit. Above all, Fish's preferred weapon is pure verbal manipulation—bluffs, lies, deal-cutting, psychological warfare, and even sexual seduction. At the age of five, Fish receives an assignment from his masters to kill a lion. Instead of engaging the animal, he tricks it into attacking his teachers, after which he explains, "Why would you try to outrun an enemy you can outsmart?" The bulk of the novel takes the reader through endless array of similar episodes in which Fish appears to be caught in hopeless situations, cornered by deadly enemies, or fighting lost causes, but somehow manages to outsmart his opponents and accomplishes the impossible mission. Gu Long is a gifted storyteller, and every one of Fish's dilemmas and solutions is created and explained with sound logic and rendered with vigor and detail. The pleasure of the text is not derived from the plot twists; rather, it comes from the plausibility of the events and the construction of Fish's character—his resourcefulness, his nonconformist attitude, and his social marginality.

Legendary Siblings is a novel about plots and plotting, but like the Deer Carver in *The Eleventh Son*, "the letter never reaches its destination" (as Derrida says of the signifier). The original plot centers on a fated fratricide, but the ostensible design and intention of the narrative are ultimately thwarted by the energy of the work itself. The force of the revenge plot (as social horror) is only understandable in the schemes of the Confucian prohibition against fratricide. The text therefore appears at first to be a story of the importance, moral priority, and inviolable nature of the Confucian hierarchy and order of human relations. What complicates the story's moral signification, and prevents interpretation of the story as a simplistic homage to filial relations, is the fact that the scene the reader waits for in this long novel never actually arrives. After thousands of pages, the anticipated duel never happens. It suddenly dissipates. What we have instead is the introduction of a new villain, Mouse, a blocking character in the romantic encounter between Fish and the last female protagonist in the novel. The struggle between Fish and Mouse takes over, replacing the original opposition between the brothers (or their teachers and protectors) and recentering the moral economy of the text.

The lack of foreshadowing for this plot twist makes it seem like a derailment of narrative energy and emotional investment, a catastrophe for the text and its chain of signification, an implosion from within where all the things that are built up so carefully by the text suddenly cease to matter. Yet, the emergence of Mouse as the sudden but final villain (or negative signifier) in the text is not random or poor writing. Since Ox and other Zodiac heroes are the first thugs who assassinate Fish's parents, the presentation of characters is arranged in accordance with the Chinese zodiac system, and the emergence of Mouse as the final, and true, villain of the text is part of the author's intentional design and artistic craft.

The rise and fall of Mouse assumes the narrative position of textual closure and resolution. The placement of Mouse is therefore part of *Legendary Siblings'* coherent design and symbolic structure.

The narrative of the threat of fratricide, and the strange displacement and evaporation of such textual force, suggests the importance of biological kinship only to displace it onto a different social plane. The juxtaposition of these two kinds of values—the dooming weight of the kinship narrative and the levity of the instant-gratification of the romantic plot—allows for the contrastive relation between filiation and affiliation to emerge. History, conceived as affiliation, offers a paradoxically promising way of narrating a different future as well.

Conclusion: The Orphan of Asia

The historical background for the rise of postwar martial arts fiction in Taiwan has profound implications for postcolonial literary studies. To begin with, the great colonial conflicts between the East Asian states are not typically recognized as a legitimate object of postcolonial studies. Many important scholarly works on the worldwide decolonization movement make no mention of non-European colonizers such as Japan.[23] In the popular media as well as in professional writings by liberal thinkers such as Francis Fukuyama, the barbaric institution of colonialism, like that of slavery, becomes a matter of mankind's preenlightened past, nightmares we have successfully overcome after "the end of history." The status of Hong Kong and Macau as European colonies until 1997 and 1999, respectively, do not seem to mar the conscience of the globe, nor does this fact bother the many historians who identify decolonization as a project that was completed in the 1960s.

An even more difficult problem for reconciling postcolonial studies with the cultural and political realities of life in Hong Kong, or, here especially, Taiwan, lies in a growing tendency to interpret Chineseness as colonialism, against which Americanism appears as the passage to freedom, a kind of postcolonial resistance. That this discourse is possible designates the limits of a conventional postcolonial theory derived from the historical experiences and analytical models of South Asia, Africa, and Latin America. Indeed, the violent historical theater of inter-Asian colonization, hierarchy, and exploitation in which those who control most of the guns are not the ones in control of most of the capital, the oppressors are not always white, and the victims are not always complaining, indicates that domination and resistance do not always operate along racially divided lines. Furthermore, the relation between the two Chinas involves the mediation of the United States, without which the Republic of China on Taiwan would not have existed at all.

While both U.S. hegemony and Sinocentrism are commonly described as neocolonial operations, the triangulation of power between the United States, the People's Republic of China, and the Republic of China on Taiwan defies postcolonial categorization of domination and resistance, which is often quickly elided with an encounter between a technologically advanced power and primitive natives. This interpretive difficulty is compounded by the fact that the United States' operation as "the empire without colonies" depends on securing proxies rather than antipodes, satellites rather than vassals. In contradistinction to seventeenth- to nineteenth-century European forms of colonialism, which focused on the expansion of territories, extraction of colonial wealth, acquisition of sources of labor-power, and direct administration, twentieth-century American power functions through the cooperation of notionally sovereign states in East Asia.[24] Progressive critics have analyzed the modes whereby U.S. colonialism presents itself, paradoxically, as an endorsement of Asian national self-determination, since the preservation of the sovereignty of China is compatible with the interests of late-arriving empires.[25] In fact, imperialism is often morally justified and disguised as support for the principle of national self-determination in newly independent third-world nations.[26] I propose to consider Taiwan as a prime example of an "anomalous colony," a political condition that Gu Long's martial arts novels explore and engage in a critical fashion.

Historically, Gu Long's literary career as an author of martial arts fiction (1964–1985) coincided with the political tale of the two Chinas. Until the late 1980s, Taiwan saw itself as China or, more accurately, as the seat of the legitimate government for the whole of China, most of which had "fallen" into the hands of the Communist Party in the form of the PRC. With the lifting of martial law (1987), democratization (1991), and the rise of the Taiwanese independence and "de-Sinicization" movements, Taiwan's identification with China and Chineseness became an attenuated and, by the twenty-first century, a politically incorrect tradition.

Taiwan cultural critic Liu Jihui defines Taiwan's early political consciousness before the 1980s as an "orphan mentality," which was eventually replaced by a new cultural semiotics she terms "goddess mentality" that reconfigures Taiwan's native soil as a life-giving, generative earth-mother.[27] As captured by Wu Zhuoliu's famous novel, *Yaxiya de gu'er* (*The Orphan of Asia*), the problem of Taiwan is that it is a state without statehood, a state that has been multiply colonized ("adopted") and abandoned by China and Japan. Peng Ruijin maintains that Wu's "orphan consciousness ... captures the soul of every person who has ever lived in Taiwan, standing as a synonym for a Taiwanese person."[28] Taiwan is a state with no international recognition, a state with *de facto* but not *de jure* independence or sovereignty. Taiwan's predicament is dramatically manifest in the Club 51 movement, which contends that Taiwan's only hope for becoming a sovereign "state" with guaranteed prosperity, security, and democracy is to become the fifty-first "state" of the United States. Their slogan is "Statehood for Taiwan—Save Taiwan—Say Yes to America." Taiwanese independence is therefore a paradoxical political project that requires a dual move: the renunciation of ties to China (which must be construed as an alien power), and the mystification and naturalization of American intervention in Asian national affairs. According to this logic, the identification of Taiwan as Chinese is essentializing, oppressive, and nationalistic, while the Americanization of Taiwan is pluralizing, liberating, and democratizing.

Today, Taiwan's claim to "reclaim the mainland and liberate

our brethren behind the iron curtain" is, needless to say, an artifact of Cold War history. However, while Taiwan's discursive identity as "the real China" has been rendered obsolete by the détente between the United States and the People's Republic of China in the wake of the political and moral bankruptcy of Washington's "strategy of containment," the question of whether there ought to be one or two Chinas continues to structure the lives and identities of one-third of the world's population, who passionately embrace, adamantly oppose, or remotely identify with the One-China policy. If we adopt the Eurocentric definition of the Cold War as the ideological and military struggle between the United States and the Soviet Union, this conflict may indeed seem to have ended with the collapse of the Soviet Union. On the contrary, from the non-Eurocentric, East Asian perspective, the Cold War is anything but finished business. The coexistence of two Chinas, like the two Koreas, defines the present reality and world order for the citizens of East Asia. Contemporary scholarship on Taiwan's martial arts fiction tends to evaluate Gu Long and his achievements in terms of a putatively distinctive and indigenous Taiwanese culture instead of a shared, even if fragmented and contested, life-world between the People's Republic of China, Hong Kong, and Taiwan. The tendency to interpret Gu Long as a representative figure of Taiwanese culture denies his affinity and contributions to Chinese literature as a whole and generates characterizations of Gu Long and his works as a lighthearted, depoliticized, and libidinal product of Taiwan's "bourgeois consumer society" in contrast to "serious" forms of literary writings on the mainland. Against this common perception, I have argued in the chapter that Gu Long's novels are neither free-floating objects dissociated from politics nor playful texts written purely for entertainment and mass consumption that embody the principle of noninterference characteristic of "Taiwanese and Hong Kong bourgeois culture." Rather, his texts are burdened with their occasion, saturated with circumstantial reality, and for that reason eminently worldly. Firmly anchored in the historical contingency of the political culture of two Chinas, Gu Long's novels contain a powerful engagement with cross-strait politics that he elaborates through a novelistic proposal of nonbiological kinship as the basis of political community. Instead of seeing Gu Long as a representative figure of an indigenous, hermetically sealed literary culture that is distinctively Taiwan's own, I suggest that it is more profitable and historically accurate to view his accomplishments as the adumbration of a universal theory of human affinity and sociality centered on the concept of historical constraint. By expanding the meaning of kinship from the natural bonds afforded by biology to a communally defended and disseminated mode of historical consciousness, Gu Long proposes a new affiliative form of human relations that resists the social atomization and alienation that attend the traumatic outcomes of the Chinese civil war, empty political slogans, and usurped ideals.

Through a reading of Gu Long, I have also attempted to expand the vocabulary of postcolonial theory. It is my sense that a traditional reliance on the language of domination and resistance in postcolonial theory fails to explain how it was possible for the citizens of Hong Kong and Taiwan to bemoan the end of British rule as the end of democracy and human rights or, indeed, as the reannexation of Hong Kong to China. When applied to Taiwan, postcolonial theory cannot currently account for the ways decolonization at the end of the Pacific War returned Japan's imperial possessions not to their precolonial positions, but to a new world that the Cold War created.[29] As Kuan-Hsing Chen has recently argued, the exceptional character of East Asian colonial history lies in part in the fact that decolonization was *intercepted* by the installment of a Cold War structure of feeling that divides the region into Communist and anti-Communist states.[30] The era of Japanese colonialism in Taiwan (1895–1945) is remembered by many of its inhabitants, including former President Lee Tenghui, as a golden age of economic and educational development that was brutally interrupted by the dictatorship of the KMT at the end of the Pacific War. During the colonial period, Japan brought similar facilities and developments to Korea and Taiwan—railways, a plumbing system, public sanitation, telegraph, electricity, trolley cars. However, whereas South Korea remembers Japan as a colonizer, Taiwan remembers Japan as a modernizer.[31]

Supporters of the Taiwanese Independence movement either tolerate Japanese colonialism as a reasonable interlude between the ineffectual Qing dynasty and the brutal dictatorship of the KMT, or enthusiastically embrace it for having provided a much needed infrastructural foundation that transformed Taiwan into the great material success story of the 1970s—one of the East Asian Economic Miracles. Today the appreciation for Japanese colonialism intertwines with a desire for America. However, despite the Taiwan Relations Act, the United States remains less interested in the sovereignty of Taiwan per se than in containing the rise of China and protecting U.S. business networks in a politically stable Asia. Yet, the United States cannot be acknowledged as a foreign power in Asian affairs, since Taiwan's material dependency on the United States is precisely the means to Taiwanese independence.[32] These particularities render the structure of domination in the region highly illegible, complicate our ability to distinguish between friend and foe, and obscure the routes of ideological persuasion. Reading Gu Long—and martial arts fiction in general—critically constitutes an imaginative exercise against the geopolitical map of ideologically divided nation-states that we have inherited from the Cold War. To reclaim such wisdom afforded by Chinese martial arts fiction is not a nationalist endeavor, but quite the opposite.

NOTES

1. On this point, see the important published exchanges between four of Taiwan's prominent intellectuals—Hou Hsiao-Hsien, Chu Tien-Hsin, Tang Nuo, and Hsia Chu-Joe. The English translation (Hou et al., "Tensions in Taiwan") has appeared in *New Left Review*.

2. For an analysis of the affinity between Taiwan-based and Republican Chinese martial arts fiction, see Liu Xiumei, *Wushi nianlai de Taiwan tongsu xiaoshuo*, 103.

3. For details of these reasons, documents, and calculations, see Guo Lianqian, 1–2, and Su Zifei, 28–30.

4. See Cao Zhengwen, *Zhongguo xia wenhua shi*; Gong Pengcheng, *Taiwan*

wenxue zai Taiwan; Ye Hongsheng, *Wuxia xiaoshuo tan yilu*; Zhou Qinglin, *Gu Long shumu*; Tan Xianmao, *Gu Long zhuan*; Yu Zhihong, "Gu Long wuxia xiaoshuo chuban nianbiao"; Chen Ying, *Zhongguo yingxiong xiayi xiaoshuo tongzhi*; and Hu Zhongquan, *Wuxia xiaoshuo yanjiu cankao ziliao.*

5. Lin Fushi, 104.

6. For a fuller discussion of the erasure of history in Gu Long, see Gong Pengcheng, *Taiwan wenxue zai Taiwan*, 105–106.

7. For a further analysis of the social implications of Gu Long's representations of clans and martial styles, see my "Cultural Bodies in Gu Long."

8. For an insight of the ideology of fictive kinship (the substitution of martial arts masters for biological fathers) in Jin Yong, see Song Weijie, *Cong yule xingwei dao wutuobang chongdong*, 95–106.

9. Teri Silvio, "Remediation and Local Globalizations: How Taiwan's 'Digital Video Knight-errant Puppetry' Writes the History of New Media in Chinese."

10. The Center was moved to National Taiwan University with Lin Baochun's new appointment in 2006.

11. Lianjing chuban gongsi, ed., *Jindai Zhongguo wuxia xiaoshuo mingzhu daxi*, 25 vols. (Taipei: Lianjing chuban gongsi, 1984).

12. The international conference proceedings were published in book form as *Aoshi guicai—Gu Long: Gu Long yu wuxia xiaoshuo guojia xueshu yantaohui* in 2006.

13. Liang Liang, ed., *Zhonghua minguo shangying dianying zongmu.*

14. Qin Tiannan, *Xianggang yinghua*, Vol. 139, June 1977, 42–43.

15. Johannes Fabian, *Time and the Other.*

16. Chen, 31.

17. Ibid., 49, 137.

18. Yang Zhao, "Xipu de pohuai yu chongjian—lun Gu Long de wulin yu jianghu," 113–126.

19. Unlike Adorno and Horkheimer's elitist, wholesale rejection of the "culture industry" or Benjamin's nostalgia for an authentic aura that was lost to the advent of mechanical reproduction, my position on Gu Long's film-like texts is closer to Jameson's evaluation of the simulacrum in *Postmodernism, or, The Cultural Logic of Late Capitalism*. Dialectically comprehending late capitalism as both catastrophe and progress, Jameson proposes a more nuanced assessment of film that neither condemns nor rationalizes it. Instead, he sees postmodernism as both a symptom of late capitalism and an occasion for its undoing. Jameson's cognitive mapping provides a useful model for recovering the inherent contradiction and Utopian impulse within the "culture industry," which propels an older mode of high art into complex and interesting new

formal inventiveness, as well as a new field of political possibilities.

20. Gu Long, preface to *Xiao Shiyilang*, 1.

21. On "zhengyan ruofan," see Liu Qiaoyun, 67–90, and Chen Kangfen, 42–48.

22. Su Zifei, 40.

23. For example, Neil Lazarus's *The Cambridge Companion to Postcolonial Literary Studies*.

24. See Giovanni Arrighi, "The Rise of East Asia and the Withering Away of the Interstate System."

25. See Mark Berger, *The Battle for Asia*, 1–55.

26. See Colleen Lye, *America's Asia*.

27. Liu Jihui, 71–107.

28. Peng Ruijin, "Wu Zhuoliu, Chen Ruoxi, Yaxiya de gu'er," 94.

29. James Cronin, *The World the Cold War Made*, 1–45.

30. Chen, Kuan-Hsing, *Yazhou zuoiwei fangfa*.

31. Bruce Cumings argues that Korea's and Taiwan's attitudes toward the colonial legacies of Japan do not simply reflect their differential treatment at the hands of the Japanese. Rather, their different responses must be explained by each nation's pre-colonial history (the fact that Taiwan was never a nation before 1895) and postcolonial economic development (the failures of the KMT regime after 1945). *Parallax Visions*, 69–94.

32. In a commentary on the 2004 election published in Chinese and English, Perry Anderson identifies several particularities that set Taiwanese nationalism apart from (other) historical settler-nationalisms. Anderson concludes that the prospect of an independent Taiwanese state is unlikely due to the lack of historical precedents for the a separation from the motherland that is caused by neither revolt nor negotiation. "Standoff in Taiwan."

Bibliography

Ah Cheng 阿城, "Wenhua zhiyue de renlei" 文化製約的人類 (The cultural conditioning of humanity), *Wenyi bao* (1985, July 6): 2–3.

Altenburger, Roland. *The Sword or the Needle: The Female Knight-Errant (xia) in Traditional Chinese Narrative*. Bern: Peter Lang Publishing, 2009.

Anderson, Marston. *The Limits of Realism: Chinese Fiction in the Revolutionary Period*. Berkeley: University of California Press, 1990.

Anderson, Perry. "Stand-off in Taiwan." *London Review of Books* 26.11 (June 2004): 12–17.

Arrighi, Giovanni. "The Rise of East Asia and the Withering Away of the Interstate System." *Marxism, Modernity, and Postcolonial Studies*. Eds. Crystal Bartolovich and Neil Lazarus. Cambridge: Cambridge University Press, 2002. 21–42.

———. *The Long Twentieth Century*. London: Verso, 2000.

Barlow, Tani, ed. *Gender Politics in Modern China: Writing and Feminism*. Durham: Duke University Press, 1993.

———, ed. *New Asian Marxisms*. Durham: Duke University Press, 2002.

———. *The Question of Women in Chinese Feminism*. Durham: Duke University Press, 2004.

Barlow, Tani, and Angela Zito, eds. *Body, Subject, and Power in China*. Chicago: University of Chicago Press, 1994.

Berry, Chris. "Stellar Transit: Bruce Lee's Body, or, Chinese Masculinity in a Transnational Frame." *Embodied Modernities*. Eds. Larissa Heinrich and Fran Martin. Honolulu: Hawaii University Press, 2006. 218–234.

Billeter, Jean-Francois. "The System of 'Class-Status.'" *The Scope of State Power in China*. Ed. Stuart Schram. London: School of Oriental and African Studies. 127–169.

Blue, Gregory, and Timothy Brook, eds. *China and Historical Capitalism*. Cambridge: Cambridge University Press, 1999.

Bordwell, David. *Planet Hong Kong: Popular Cinema and the Art of Entertainment*. Cambridge: Harvard University Press, 2000.

———. "Hong Kong Martial Arts Cinema." *Crouching Tiger, Hidden*

Dragon: A Portrait of the Ang Lee Film. Ed. Linda Sunshine. New York: New Market Press, 2000.

Brook, Timothy, ed. *The Asiatic Mode of Production in China.* Armonk: M.E. Sharpe, 1989.

Cai, Rong. "Gender Imaginations in *Crouching Tiger, Hidden Dragon* and the Wuxia World." *positions: east asia cultures and critique* 13.2 (2005): 441–471.

Cao, Yibing 曹亦冰. *Xiayi gong'an xiaoshuo shi* 俠義公案小說史 (A history of Chinese tales of chivalry and justice). Zhejiang: Zhejiang guji, 1998.

Cao, Zhengwen 曹正文. *Xia wenhua* 俠文化 (The culture of *xia*). Taipei: Yunlong, 1997.

Chan, Adrian. *Chinese Marxism.* London: Continuum, 2003.

Chan, Stephen Ching-kiu. "Figures of Hope and the Filmic Imaginary of Jianghu in Contemporary Hong Kong Cinema." *Cultural Studies* 15 (3/4), 2001: 486–514.

Chan Ching-kiu, Li Siu-leung, and Wong Wang-chi 陳清橋, 李小良, 王宏志. *Fouxiang xianggang* 否想香港 (Hong Kong un-imagined: History, culture, and the future). Taipei: Rye Field, 1997.

Chan, Kenneth. "The Global Return of the *Wu Xia Pian* (Chinese Sword-Fighting Movie): Ang Lee's *Crouching Tiger, Hidden Dragon.*" *Cinema Journal* 43:4 (Summer 2004): 3–17.

Chang, Kang-I Sun, and Ellen Widmer, eds. *Writing Women in Late Imperial China.* Stanford: Stanford University Press, 1997.

Chang, Hsiao-hung 張小虹. "Wen Jin Yong qing shi he wu—liwu, xinwu, zhengwu," 問金庸情是何物—禮物, 信物, 証物 (Asking Jin Yong what love is—gifts, tokens, and evidence). *Jin Yong xiaoshuo guoji xueshu yantao hui lunwen ji* 金庸小說國際學術研討會論文集. Ed. Wang Qiugui. Taipei: Yuanliu, 1999. 153–179.

Chatterjee, Partha. *The Nation and Its Fragments.* Princeton: Princeton University Press, 1993.

———. *Nationalist Thought and the Colonial World: A Derivative Discourse?* London: Zed Books, 1986.

Chen Duxiu. "Wenxue geming lun" (On literary revolution). *Zhongguo xin wenxue daxi* (Compendium of modern Chinese literature, Vol. I). Ed. Zhao Jiabi. Shanghai: Liangyou tushu gongsi, 1935.

Chen, Kang-fen 陳康芬. *Gu Long Wuxia xiaoshuo yanjiu* 古龍武俠小說研究 (A study of Gu Long's fiction). M.A. Thesis, Graduate Institute of Chinese Literature, Tamkang University, 1999.

Chen, Mo 陳墨. *Qing ai Jin Yong* 情愛金庸 (Love in Jin Yong). Taipei: Yunlong, 1997.

———. *Zhengjiao Jin Yong* 政教金庸 (Politics in Jin Yong). Taipei: Yunlong, 1997.

———. *Wuxia wudajia pingshang* 武俠五大家評賞 (Commentary on five major martial arts novelists). Taipei: Fengyun Shidai, 2001.

———. *Wuren buyuan youqing jienie—xishuo Tianlong babu* 無人不冤有情皆孽—細說天龍八部 (Close reading of *Tianlong babu*). Taipei: Yuanliu, 2005.

———. *Zhongguo wuxia dianying shi* 中國武俠電影史 (History of the Chinese martial arts film). Taipei: Fengyun, 2006.

Chen, Pingyuan 陳平原. *Qiangu wenren xiake meng: wuxia xiaoshuo leixing yanjiu* 千古文人俠客夢：武俠小說類型研究 (The dreams of the scholars and the *xia* since ancient times—toward a typology of martial arts fiction). Beijing: Renmin wenxue, 1992.

Chen Shuo 陳碩. *Jingdian zhizao* 經典制造 (Canon-formation). Guilin: Guangxi shifan daxue, 2004.

Chen, Ying 陳穎. *Zhongguo yingxiong xiayi xiaoshuo tongshi* 中國英雄俠義小說通史 (A history of Chinese chivalrous literature). Jiangsu: Jiangsu jiaoyu chubanshe, 1998.

Cheung, Kwai-Yeung 張圭陽. *Jin Yong yu bao ye* 金庸與報業 (Jin Yong and the press). Hong Kong: Ming Pao, 2000.

Chou, Wah-shan 周華山. *Houzhimin Tongzhi* 後殖民同志 (The postcolonial tongzhi). Hong Kong: Hong Kong tongzhi yanjiushe, 1997.

———. *Tongzhi lun* 同志論 (Theory of the Chinese queer). Hong Kong: Xianggang Tongzhi Yanjiushe, 1995.

Chow, Rey. *Woman and Chinese Modernity: The Politics of Reading between West and East*. Minnesota: University of Minnesota Press, 1991.

Chow, Tse-tsung. *The May Fourth Movement: Intellectual Revolution in Modern China*. Stanford: Stanford University Press, 1967.

Cohen, Paul A. *History in Three Keys: The Boxers as Event, Experience, and Myth*. New York: Columbia University Press, 1998.

Cronin, James E. *The World the Cold War Made: Order, Chaos, and the Return of History*. London: Routledge, 1996.

Cui, Fengyuan 崔奉源. *Zhongguo gudian duanpian xiayi xiaoshuo yanjiu* 中國古典短篇俠義小說研究 (A study of classical Chinese short *xiayi* tales). Taipei: Lianjing, 1986.

Culler, Jonathan. *The Pursuit of Signs*. Ithaca: Cornell University Press, 1983.

Cumings, Bruce. *Parallax Visions: Making Sense of American-East Asian Relations at the End of the Century*. Durham: Duke University Press, 1999.

Danjiang daxue Zhongguo wenxue xi 淡江大學中國文學系 (The Chinese Department of Tamkang University), ed. 人物類型與中國市井文化 *Renwu leixing yu Zhongguo shijing wenhua* (Character types and Chinese subcultures). Taipei: Xuesheng, 1995.

———. *Xia yu zhongguo wenhua* 俠與中國文化 (*Xia* and Chinese culture). Taipei: Xuesheng, 1993.

———. *Zongheng wulin: Zhongguo wuxia xiaoshuo guoji xueshu yantao hui lunwen ji* 縱橫武林：中國武俠小說國際學術研討會論文集 (Proceedings of the International Conference on martial arts fiction). Taipei: Xuesheng, 1998.

DeFrancis, John. *Nationalism and Language Reform in China*. Princeton: Princeton Universtiy Press, 1950.

Dirlik, Arif. *The Origins of Chinese Communism*. New York: Oxford University Press, 1989.

———. *Revolution and History: Origins of Marxist Historiography in China, 1919–1937*. Berkeley: University of California Press, 1978.

Dittmer, Lowell, and Samuel Kim. *China's Quest for National Identity*. Ithaca: Cornell University Press, 1993.

Doleželová-Velingerová, Milnea, and Kárl Oldřich, eds. *The Appropriation of Cultural Capital: China's May Fourth Project*. Cambridge: Harvard University Press, 2001.

Duara, Prasenjit. *Rescuing History from the Nation: Questioning Narratives of Modern China*. Chicago: University of Chicago Press, 1995.

Eng, David. *Racial Castration: Managing Masculinity in Asian America*. Durham: Duke University Press, 2001.

Eng, Robert. "Is Hero a Paean to Authoritarianism? www.asiamedia. ucla.edu/article.asp, accessed on June 2005.

Eperjesi, John. "Crouching Tiger, Hidden Dragon: Kung Fu Diplomacy and the Dream of Cultural China." *Asian Studies Review* 28.1 (March 2004): 25–39.

Fabian, Johannes. *Time and Other: How Anthropology Makes Its Object*. New York: Columbia University Press, 1983.

Fan, Boqun 范伯群, ed. *Zhongguo jinxiandai tongsu wenxue shi* 中國近現代通俗文學史 (A history of modern Chinese popular literature). Nanjing: Jiangsu jiaoyu, 1999.

Fei, Yong, and Xiaoyi Zhong 費勇, 鍾曉毅. *Gu Long chuanqi* 古龍傳奇 (The legend of Gu Long). Guangzhou: Guangdong renmin chubanshe, 1996.

————. *Jin Yong chuanqi* 金庸傳奇 (The legend of Jin Yong). Banqiao: Yashutang, 2002.

Feuerwerker, Albert, ed. *History in Communist China.* Cambridge: MIT Press, 1968.

Feuerwerker, Yi-Tsi Mei. *Ideology, Power, Text: Self-Representation and The Peasant Other in Modern Chinese Literature.* Stanford: Stanford University Press, 1998.

Fitzgerald, John. *Awakening China: Politics, Culture, and Class in the Nationalist Revolution.* Stanford: Stanford University Press, 1998.

Frank, Andre Gunder. *ReOrient: Global Economy in the Asian Age.* Berkeley: University of California Press, 1998.

Freud, Sigmund. "Instincts and Their Vicissitudes." *The Standard Edition of the Complete Works of Sigmund Freud,* Vol. 14. London: The Hogarth Press and the Institute of Psychoanalysis, 1953–1974.

————. "On Narcissism," *Standard Edition,* Vol. 14.

————. "Three Essays on the Theory of Sexuality," *Standard Edition,* Vol. 7.

Fung, Edmund. *The Intellectual Foundations of Chinese Modernity.* Cambridge: Cambridge University Press, 2010.

Garber, Marjorie. *Vested Interests: Cross-Dressing and Cultural Anxiety.* New York: Routledge, 1992.

Ge Tao 葛濤. *Jin Yong pingshuo wushi nian* 金庸評說五十年 (Fifty years of Jin Yong criticism). Beijing: Wenhuayishu chubanshe, 2007.

Gilmartin, Christina, et al., eds. *Engendering China: Women, Culture, and the State.* Cambridge: Harvard University Press, 1994.

Gipoulon, Catherine. "The Emergence of Women in Politics in China, 1898–1927." *Chinese Studies in History* (Winter 1989–1990).

Gong, Pengcheng 龔鵬程. *Taiwan wenxue zai Taiwan* 台灣文學在台灣 (Taiwan literature in Taiwan). Taipei: Luotuo, 1997.

————. *Renzai jianghu* 人在江湖 (The Martial Order). Taipei: Jiuge, 1994.

Gong, Pengcheng, and Lin Baochun 龔鵬程, 林保淳. *Ershisi shi xiake ziliao huibian* 二十四史俠客資料匯編 (Compendium of *xia* in Chinese dynastic histories). Taipei: Xuesheng, 1995.

Goodman, David, and Yixu Lu, *Germany in China: Colonial Interactions, Qingdao 1897–1914.*

Gu, Mingdao 顧明道. *Huangjiang nuxia* 荒江女俠 (A female *xia* from Huagjiang). Taipei: Lianjing, (1928) 1985.

Gu, Yi. "Qiantan zhanhou gongfu xiaoshuo zai Yingdunixiya" (On the postwar kung fu novel in Indonesia). *Zhongguo chuantong xiaoshuo zai Ya*

Zhou (The Chinese traditionalist novel in Asia). Beijing: Guoji wenhua, 1989. 458–472.

Gu, Yuanqing 古遠清. *Xianggang dangdai wenxue piping shi* 香港當代文學批評史 (A history of contemporary Hong Kong literary criticism). Hubei: Jiaoyu, 1997.

Guha, Ranajit. *Dominance without Hegemony*. Cambridge: Harvard University Press, 1997.

Guillory, John. *Cultural Capital: The Problem of Literary Canon Formation*. Chicago: The University of Chicago Press, 1993.

Guo, Lianqian 郭璉謙. "Gu Long xiaoshuo mulu ji chuangzuo niandai shangque" 古龍小說目錄及創作年代商榷 (On the exact dates and catalogue of Gu Long's martial arts fiction). Ed. Lin Baochun, *Aoshi guicai, Aoshi guicai—Gu Long: Gu Long xiaoshuo yu wuxia xiaoshuo guojia xueshu yantaohui* 傲世鬼才―古龍： 古龍小說與武俠小說國家學術研討會 (The prodigy of martial arts literature—Gu Long: proceedings of the international conference on Gu Long). Taipei: Xuesheng shuju, 2006. 1–24.

Gunn, Edward. *Unwelcome Muse: Chinese Literature in Shanghai and Peking, 1937–1945*. New York: Columbia University Press, 1980.

――――. *Rewriting Chinese: Style and Innovation in Twentieth-Century Chinese Prose*. Stanford: Stanford University Press, 1991.

――――. *Rendering the Regional: Local Language in Contemporary Chinese Media*. Honolulu: University of Hawaii Press, 2006.

Hardt, Michael, and Antonio Negri. *Empire*. Cambridge: Harvard University Press, 2001.

Hamm, John Christopher. *Paper Swordsmen: Jin Yong and the Modern Chinese Martial Arts Novel*. Honolulu: University of Hawaii Press, 2005.

Han, Shaogong, "Wenxue de gen" (The roots of literature). *Zuojia* 4 (1985): 2–5.

Han, Shaogong, and Xia Yun. "Da Meizhou *Huaqiao ribao* jizhe wen" (Response to the American *Overseas Chinese Journal*). *Zhongshan* 5 (1987): 12–15.

Ho, Josephine, and Yin-Bin Ning 何春蕤, 卡維波. *Weishenme tamen bu gaosu ni* 為什麼他們不告訴你 (Why wouldn't they tell you). Taipei: Fangzhi, 1990.

Heinrich, Larissa. "Handmaids to the Gospel: Lam Qua's Medical Portraiture." *Tokens of Exchange: The Problem of Translation in Global Circulations*. Ed. Lydia Liu. Durham: Duke University Press, 1999. 239–275.

Hershatter, Gail. *Women in China's Long Twentieth Century*. Berkeley: University of California Press, 2007.

Hinsch, Bret. *Passions of the Cut Sleeve: The Male Homosexual Tradition in China.* Berkeley: University of California Press, 1990.

Hong Qingtian 洪清田. "Jin Yong zuopin yu zhonggang shehui" 金庸作品與中港社會 (Jin Yong's writings and Chinese and Hong Kong societies), *Jiefang Jin Yong* 解放金庸 (Liberate Jin Yong). Taipei: Yuanjing, 2002. 187–191.

Hou, Hsiao-Hsien, Chu Tien-Hsin, Tang Nuo, and Hsia Chu-Joe. "Tensions in Taiwan." *New Left Review* 28 (July/August 2004): 19–42.

Hu, Ying. *Tales of Translation: Composing the New Woman in China, 1898–1918.* Stanford: Stanford University Press, 2000.

Hu, Zhongquan 胡仲權. *Wuxia xiaoshuo yanjiu cankao ziliao* 武俠小說研究參考資料 (Research materials on *wuxia xiaoshuo*). Taipei: Wanjuan lou, 1998.

Huang, Zonghui 黃宗慧. "Ta bukan ta shi ta zai ma?" 他不看她時她在嗎? (Does she exist without his gaze?)" *Jin Yong xiaoshuo guoji xueshu yantao hui lunwen ji* 金庸小說國際學術研討會論文集. Ed. Wang Qiugui. Taipei: Yuanliu, 1999. 181–206.

Huangzhu louzhu 還珠樓主. *Shushan jianxia zhuan* 蜀山劍俠傳, *1932–1949.* Taipei: Lianjing, 1984.

Hung, Chang-tai. *War and Popular Culture: Resistance in Modern China, 1937–1945.* Berkeley: University of California Press, 1994.

———. *Going to the People: Chinese Intellectuals and Folk Literature.* Cambridge: Harvard University Asia Center, 1986.

Hunt, Leon. *Kung Fu Cult Masters: From Bruce Lee to Crouching Tiger.* London: Wallflower Press, 2003.

Huss, Ann, and Jianmei Liu, eds. *The Jin Yong Phenomenon: Chinese Martial Arts Fiction and Modern Chinese Literary History.* New York: Cambria Press, 2007.

Jayamanne, Laleen. "Let's Miscegenate: Jackie Chan and His African-American Connection." *Hong Kong Connections: Transnational Imagination in Action Cinema.* Eds. Meaghan Morris et al. Durham: Duke University Press, 2005. 151–162.

Jencks, Harlan. *From Muskets to Missiles: Politics and Professionalization in the Chinese Army, 1945–1981.* Boulder: Westview Press, 1972.

Jameson, Fredric. *The Ideologies of Theory: Essays 1971–1986, Vol. 2: The Syntax of History.* Minneapolis: University of Minnesota Press, 1988.

Jauss, Hans Robert. "Literary History as a Challenge to Literary Theory." *New Directions in Literary History.* Ed. Ralph Cohen. Baltimore: Johns Hopkins University Press, 1974. 11–41.

Jia, Leilei 賈磊磊. 武之舞—中國武俠電影的形態與神魂 *Wuzhiwu— Zhongguo wuxia dianying de xingtai yushenhun* (The Chinese martial arts film and its cultural spirit). Henan: Henan renmin chubanshe, 1998.

———. *Zhongguo wuxia dianying shi* 中國武俠電影史 (A history of the Chinese martial arts film). Beijing: Wenhua yishu chubanshe, 2005.

Jin, Yong 金庸 (Louis Cha). *Jin Yong zuopinji* 金庸作品集 (Collected works of Jin Yong), 36 vols. Taipei: Yuanliu, 1987.

———. *The Book and the Sword*. Trans. Graham Earnshaw. Hong Kong: Oxford University Press, 2005.

Jing, Tsu. *Failure, Nationalism, and Literature: The Making of Modern Chinese Identity, 1895–1937*. Stanford: Stanford University Press, 2005.

Karl, Rebecca. *Staging the World: Chinese Nationalism at the Turn of the Twentieth Century*. Durham: Duke University Press, 2002.

Kay, Geoffrey. *The Economic Theory of the Working Class*. London: Macmillan, 1979.

Keulemans, Pieter (Paize). "Sounds of the Novel: Storytelling, Print-culture, and Martial-arts Fiction in Nineteenth-century Beijing." Ph.D. Dissertation, University of Chicago, 2004.

Klein, Christina. "*Crouching Tiger, Hidden Dragon*: A Diasporic Reading," *Cinema Journal* 43.4 (Summer 2004): 18–42.

Ko, Dorothy. *Teachers of the Inner Chamber: Women and Culture in Seventeenth China*. Stanford: Stanford University Press, 1994.

Kong, Qingdong 孔慶東. *Jin Yong pingzhuan* 金庸評傳 (Commentaries on Jin Yong). Zhengzhou: Zhengzhou University Press, 2004.

Kubin, Wolfgang. "Ban the Poet Lu Xun! Or, New Epochs of Indignation: Reflections on the Problem of Law and Memory," *Minima Sinica* (February 2007): 15–26.

Lai, Sharon. "Translating Jin Yong: A Review of Four English Trans-lations." *Jin Yong xiaoshuo guoji xueshu yantao hui lunwen ji* 金庸小說國際學術研討會論文集. Ed. Wang Qiugui. Taipei: Yuanliu, 1999. 355–384.

Laplanche, Jean. *Life and Death in Psychoanalysis*. Baltimore: Johns Hopkins University Press, 1976.

Lazarus, Neil, ed. *The Cambridge Companion to Postcolonial Literary Studies*. New York: Cambridge University Press, 2004.

Lee, Chisu. "Zhongguo wuxia xiaoshuo zai Hanguo de jieshao yu yingxiang" (The translations and influences of the Chinese martial arts novel in Korea). *Xia yu Zhongguo wenhua* 俠與中國文化 (*Xia* and Chinese culture). Taipei: Xuesheng, 1993. 77–90.

Lee, Haiyan. "Governmentality and the Aesthetic State: A Chinese

Fantasia," *positions: east asia cultures critique* 14.1 (2006): 99–129.

———. *Revolution of the Heart: A Genealogy of Love in China, 1900–1950.* Stanford: Stanford University Press, 2007.

Lee, Leo Ou-fan. *The Romantic Generation of Modern Chinese Writers.* Cambridge: Harvard University Press, 1973.

———. *Shanghai Modern: The Flowering of a New Urban Culture in China, 1930–1945.* Cambridge: Harvard University Press, 1999.

Lee, Leo Ou-fan, and Andrew J. Nathan. "The Beginnings of Mass Culture: Journalism and Fiction in the Late Ch'ing and Beyond." *Popular Culture in Late Imperial China.* Eds. David Johnson, Andrew J. Nathan, and Evelyn S. Rawski. Berkeley: University of California Press, 1985. 360–395.

Leng Xia 冷夏. *Jin Yong zhuan* 金庸傳 (A biography of Jin Yong). Hong Kong: Ming Pao, 1995.

Lenin, V. I. *Imperialism: The Highest Stage of Capitalism.* New York: International Publishers, 1939.

Lévi-Strauss, Claude. *The Elementary Structures of Kinship.* Boston: Beacon Press, 1969.

Li, Siu Leung. "Kung Fu: Negotiating Nationalism and Modernity." *Cultural Studies* 15 (3/4) 2001: 515–542.

———. "The Myth Continues: Cinematic Kung Fu in Modernity." *Hong Kong Connections: Transnational Imagination in Action Cinema.* Eds. Meaghan Morris, Siu-Leung Li, and Stephen Ching-kiu Chan. Durham: Duke University Press, 2005. 49–62.

Li, Tuo. "The Language of Jin Yong's Writing: A New Direction in the Development of Modern Chinese." Eds. Ann Huss and Jianmei Liu. *The Jin Yong Phenomenon: Chinese Martial Arts Fiction and Modern Chinese Literary History.* New York: Cambria Press, 2007. 39–54.

Li, Xiaojiang. *Xingbie yu Zhongguo* 性別與中國 (Gender and China). Beijing: Sanlian, 1994.

Li, Yi 李軼. *Gu Long zhimi* 古龍之謎 (The mystery of Gu Long). Qingdao: Qingdao renmin chubanshe, 1996.

Li, Yinhe 李銀河. *Zhongguo nüxing de xing yu ai* 中國女性的性與愛 (The love and sex of Chinese women). Hong Kong: Oxford, 1996.

Li, Zude 李祖德, et al. *Ping Weitefu de dongfang zhuanzhi zhuyi* 評魏特夫的東方專制主義 (Essays on Wittfogel's *Oriental Despotism*). Beijing: Zhongguo sheihuikexue, 1997.

Liang, Liang 梁良, ed. *Zhonghua minguo shangying dianying zongmu* 中華民國上映電影總目 (Complete catalogue of films shown in the Republic of China). Taipei: Zhonghua minguo dianying tushuguan, 1984.

Liang, Qichao 梁啟超. *Zhongguo zhi wushidao* 中國之武士道 (China's *bushido*). 1904. Taipei: Chung Hwa Book Company, 1971.

Liang, Shouzhong 梁守中. 武俠小說話古今 *Wuxia xiaoshuo hua gujin* (Martial arts fiction today and yesterday). Taipei: Yuanliu, 1990.

Lieu, Samuel N.C. "Fact or Fiction: Ming-chiao (Manichaeism) in Jin Yong's *I-t'ien t'u-lung chi*." *Jin Yong xiaoshuo yu ershi shiji Zhongguo wenxue guoji xueshu yantaohui lunwen ji*. Ed. Lijun Lin. Hong Kong: Mingheshe, 2000. 43–66.

Lin, Baochun 林保淳. *Jiegou Jin Yong* 解構金庸 (Deconstructing Jin Yong) Taipei: Yuanliu, 2000.

———. "Zhongguo gudian xiaoshuo zhong de nüxia xingxiang" 中國古典小說中的女俠形象 (The images of "nüxia" in Classical Chinese tales). *Zhongguo wenzhe yanjiu jikan* 11 (1997): 43–88.

Lin, Baochun, and Ye Hongsheng 葉洪生. *Taiwan wuxia xiaoshuo fazhan shi* 臺灣武俠小說發展史 (The development of martial arts literature in Taiwan). Taipei: Yuanliu, 2005.

Lin, Baochun, ed. *Aoshi guicai—Gu Long: Gu Long xiaoshuo yu wuxia xiaoshuo guojia xueshu yantaohui* 傲世鬼才—古龍：古龍小說與武俠小說國家學術研討會 (The prodigy of martial arts literature—Gu Long: Proceedings of the international conference on Gu Long). Taipei: Xuesheng shuju, 2006.

Lin, Boyuan 林伯原. *Zhongguo wushu shi* 中國武術史 (A history of martial arts in China). Taipei: Wuzhou, 1996.

Lin, Fushi 林富士. "*Wuxia shijie zhong de yizhe*" 武俠世界中的醫者 (Healers in the world of martial arts). *Jin Yong xiaoshuo yu ershi shiji Zhongguo wenxue guoji xueshu yantaohui lunwen ji*. Ed. Lijun Lin. Hong Kong: Mingheshe, 2000. 85–104.

Lin, Lijun 林麗君, ed. *Jin Yong xiaoshuo yu ershi shiji Zhongguo wenxue guoji xueshu yantaohui lunwen ji* 金庸小說與二十世紀中國文學國際學術研討會論文集 (Collected papers from the international conference on Jin Yong's fiction and twentieth-century Chinese literature). Hong Kong: Mingheshe, 2000.

Lin, Yaode 林耀德. "Dangdai Taiwan wuxia xiaoshuo de chengren tonghua" "當代台灣武俠小說的成人童話" (The adult fairy tale of contemporary Taiwan martial arts fiction). *Liuxing tianxia—dangdai Taiwan tongsu wenxue lun* 流行天下—當代台灣通俗文學論 (On contemporary popular fiction in Taiwan). Taipei: Shibao, 1992.

Lin, Wushu 林悟殊. *Monijiao ji qi dongjian* 摩尼教及其東漸 (Manichaeism and its eastward expansion). Taipei: Shuxing, 1997.

———. "Jin Yong's Manichaeism versus Historical Reality." *Historical Monthly* 3 (1996): 66–67.

Link, Perry. "Traditional-Style Popular Urban Fiction." Ed. Merle Goldman. *Modern Chinese Literature in the May Fourth Era*. Cambridge: Harvard University Press, 1977. 327–349.

———. *Mandarin Ducks and Butterflies: Popular Fiction in Early Twentieth Century Chinese Cities*. Berkeley: University of California Press, 1981.

Link, Perry, Richard Madsen, and Paul Pickowicz, eds. *Unofficial China: Popular Culture and Thought in the People's Republic*. Boulder: Westview Press, 1989.

Liu, Bingze, and Chunggui Wang 劉炳澤, 王春桂. *Zhongguo tongsu xiaoshuo gailun* 中國通俗小說概論 (An overview of popular literature in Chinese). Taiyuan: Beiyue wenyi, 1993.

Liu, James. J.Y. *The Chinese Knight-Errant*. London: Routledge, 1967.

Liu, Jen-peng 劉人鵬. *Jindai Zhongguo nüquan lunshu* 近代中國女權論述 (The discourse of women's rights in modern China). Taipei: Taiwan Xuesheng Shuju, 2000.

Liu, Jihui 劉紀蕙. *Gu'er, nüshen, fumianshuxie* 孤兒, 女神, 負面書寫 (Orphan, goddess, and the writing of the negative). Taipei: Lixu, 2000.

Liu, Jingyao 劉經瑤. "Xia'nü, meinü yu yaonü—Jin Yong wuxia xiaoshuo zhong de xingbie zhengzhi" 俠女美女與妖女─金庸武俠小說中的性別政治 (Female knights-errant, beautiful women, and female monsters—sexual politics in Jin Yong's fiction). *Ming Pao yuekan* 31.2, 1996.

Liu, Lydia. *The Clash of Empires: The Invention of China in Modern World Making*. Cambridge: Harvard University Press, 2006.

———. "Desire and Sovereign Thinking." *Grounds of Comparison: Around the Work of Benedict of Anderson*. Eds. Jonathan Culler and Pheng Cheah. New York: Routledge, 2003. 191–219.

———, ed. *Tokens of Exchange: The Problem of Translation in Global Circulations*. Durham: Duke University Press, 1999. 239–275.

———. *Translingual Practice: Literature, National Culture, and Translated Modernity—China, 1900–1937*. Stanford: Stanford University Press, 1995.

———. *Yujishuxie* (Translingual practice). Hong Kong: Tiandi chubanshe, 1997.

Liu, Petrus. "Review of Taiwan *wuxia xiaoshuo fazhangshi* (On the historical development of martial arts fiction criticism in Taiwan) by Lin and Ye." *Zhongguo wenzhe yanjiu qikan* (Bulletin of the Institute of Chinese

Literature and Philosophy), 30 (March 2007): 406–409.

———. "Cultural Bodies in Gu Long." *Aoshi guicai—Gu Long: Gu Long xiaoshuo yu wuxia xiaoshuo guojia xueshu yantaohui*. Ed. Lin Baochun. Taipei: Taiwan xuesheng shuju, 2006. 91–112.

Liu, Qiaoyun 劉巧雲. "Zhengyan ruo fan—lun Gu Long wuxia xiaoshuo de tese." Ed. Lin Baochun. *Aoshi guicai—Gu Long: Gu Long xiaoshuo yu wuxia xiaoshuo guojia xueshu yantaohui*. Taipei: Taiwan xuesheng shuju, 2006. 67–90.

Liu, Xiumei 劉秀美. *Wushi nianlai de Taiwan tongsu xiaoshuo* 五十年來的台灣通俗小説 (Popular fiction in Taiwan in the past fifty years). Taipei: Wenjing, 2001.

Liu, Yitang 劉義棠. *Zhongguo xiyu yanjiu* 中國西域研究 (A study of China's western regions). Taipei: Zhengzhong, 1997.

Lu, Sheldon. "Crouching Tiger, Hidden Dragon, Bouncing Angels: Hollywood, Taiwan, Hong Kong, and Transnational Cinema." *Chinese-Language Film: Historiography, Poetics, Politics*. Eds. Sheldon Lu and Emilie Yueh-yu Yeh. Honolulu: University of Hawaii Press, 2005. 220–233.

Lu, Sheldon, and Emilie Yueh-Yu Yeh, eds. *Chinese-Language Film: Historiography, Poetics, Politics*. Honolulu: University of Hawaii Press, 2005.

Lu, Xun 魯迅. *Lu Xun quanji* 魯迅全集 (Complete works of Lu Xun), 16 vols. Beijing: Renmin chubanshe, 1981.

———. *Diary of a Madman and Other Stories*. Trans. William Lyell, Honolulu: University of Hawaii Press, 1990.

Lu, Yanzhen 盧燕貞. *Zhongguo jindai nüzi jiaoyu shi* 中國近代女子教育史 (1895–1945) (A history of women's education in modern China, 1895–1945). Taipei: Wenshizhe, 1989

Lukács, Georg. *History and Class Consciousness*. Cambridge: MIT Press, 1972.

Luo Ka, Wu hao, Zuo Botang 羅卡、吳昊、卓伯棠 *Xianggang dianying leixing lun* 香港電影類型論 (Genres of Hong Kong cinema). Oxford: Oxford University Press, 1997.

Luo, Liqun 羅立群. *Zhongguo wuxia xiaoshuo shi* 中國武俠小說史 (A history of Chinese martial arts fiction). Shenyang: Liaoning renmin, 1990.

Luo, Xianshu 羅賢淑. *Jianguang xiaying lun Jin Yong* 劍光俠影論金庸 Jin Yong (Sword's shine, *xia*'s shadow: On Jin Yong). Taipei: Wanjuanlou, 2003.

Lye, Colleen. *America's Asia: Racial Form and American Literature: 1893–1945*. Princeton: Princeton University Press, 2005.

Ma, Kwok-ming 馬國明. "*Jin Yong de wuxia xiaoshuo yu Xianggang*" (Jin Yong's martial arts fiction and Hong Kong). Xianggang de liuxing wenhua 香港的流行文化 (Hong Kong popular culture). Ed. Liang Bingjun

梁秉鈞. Hong Kong: Joint Publishing, 1993. 84–94.

Ma, Yuxin. "Women Journalists in the Chinese Enlightenment, 1915–1923." *Gender Issues* 22:1 (December 2005): 56–87.

Macpherson, Crawford Brough. *The Political Theory of Possessive Individualism: Hobbes to Locke*. New York Oxford University Press, 1962.

Madsen, Deborah. "Transcendence through Violence: Women and the Martial Arts Motif in Recent American Fiction and Film." *Literature and the Visual Media*. Ed. David Seed. Rochester: D.S. Brewer, 2005. 163–180.

Mandel, Ernest. *Late Capitalism*. London: Verso, 1999.

Mann, Susan. *Precious Records: Women in China's Long Eighteenth Century*. Stanford: Stanford University Press, 1997.

Mao Dun (Shen Yanbing) 矛盾 （沈雁冰）. "Fengjian de xiao shimin wenyi" "封建的小市民文藝" (The literature of the feudal petty bourgeoisie). *Dongfang zazhi* 30.3 (1933): 21.

Mao, Tse-Tung [Zedong]. *Selected Works of Mao Tse-tung*. Beijing: Foreign Language Press, 1967.

Marchetti, Gina. "Jackie Chan and the Black Connection." *Keyframes: Popular Cinema and Cultural Studies*. Eds. Matthew Tinkcom and Amy Villarejo. London: Routledge, 2003. 137–158.

Marx, Karl. *Capital*, Vol. 1. Trans. Ben Fowkes. Harmondsworth: Penguin Books, 1976.

———. *Capital*, Vol. 2. Trans. David Fernbach. Harmondsworth: Penguin Books, 1978.

———. *Capital*, Vol. 3. Trans. David Fernbach. Harmondsworth: Penguin Books, 1981.

———. *Grundrisse*. Trans. Martin Nicolaus. Harmondsworth: Penguin Books, 1973.

———. *Theories of Surplus-Value*. Moscow: Progress Publishers, 1971.

Mbembe, Achille. "The Banality of Power and the Aesthetics of Vulgarity in the Postcolony." *Public Culture* 4.2 (1992): 1–30.

McLellan, David. *Marxism after Marx*. Boston: Houghton Mifflin, 1979.

Meisner, Maurice. *Mao's China and After*. New York: Free Press, 1986.

Meng, Quan 孟銓. *Haoxia zhuan* 豪俠傳 (Biographies of great *xia*). Taipei: Zhuangyan, 1978.

Minford, John. "Louis Cha through the Translator's Eyes." *Jin Yong xiaoshuo guoji xueshu yantao hui lunwen ji* 金庸小說國際學術研討會論文集. Ed. Wang Qiugui. Taipei: Yuanliu, 1999. 305–354.

Mok, Olivia. "Translational Migration of Martial Arts Fiction East and West." *Target* 13.1 (2001): 81–102.

Morris, Meaghan. "Transnational Imagination in Action Cinema: Hong Kong and the Making of a Global Popular Culture." *Inter-Asia Cultural Studies*, Vol. 5, Number 2, 2004.

———. "Learning from Bruce Lee: Pedagogy and Political Correctness in Martial Arts Cinema." *Keyframes: Popular Film and Cultural Studies*. Eds. Matthew Tinkcom and Amy Villarejo. London: Routledge, 2001. 171–186.

Morris, Meaghan, Siu Leung Li, and Stephen Chan Ching-kiu, eds. *Hong Kong Connections: Transnational Imagination in Action Cinema*. Durham: Duke University Press, 2005.

Nai Rong 乃榕. *Jin Yong xiaoshuo zhi banghui chuanqi* 金庸小說之幫會傳奇 (Legends of sects and secret societies in Jin Yong). Taipei: Yinghan, 2003.

Nealon, Christopher. *Foundlings: Lesbian and Gay Historical Emotion before Stonewall*. Durham: Duke University Press, 2001.

Ng, Mau-sang. *The Russian Hero in Modern Chinese Fiction*. Albany: State University of New York Press, 1988.

Ongiri, Amy. "He Wanted to Be Just Like Bruce Lee: African Americans, Kung Fu Theater, and Cultural Exchange at the Margins." *JAAS* (February 2002): 31–40.

———. *Spectacular Blackness: The Cultural Politics of the Black Power Movement and the Search for a Black Aesthetic*. Charlottesville: University of Virginia Press, 2010.

Pashukanis, E.B. *The General Theory of Law and Marxism*. New Brunswick: Transaction Books, 2001.

Pateman, Carole. *The Sexual Contract*. Stanford: Stanford University Press, 1988.

Pei Si-lan 裴思蘭 (Prisana Utthachat). *Lu Xun he Jin Yong zai Taiguo de jieshou bijiao* 魯迅和金庸在泰國的接受之比較 (A comparison of the reception history of Lu Xun and Jin Yong in Thailand). M.A. Thesis, Qingdao University, 2004.

Peng, Hsiao-yen 彭小妍. *Chaoyue xieshi* 超越寫實 (Beyond realism). Taipei: Lianjing, 1993.

———. "*Wusi de xinxingdaode: nüxing qingyu lunshu yu jiangou minzuguojia*" 五四的新性道德：女性情慾論述與建構民族國家 (May Fourth "new sexual ethics": The discourse of female desire and nation-building). *Haishang shuo qingyu* 海上說情慾 (Talking about love and desire on the sea). Taipei: Zhongyang yanjiu yuan, 2001. 1–26.

Peng, Hua 彭華. *Xiagu rouqing: Gu Long de jinshi jinsheng* 俠骨柔情：古龍的今世今生 (A biography of Gu Long). Taipei: Daduhui, 2004.

———. *Fenghua zaixian: Jin Yong zhuan* 風華再現:金庸傳 (A biography of Jin Yong). Taipei: Daduhui, 2003.

Peng, Hua, and Zhao Jingli 彭華, 趙敬立. *Daoguang, jianying, xiake meng: mantan jinyong* 刀光, 劍影, 俠客夢:漫談金庸 (Flash of the blade, shadow of the sword, dreams of the *xia*: On Jin Yong). Taipei: Daduhui, 2002.

Peng, Ruijin 彭瑞金. "Wu Zhuoliu, Chen Ruoxi: Yaxiya de gu'er," 吳濁流, 陳若曦:亞細亞的孤兒. *Wenxue jie*, 14: 93–104.

Pham, Minh-Ha T. "The Asian invasion (of Multiculturalism) in Hollywood." *Journal of Popular Film and Television*, 32:3 (Fall 2004): 121–131.

Pingjiang Buxiaosheng (Xiang Kairan) 平江不肖生 (向愷然). *Jianghu qixia zhuan* 江湖奇俠傳 (An extraordinary *xia* in the world of martial arts), 1923. Taipei: Shijie, 2004.

———. *Jindai xiayi yingxiong zhuan* 近代俠義英雄傳 (Chronicles of a modern-day hero), 1923. Taipei: Shijie, 2004.

———. *Yujue jinhuan lu* 玉玦金環錄 (Record of the jade ring and the gold ring), 1925. Taipei: Lianjing, 1984.

Pletsch, Carl. "The Three Worlds, or the Division of Social Scientific Labor, circa 1950–1975." *Comparative Studies in Society and History* 23.4 (October 1981): 565–590.

Pomeranz, Kenneth. *The Great Divergence*. Princeton: Princeton University Press, 2000.

Postone, Moishe. *Time, Labor, and Social Domination*, Cambridge: Cambridge University Press, 1996.

———. "Anti-Semitism and National Socialism." *Germans and Jews Since the Holocaust*. Eds. Anson Rabinbach and Jack Zipes. New York: Holmes and Meier, 1986. 302–314.

Poulantzas, Nicos. *State, Power, Socialism*. London: Verso, 1980.

Prasad, Madhava. *Ideology of the Hindi Film: A Historical Construction*. New Delhi: Oxford University Press, 1998.

Prashad, Vijay. *Everybody Was Kung Fu Fighting: Afro-Asian Connections and the Myth of Cultural Purity*. Boston: Beacon Press, 2001.

Pusey, James. *China and Charles Darwin*. Cambridge: Harvard University Press, 1983.

———. *Lu Xun and Evolution*. Albany: State University of New York Press, 1998.

Qin, Tiannan 秦天南. "Weimei, zuguan, langman, chaoxianshi: Chu Yuan yu Gu Long: jingshen shang yidui luanshengzi" 唯美, 主觀, 浪漫, 超現實:楚原與古龍 精神上一對孿生子 (Chu Yuan yu Gu Long: Spiritual twins). *Xianggang yinghua* 香港影畫 139 (June 1977): 42–43.

Qu, Qiubai 瞿秋白. "Jihede de shidai" 吉訶德的時代 (The era of Don Quixote). *Beidou*, Vol. 1, No. 2 (October 1931): 82–83.

Qi, Yukun, and Chen Huiqin 齊裕焜, 陳惠琴. *Jing yu jian: Zhongguo fengci xiaoshuo lue* 鏡與劍:中國諷刺小說史略 (The sword and the mirror: A brief history of the Chinese satire). Taipei: Wenjin, 1995.

Riley, Denise. "The Right to be Lonely." *Difference: A Journal of Feminist Cultural Studies* 13.1 (Spring 2002): 1–13.

Reed, Christopher. *Gutenberg in Shaghai: Chinese Print Capitalism, 1876–1937.* Vancouver: University of British Columbia Press, 2004.

Rojas, Carlos. "Jin Yong and Picturing Nationalism." *The Naked Gaze: Reflections on Chinese Modernity.* Cambridge: Harvard University Asia Center, 2008.

Rubin, Gayle. "Thinking Sex: Notes for a Radical Theory of the Politics of Sexuality." *Pleasure and Danger: Exploring Female Sexuality.* Ed. Carole S. Vance. London: Pandora. 1992. 267–293.

Rui, Heshi 芮和師 et al., eds. *Yuanyang hudie pai wenxue ziliao* 鴛鴦蝴蝶派文學資料 (Materials on mandarin duck and butterfly fiction). Fuzhou: Fujian renmin, 1984.

Russo, Alessandro. "The Probable Defeat: Preliminary Notes on the Chinese Cultural Revolution." *New Asian Marxisms.* Ed. Tani E. Barlow. Durham: Duke University Press, 2002. 311–332.

Said, Edward. *Covering Islam.* New York: Vintage, 1997.

Sakamoto, Hiroko. "The Cult of 'Love and Eugenics' in May Fourth Movement Discourse." *positions: east asia cultures and critique* 12.2 (2004): 329–376.

Samsamsha 小明雄. *Zhongguo tongxing ai shilu* 中國同性愛史錄 (A history of same-sex desire in China). Hong Kong: Rosa Winkel Press, 1984.

San Mao 三毛. *Zhuzi baijia kan Jin Yong* 諸子百家看金庸 (Perspectives on Jin Yong's fiction). Taipei: Yuanjing, 1984.

Sang, Tze-lan D. *The Emerging Lesbian.* Chicago: University of Chicago Press, 2003.

———. "Women's Work and Boundary Transgression in Wang Dulu's Popular Novels." *Gender in Motion: Divisions of Labor and Cultural Change in Late Imperial and Modern China.* Ed. Bryna Goodman and Wendy Larson. Lanham: Rowman and Littlefield, 2005. 287–308.

———. "The Transgender Body in Wang Dulu's *Crouching Tiger, Hidden Dragon.*" *Embodied Modernities.* Larissa Heinrich and Fran Martin. Honolulu: Hawaii University Press, 2006. 218–234.

Schwartz, Vera. *The Chinese Enlightenment: Intellectuals and the Legacy of the May Fourth Movement of 1919.* Berkeley: Center for Chinese Studies, 1986.

Sedgwick, Eve. *Between Men: English Literature and Male Homosocial Desire.* New York: Columbia University Press, 1985.

———. *Epistemology of the Closet.* Berkeley: University of California Press, 1990.

Shahar, Meir. *Crazy Ji: Chinese Religion and Popular Culture.* Cambridge: Harvard University Press, 1998.

Shih, Shu-mei. *Visuality and Identity: Sinophone Articulations across the Pacific.* Berkeley: University of California Press, 2007.

Sieber, Patricia. *Red Is Not the Only Color: Contemporary Chinese Fiction on Love and Sex between Women, Collected Stories.* Lanham: Rowman & Littlefield Publishers, 2001.

Silverman, Kaja. *Male Subjectivity at the Margins.* New York: Routledge, 1992.

Sommer, Matthew. *Sex, Law, and Society in Late Imperial China.* Stanford: Stanford University Press, 2000.

Song, Weijie 宋偉杰. *Cong yule xingwei dao wutuobang chongdong: Jin Yong xiaoshuo zaijiedu* 從娛樂行為到烏托邦衝動：金庸小說再解讀 (From entertainment activity to utopian impulse: Rereading Jin Yong's fiction). Nanjing: Jiangsu renmin chubanshe, 1999.

———. "The Reproduction of a Popular Hero." *Rethinking Modern Chinese Popular Culture: Literature and Its Discontents.* Eds. Carlos Rojas and Eileen Chow. London: Routledge, 2009. 179–189.

———. "Cinematic Geography, Martial Arts Fantasy, and Tsui Hark's Wong Fei-hung Series." *Asian Cinema* 19.1 (2008): 123–142.

Srinivas, S.V. "Kung Fu Hustle: A Note on the Local." *Inter-Asia Cultural Studies,* Vol. 6, No. 2 (2005): 289–295.

Su Min 素民. "Huoshao guopian" 火燒國片 (Burn the Chinese film). *Baiman* 百幔, No. 6, 1931.

Sun, Yixue 孫宜學. *Jin Yong zhuan* 金庸傳 (A biography of Jin Yong). Taipei: Fengyun shidao, 2004.

Tan Xianmao 覃賢茂. *Gu Long zhuan* 古龍傳 (A biography of Gu Long). Sichuan: Sichuan renmin chubanshe, 1995.

Tang, Xiaobing. *Chinese Modern: The Heroic and the Quotidian.* Durham: Duke University Press, 2000.

Teo, Stephen. *Hong Kong Cinema: The Extra Dimensions.* London: British Film Institute, 1997.

———. "*Wuxia* Redux: Crouching Tiger, Hidden Dragon as a Model of Late Transnational Production." *Hong Kong Connections: Transnational Imagination in Action Cinema*. Eds. Meaghan Morris, Siu-Leung Li, and Stephen Ching-kiu Chan. Durham: Duke University Press, 2005. 191–204.

———. *Chinese Martial Arts Cinema: The Wuxia Tradition*. Edinburgh: Edinburgh University Press, 2009.

Tinkcom, Matthew, and Amy Villarejo, eds. *Keyframes: Popular Film and Cultural Studies*. New York: Routledge, 2001.

Tu, Weiming. *Confucian Ethics Today: The Singapore Challenge*. Singapore: Federal Publications, 1984.

Van Gulik, R.H. *Sexual Life in Ancient China*. Leiden: E.J. Brill, 1961.

Wakeman, Frederic Jr., and Xi Wang. *China's Quest for Modernization: A Historical Perspective*. Berkeley: Institute for East Asian Studies, 1997.

Wagner, Rudolf. "The Canonization of May Fourth." *The Appropriation of Cultural Capital: China's May Fourth Project*. Eds. Milnea Doležzelová-Velingerová and Kárl Oldřich. Cambridge: Harvard University Press, 2001. 66–120.

Wang, David. *Fictional Realism in 20th-Century China*. New York: Columbia University Press, 1992.

———. *Fin-de-siècle Splendor: Repressed Modernities of Late Qing Fiction, 1849–1911*. Stanford: Stanford University Press, 1997.

Wang, Dulu 王度盧. *Baojian jinchai* 寶劍金釵 (Precious sword, golden hairpin), 1938. Taipei: Yuanjing, 2001.

———. *Jianqi zhuguang* 劍氣珠光 (Sword energy, pearl shine), 1939. Taipei: Yuanjing, 2001.

———. *Hejing Kunlun* 鶴驚崑崙 (Crane startles Kunlun), 1940. Taipei: Yuanjing, 2001.

———. *Wohu canglong* 臥虎藏龍 (Crouching tiger, hidden dragon), 1941. Taipei: Yuanjing, 2001.

——— *Tieji yinping* 鐵騎銀瓶 (Iron knight, silver vase), 1942. Taipei: Yuanjing, 2001.

Wang, Hailin 王海林. *Zhongguo wuxia xiaoshuo shi lue* 中國武俠小說史略 (A brief history of Chinese martial arts fiction). Shangxi: Taiyuan beiyue wenyi, 1988.

Wang, Hui 汪輝. *Xiandai Zhongguo sixiang de xingqi* 現代中國思想的興起 (The rise of modern Chinese thought). Beijing: Sanlian shudian, 2004.

Wang, Qiugui 王秋桂, ed. *Jin Yong xiaoshuo guoji xueshu yantaohui lunwenji* 金庸小說國際學術研討會論文集. (Proceedings of the international conference on Jin Yong's novels). Taipei: Yuanliu, 1999.

Wang, Shuo 王朔. "Wo kan Jin Yong" (My reading of Jin Yong). *Jin*

Yong xiaoshuo lunzhan ji 金庸小說論戰集 (Collected debates on Jin Yong's works). Ed. Liao Kebin 廖可斌. Hangzhou: Zhejiang daxue chubanshe, 2000. 3–7.

Wang, Yue 王月. *Jin Yong xiaoshuo zhi lishi qingyuan* 金庸小說之歷史情緣 (Jin Yong's emotional ties to "history"). Taipei: Yinghan, 2003.

Wang, Zheng. *Women in the Chinese Enlightenment.* Berkeley: University of California Press, 1999.

Wei, Shaochang 衛紹昌, ed. *Yuanyang hudie pai yanjiu ziliao* 鴛鴦蝴蝶派研究資料 (Research materials on Mandarin Duck and Butterfly literature). Hong Kong: Sanlian, 1980.

Wen, Rui-an 溫瑞安. *Tan xiao-ao jianghu* 談笑傲江湖 (On *State of Divinity*). Taipei, Yuanliu, 1997.

Weng, Wenxin 翁文信. *Gu Long yishu shei yu zheng feng* 古龍一出誰與爭锋. Taipei: Fengyun, 2008.

West, David. *Chasing Dragons: An Introduction to the Martial Arts Film.* London: Tauris, 2006.

Widmer, Ellen. "The Rhetoric of Retrospection: May Fourth Literary History and the Ming-Qing Woman Writer." *The Appropriation of Cultural Capital: China's May Fourth Project.* Eds. Milnea Doleželová-Velingerová and Kárl Oldřich. Cambridge: Harvard University Press, 2001. 193–225.

Wittfogel, Karl. *Dongfang zhuanzhi zhuyi* 東方專制主義 (Oriental Despotism). Trans. Shigu Xu 徐式谷, et al. Beijing: Zhongguo shehuikexue, 1989.

Wong, Bin. *China Transformed: Historical Change and the Limits of European Experience.* Ithaca: Cornell University Press, 1997.

Wu, Yiching. *The Other Cultural revolution: Politics and practice of class in the Chinese Cultural Revolution, 1966—1969.* Ph.D. Dissertation, University of Chicago, 2007.

Xia, Xiaohong. 夏曉虹. *Wan qing funü wenren guan* (Late Qing women literati's view). Beijing: Zhuojia chubanshe, 1995.

———. "*Cong nannü pingdeng dao nüquan yishi—wan qing de funü sichao*" 從男女平等到女權意識—晚清的婦女思潮 (From equality between men and women to the consciousness of women's rights—women's movement in the Late Qing period), *Beijing daoxue xuebao* 4, 1995.

Xia, Yan. *Shanghai Wuyan xia* 上海屋簷下 (Under Shanghai roofs). Shanghai: Kaiming shudian: 1949.

Xiao, Sa. 蕭颯. *Danshenyihui* 單身薏惠 (The single lady). Taipei: Jiuge, 1993.

Xu, Sinian 徐斯年. *Xia de zongji* 俠的蹤跡 (Footsteps of *xia*). Beijing: renminwenxue, 1995.

Xu, Wenying 徐文瀅. "Minguo yilai de zhanghui xiaoshuo" 民國以來的章回小說. *Wanxiang* 1941: 6.

Yang, Lige 楊莉歌. *Jin Yong chuanshuo* 金庸傳說 (The legend of Jin Yong). Taipei: Yanjing, 1997.

Yan, Jiayan 嚴家炎. *Jin Yong xiaoshuo lun gao* 金庸小說論稿 (Essays on Jin Yong's fiction). Beijing: Beijing daxue, 1999.

———. Yan Jiayan, *Shiji de zuyin* 世紀的足音. Hong Kong: Tiandi, 1995.

Yang, Zhao 楊照. "Xipu de pohuai yu chong jian—lun Gu Long de wulin yu jiang hu" 系譜的破壞與重建—論古龍的武林與江湖. *Aoshi guicai—Gu Long: Gu Long yu wuxia xiaoshuo guoji xueshu yantaohui*. Ed. Lin Baochun. Taipei: Xuesheng shuju, 2006. 113–126.

Ye, Hongsheng 葉洪生. *Wuxia xiaoshuo tan yi lu—Ye Hongsheng lun jian* 武俠小說談藝錄—葉洪生論劍 (Martial arts fiction and aesthetics—Ye Hongsheng on the sword). Taipei: Lianjing, 1994.

———. "*Beiju xiaqing zhizu*" 悲劇俠情之祖 (The founding father of a tragic, chivalrous kind of love), *Minsheng bao*, June 1982.

———. "Dangdai Taiwan wuxia xiaoshuo de chengren tonghua shijie" 當代台灣武俠小說的成人童話世界 (The world of adult fairy tales in contemporary martial arts literature in Taiwan). Eds. Lin Yaode and Meng fan. Taipei: Shibao wenhua, 1992.

Yeh, Catherine Vance. "Root Literature of the 1980s: May Fourth as a Double Burden." *The Appropriation of Cultural Capital: China's May Fourth Project*. Cambridge: Harvard University Press, 2001. 229–256.

Yeh, Wen-Hsin. *The Alienated Academy: Culture and Politics in Republican China, 1919–1937*. Cambridge: Harvard University Press, 1990.

Ying, Hu. *Tales of Translation: Composing the New Woman in China, 1898–1918*. Stanford: Stanford University Press, 2000.

Yu, Ying-shih. "Neither Renaissance nor Enlightenment: a historian's reflections on the May Fourth Movement." *The Appropriation of Cultural Capital: China's May Fourth Project*. Eds. Milnea Doleželová-Velingerová and Kárl Oldřich. Cambridge: Harvard University Press, 2001. 300–324.

Zhang, Gansheng 張贛生. "Zhongguo wuxia xiaoshuo de xingcheng yu liubian" 中國武俠小說的形成與流變. *Hebei daxue xuebao* 1987.4: 38–45.

Zhang, Jingyuan 張京媛. *Houzhimin lilun yu wenhua rentong* 後殖民理論與文化認同 (Postcolonial criticism and cultural identity). Taipei: Rye Field, 1995.

Zhang, Xudong. *Chinese Modernism in the Era of Reforms: Cultural Fever, Avant-Garde Fiction, and the New Chinese Cinema*. Durham: Duke University Press.

Zhang Zhen, *An Amorous History of the Silver Screen: Shanghai Cinema, 1896–1937*. Chicago: The University of Chicago Press, 2005.

———. "Bodies in the Air." *Chinese-Language Film: Historiography, Poetics, Politics*. Eds. Sheldon Lu and Emilie Yeh. Honolulu: University of Hawaii Press, 2005. 52–75.

Zhang, Zhihe, and Chunyuan Zheng 張志和, 鄭春原. *Zhongguo wenshi zhong de xiake* 中國文史中的俠客 (*Xia* in Chinese literary history). Beijing: Chinese Social Science, 1994.

Zhao, Xifang 趙稀方. "Shichang xiaofei yu wenhua tisheng: lun Xianggang xinpai wuxia xiaoshuo" 市場消費與文化提升—論香港新派武俠小說. 中國社會科學院研究生院學報   Beijing: Graduate School of Chinese Academy of Social Science, May 2000: 53–59.

Zheng, Yimei 鄭逸梅. *Wuxia xiaoshuo de tongbing* 武俠小說的通病 (Martial arts fiction's common problems). Ed. *Yuanyang hudie pai wenxue ziliao* 鴛鴦蝴蝶派文學資料.   Fujian: Fujian renmin chubanshe, 1984.

Zheng, Zhenduo 鄭振鐸.   *Lun wuxia xiaoshuo* 論武俠小說 (On martial arts fiction). Shanghai: Xinzhongguo shudian, 1932.

———. *Zhongguo su wenxue shi* 中國俗文學史 (History of Chinese popular fiction). Beijing: Zuojia, 1938; reprinted 1954.

Zheng, Zhengyin 鄭證因. *Yingzhua wang* 鷹爪王 (King of the eagle talon). Taipei: Lianjing, 1984.

Žižek, Slavoj. *Welcome to the Desert of the Real*. New York: Routledge; London: Verso, 2002.

Index

CORNELL EAST ASIA SERIES

CORNELL
East Asia Series

www.einaudi.cornell.edu/eastasia/publications